A STUDY OF
BABA YAGA

RONESA AVEELA

BENDIDEIA
PUBLISHING

I0096519

Copyright © 2022 Ronesa Aveela

December 2022

Ebook ISBN: 978-1-949397-37-6
Paperback ISBN: 978-1-949397-38-3
Hardback ISBN: 978-1-949397-39-0

All rights reserved.

All rights reserved. Except for the quotation of short passages for the purposes of criticism and review, no part of this publication may be reproduced, stored in a retrieval system, or transmitted in whole or in part in any form by any electronic, mechanical, or other means, now known or hereafter invented, including xerography, photocopying and recording, without the written permission of the publisher: Bendideia Publishing, www.bendideia.com.

Cover Design by Nelinda, www.nelindaart.com.
Cover Illustration by Alexander Petkov, https://www.facebook.com/alexander.petkov1.
Series interior layout design by Nicole Lavoie, www.JustSayingDezigns.com.
Vecna font is used in the book's title. It is available for commercial use from Pixel Sagas at www.pixelsagas.com.

Contents

Editorial Review

The black and white view of Baba Yaga is wrenched into brilliant greys by the keen research and writing of Ronesa Aveela. You don't have to forget what you might know about this misunderstood figure of Slavic folklore, but you must be ready to learn, at the very least, several new aspects of the character. What other sources outline in broad strokes, Ronesa colors in with details and features in a brilliant masterpiece of information, storytelling, and understanding of Baba Yaga in one volume. It's clear this figure holds a special place in the author's heart, which makes the character gleam on every page. If you're looking for a source of information, parallels to different mythologies, a thoughtful consideration of roles and heritage, plus all the chicken feet you can handle – look no further; you've found it.

— **David Flora, *Blurry Photos Podcast***
www.blurryphotos.org/podcast/

Acknowledgments

Books are never made by the authors alone. We've had some wonderful people help us along the way to make this book what it is today. We'd like to thank Alexander Petkov for his illustrations filled with expression that bring Baba Yaga to life. Many, many thanks go to Vadym Grebniev for translating yet "one more" story or article. And a special thanks to David Flora (of *Blurry Photos Podcast*, http://www.blurryphotos.org/podcast/) for taking the time to read an advance copy and providing an editorial review. And, always, thank you to our readers! We write these books for you.

A Closer Look at Baba Yaga

Who was Baba Yaga? Did she ever exist? And, more importantly, does she still exist today?

Many books have been published about Baba Yaga: academic studies and spiritual guides alike. So why something new? What makes this book one you'd want to add to your collection?

The answer is simple: the diversity of the content. It's an in-depth study that will take you beyond the tales that have terrified children throughout the ages. The book is like a liberal arts study—a little of this, a little of that. It takes all the best from the academic world and portrays the information in easy-to-understand bits. Plus, it digs deeper into her character, and we are not afraid to discuss any topic related to Baba Yaga: modern-day beliefs, controversial subjects (aliens, anyone?), and anything we can find that will give readers a well-rounded look at who this persona called Baba Yaga might actually be. You'll even discover a side of the witch as she is perceived by those who say they have had an encounter with her.

We want to tell you her story and make her come alive. By the time you finish reading this book, you'll either want to crawl back into bed with the covers over you, or you'll seek out the witch of witches for her guidance.

Baba Yaga (Баба Яга)

Good is good, and bad is bad.

Baba Yaga (singular); **Baby/Babi Yagi**, Бабы Яги (plural)
In Russian and other languages, "Yaga" is accented on the second syllable (Bába Yagá), but other languages, like Bulgarian, accent the word on the first syllable (Bába Yága).

Common name variations: Yaga Baba, Baba-Yaga, Baba Jaga, Baba Iaga, Egibaba, Yagishna, Iagishna, Yagonishna.[1]

Related names: Ježibaba (Czech, Slovak), Jezinka (Czech), Baba Roga (Bosnian, Croatian, Macedonian, Serbian – "horned old woman/grandmother"), Jezda/Ienzababa (Polish), Jazi Baba (Czech), Baba Cloanţa (Romanian – "old hag with broken teeth"), Zalizna Baba (Ukrainian – "iron woman"), Vasorrú bába (Hungarian – "iron-nosed woman").

Slang: "Baba," by itself, is a derogatory word among Russians, Ukrainians, Poles, Czechs, and others (but not Bulgarians), referring to a loud, whiny, low-class woman who is a slob and unattractive. It may also refer to a timid man, who is considered unmanly or lacking character. The term "iaga" may be hurled as an insulting word, with much the same meaning. The two words together can also refer to any old woman who lives alone.

If you're familiar with Baba Yaga, you'll likely say she's a cannibalistic witch. Many who have researched this infamous individual have called her "ambiguous," but my thought is that she is more "complex" than ambiguous. The proverb "Good is good and bad is bad" may be true of most characters in Slavic fairy tales, and fairy tales in general, but Baba Yaga is an exception. She is almost never completely one or the other—at least not if you examine the story and culture more thoroughly.

She may be the hero's enemy or friend depending on the situation. When she is "good," she may do so reluctantly, or she may assist the hero or heroine while harboring nefarious thoughts. She is a trickster, after all.

When she is "bad," the hero may have caught her on an off day, or he may be trespassing, or any other number of reasons, such as in the story of "Nikita the Footless and the Terrible Tsar," where two brothers, one with no legs and the other blind, trespass in Baba Yaga's house, eat her food, steal from her, and make a terrible mess.

> Then when all was still the door was suddenly opened and the wicked Baba-Yaga entered her cottage. When she saw the two in one she screamed out with a loud voice: "You beggars and thieves! Up to this time not even a bird or a beast had come to my lonely dwelling, and now you have come to devour my food and loosen the very props of my little cottage. But very soon, and indeed sooner than that, I will settle with you."[2]

She's had many labels besides that of witch: goddess, demon, nature spirit, healer, shaman, mother figure, cannibal, and even alien. Even within the fairy tales, she plays numerous roles: villain, helper, guide, gift-giver, mentor, sorceress, initiator, animal mistress, and more.

Etymology

Translating names of mythical characters can be a tricky business. Native speakers understand the cultural context that goes along with the names. But how do you convey that in a translation? Understanding the origin of the name can help. Scholars have a multitude of opinions about where the name Baba Yaga came from. It may not even be her actual name. It was common practice in ancient times to substitute a euphemism for demonic beings, so it may have been taboo to speak Baba Yaga's true name for fear of summoning her. Or, she could have been a goddess, in which case, her name would have been too sacred to say out loud. The following ideas about the meaning of her name will give you an idea of Baba Yaga's complexity.

Baba

Even if Baba Yaga was her one and only name, the least controversy exists about the meaning of the word "baba." Throughout the Slavic languages, it means "grandmother." Along with this, though, comes an implied reference to any woman, but in particular to an older woman. Although in olden days, this was not the case. Once a woman married, she became a "baba," regardless of her age. It was also a term used for a midwife, sorceress, or fortune teller. The word "baba" comes from the Indo-European root *b(h)āb(h)-*. This is a "consonant-vowel pattern, repeating syllables" and reflects how adults speak to children (Johns, *The Ambiguous Mother*, 9).

Yaga

Now the fun begins, trying to determine the meaning and origin of "yaga" or "iaga." To know this will take you a long way into unraveling who exactly Baba Yaga is, or where she originated from. By looking at words with a similar sound, scholars have made numerous suggestions. One is that "Yaga" is a proper noun, a form of the name Jadwiga. Other possibilities are words that have a negative connotation or type of problem, such as:

- Eza (Bulgarian) – torment, torture
- Jeza (Old Serbian) – illness, nightmare
- Jęza/jędza (Old Church Slavonic) – disease, illness
- Jeziv (Serbo-Croatian) – dangerous
- Jeza (Slovenian) – anger
- Jezinka (Czech) – evil woman, wicked wood nymph, dryad
- Jeza (Serbo-Croatian) – horror, shudder, chill
- Jězě (Old Czech) – witch, legendary evil female being
- Jędza (Polish) – witch, evil woman, fury
- Iagat' (Russian) – yell, make a noise, rage, curse, squabble
- Egat' (Russian) – burn fiercely, be angry, rage

Etymology *continued*

These definitions certainly paint a not-so-nice picture of Baba Yaga. Not all examples point to a negative origin, however. Other thoughts about the meaning of "yaga" follow:

- A large number of sources say "iaga" has been derived from the Proto-Slavic *ož* and Sanskrit *ahi* (Johns, *The Ambiguous Mother*, 10), or Latin *anguis* (Scielzo, 123), for "serpent" or "snake," making her name "snake-baba."
- Variations of the name in different languages are related to fire, flame, or heat (Baba Aga, Ega, Iga, Ga, Yaga), thereby making her name "Fiery Baba" (Ustinova, 5).
- Yagilev (Russian) – from *yagel* for "deer moss," which was once called *yag*. The theory is that Baba Yaga lived where reindeer moss grew (Peskiadmin.ru).
- The word may have Uralic origins. A suggestion says prehistoric Slavs came in contact with Samoyed people and adopted the word *nga for "god" and integrated the God of Death with Baba Yaga (Johns, *The Ambiguous Mother*, 29).
- Another theory is that the name is a derivative of the Sanskrit *yagya*, for "sacrifice," with "baba" derived from another word for "sage," "father," or "ascetic" (Nikitina).
- A less-popular theory is that the name may have come from a tribe of cannibals called *yaggas*, who were ruled by a queen. Russian sailors may have brought the tales with them from Central Africa and incorporated them into Russian fairy tales (Peskiadmin.ru).
- More in tune with nature, "yaga" may come from a word in the Komi language that means "coniferous forest" or "pinewood" (Ulasevich). Even the Russian *ekhat* for "to ride [a horse]" is a possibility (Forrester).
- An older belief was that "iaga" was from the Mongolaian *eke* for "mother," which is similar to the Turkic *ekä* for "elder sister" or "aunt." The word "baba" was added to help explain the unfamiliar word (Johns, *The Ambiguous Mother*, 10).
- In a similar vein, the designation of "baba" was a way to distinguish her from a male Yaga counterpart, with the two of them being similar to ancient Indian deities Yama and Yami (Johns, *The Ambiguous Mother*, 10). In this case, *iaga* comes from a Baltic word for "strength," "force," "understanding," or "sense" (Johns, *The Ambiguous Mother*, 10-11). This positive aspect of her name may have come from an earlier time, with the more negative meaning added later (McNeil).
- Another origin of "yaga" points toward a sleeveless coat called "yaga" or "yagushka," which was worn with the wool on the outside. In ancient Slavic mythology, this was considered an attribute of the "undead" (Ulasevich). In a Finno-Ugric ritual to be connected with deceased relatives, people created a baba doll out of sticks and dressed it in the above-mentioned *yaga* fur coat. They made for the doll a windowless and doorless wooden house and raised it above the ground to prevent animals from getting inside (Mirdinara.com). As you'll discover later, this house resembles Baba Yaga's hut.

These titles are not all mutually exclusive. Baba Yaga doesn't have to fit nicely into a single category. People's personalities differ, being kind to one person and cruel to another. Why not so for Baba Yaga herself? Ancient deities possessed diverse functions; it indicated they held great power and authority.[3]

Let's look at the extremes: a goddess and a demon. What's the difference between them? Does a goddess do "good" while a demon does "bad"? The line between good and bad is often indistinct, especially if knowledge of the intention behind the action is lacking.

Think about nature. It can be nurturing or destructive. The same applies to the immortals. On one hand, their actions can be beneficial, while on the other, they are construed as evil. As you'll discover, Baba Yaga is fickle like nature: able to nurture and destroy all within a matter of moments. She is a character who "straddles the threshold between life and death, between the promise of change and the imminent thread of destruction, between learning to cook a meal or becoming the meal."[4]

It's this complexity that makes Baba Yaga more real, rather than simply being a fairy-tale character, who is black-and-white, at least on the surface. Take the hero, for instance. Although often clueless, he's on a noble quest (at least according to him). And let's not forget about the princess. She's always beautiful and in need of a hero (even if she doesn't really want one). Not least of all of the one-dimensional characters is the villain, frequently the kidnapper of maidens. Whether he's a dragon or other monstrous being, he's always evil.

But Baba Yaga is so much more. What "real" person doesn't have conflicting actions or desires depending on the circumstances? Does the fact that she doesn't fit into the cut-and-dry fairy-tale character mold prove that she was, or even still is, something more than an imaginary being? Perhaps. Read on, so you can make up your own mind as to whom you think this Baba Yaga is or was.

Origins

Who was Baba Yaga before she became a legendary cannibalistic witch? Where did she come from? Just like there are a variety of opinions about the meaning of her name, numerous theories exist about Baba Yaga's origins—from ones many scholars agree upon to those that will raise the eyebrows of the academic world and perhaps even the non-academic one. The following brief summaries will give you a clue as to what makes up this fascinating being. You'll see her transform from goddess to wicked witch as time marches on.

Zoomorphic Aspect

The creatures that primitive mankind worshiped were giant snakes, birds, or fish that developed from ordinary animals. As time went on, people's imaginations became more vivid, and animals evolved into hybrid beasts: snakes grew wings, and birds obtained human faces. In the same way, Baba Yaga displays zoomorphic traits dating back to the earliest of times. Remnants can still be found in fairy tales, where she was known to "squeal like a snake" or "roar like an animal."

Frog

Let's start way back in time. In the earliest days, she had the appearance of a frog, with clawed, twisted arms and disheveled hair.[5] This type of frog goddess appeared in Europe during the Neolithic age (circa 7000/6000 to 3000 B.C.), but also extended to an even wider time span in the Near East, China, and the Americas.[6]

A frog goddess symbolized regeneration and, like the Egyptian goddess Heket, was considered the "primordial mother of all existence" who "controlled fecundity and regeneration after death."[7] This aspect of Baba Yaga is apparent in tales in which her children are all manner of creatures, as in the story of "The Stepdaughter and the Stepmother's Daughter," where both girls, at different times, are ordered

Baba Yaga rides on a pig to battle a "crocodile." Unknown artist, 18th century.
Lubok from the collection of D. Rovinsky. Public domain, via Wikimedia Commons.

to bathe Baba Yaga's children: "Suddenly she saw worms, frogs, rats, and all sorts of insects come crawling up to her in the bathhouse."[8] In another tale, Baba Yaga is a dragon-like creature. She bursts after drinking water from the sea to quench her thirst. Out of her come vipers, toads, lizards, spiders, worms, and all manner of vile creatures.

Snake

Baba Yaga's most popular animal connection, however, is with snakes. These, in turn, are associated with the underworld, death, and rebirth, because they live in the earth. Even the words in Russian are similar: snake (*zmeya*) and earth (*zemlya*). This underground world of the dead, however, wasn't the Hades we so often imagine. People perceived the earth, all of it, as being "a living entity whose good will must be earned and whose feelings must be respected."[9] As you'll discover, respect and worthiness are two attributes Baba Yaga demands from her visitors before she will assist them. This reinforces her link to the earth and the world below it.

In oral tradition, Baba Yaga may have first been called a "snake-baba."

> The latent significance of the name is also interesting as the first letter of the elusive "Yagá" also means the personal pronoun "I" in Russian. Because of the importance of sound value in folklore, the Latin root "anguis" or snake was doubly rich, since on Slavic ground it afforded a double suggestion. This interpretation is aided by the hyphen connecting the two parts of the name Bába-Yagá, or possibly "the (old) woman-who-is-I snake."[10]

This snake aspect made its way into fairy tales. In some stories, an enormous female snake-dragon (*zmeikha*) may be called Baba Yaga or simply be an unnamed mythical snake. Either way, listeners understood that the creature and Baba Yaga were interchangeable. This villain may be the wife or mother of multi-headed dragons who create chaos throughout the land. She has the ability to shapeshift into a mountain, storm cloud, dense forest, or endless wall, and her mouth opens so wide it touches both the ground and the clouds.

Did you know?

In Ukraine, a flying witch is called a snake (Ralston, *The Songs of the Russian People*, 162).

Other snakelike aspects of Baba Yaga show her slithering through the air in a mortar that spits out fire, while she uses a burning broom to wipe away her traces, much like the "fiery snake" (one name for the monstrous dragon-like snake) makes its way through the sky.

People also once believed that snakes loved milk. Families would set out a bowl of milk for the guardian snake, which lived under the threshold and protected the home. Not all snakes were so benevolent, however. Stories told how some would suck milk from cows, from an infant's bottle, or even from the nursing mother herself. In one fairy tale, Baba Yaga sucks milk (or blood) from a woman's breast to steal her lifeforce.

> But one day Baba Yaga with the bony legs came into the hut and sucked the blood out of the fair maiden's breast. And whenever the two knights went away on the chase, Baba Yaga came back, so that very soon the merchant's fair daughter became thin and feeble.[11]

As a giant snake, Baba Yaga was also believed to devour the sky, steal rain and dew, and consume the moon and stars, much like the dragon or storm demon Hala.[12] Peasants believed that the moon was Baba Yaga's body. Like her, the moon, at certain phases, was horned like a bull. The cannibal witch ate away at her own body in the process of regulating fertility not only of the planet, but also of women. The phases of the moon suggest "the decomposition of the body, as the self-devouring goddess moves from generation to death."[13]

Snakes, like Baba Yaga, are also the guardians of the waters of life and death, sometimes called healing and living waters, or life-giving and dead waters. These springs are hidden deep within the earth and bubble up through wells, or Baba Yaga may keep them at her home, contained within barrels. These waters demonstrate her power over life and death, and they represent death and rebirth through initiation. This dual concept of both living and dead waters appears mostly in Slavic tales, whereas in most other ethnic fairy tales, you'll read about only the water of life.

How exactly do these waters work?

Baba Yaga and her cat. Alexander Petkov, 2022.

The hero sometimes gets chopped up by the villain. In this case, his companions or others will arrange the pieces of his corpse in their proper positions. It's not always quite so drastic a death. The hero may have been killed with a sword or fire. In any case, his body is sprinkled with the dead water. This enables the dismembered corpse to grow together. The reason for doing this may be because of the belief that "the continuation of life after death and the rebirth of the deceased is possible only upon the condition of the integrity (preservation) of the body."[14] Once the body is back to its original state, it's still dead. The companions once again sprinkle their fallen hero, only this time they use the water of life, so he is reborn.

> Koshchey leaped on his horse, caught up with Ivan Tsarevich, broke him up into tiny bits, put them into a tar chest, took this chest, locked it with iron bolts and threw it into the blue sea. And he took Marya Moryevna away with him.
>
> At the same time the brothers-in-law of Ivan Tsarevich looked at their silver ornaments and found they had turned black.
>
> "Oh," they said, "evidently some disaster has befallen him!"
>
> The Eagle rushed into the blue sea, dragged out the chest to the shore, and the Hawk flew for the Water of Life, and the Crow flew for the Water of Death. Then they all three met at a single spot and broke up the chest, took out the bits of Ivan Tsarevich, washed them, laid them together as was fit. Then the Crow sprinkled him with the Water of Death, and the body grew together and was one. And the Hawk sprinkled him with the Water of Life.
>
> Ivan Tsarevich shivered, sat up and said, "Oh, what a long sleep I have had!"[15]

In cases where the hero has not been slain, but merely needs healing, before he attempts to use the waters, he will test them out on a twig to avoid Baba Yaga's deception. The living water will cause the twig to bloom, while the dead water will make it dry up or burst into flames.

> "Very well, ancient witch," said the knights, "show us the well with the waters of Life and Death."
>
> "If you'll only not beat me, I'll show you it."
>
> Then Katoma climbed onto the blind man's back, and he grabbed Baba Yaga by her hair. They traveled into the deepest part of the dense forest.
>
> There, she showed them a well and said, "This is the healing water that brings life."
>
> "Be careful, Katoma. Don't make a mistake. If she deceives us this time, we might not recover from it for our entire lives."
>
> Katoma broke off a twig. It had hardly fallen into the water before it flamed up. "Ah! that was another deceit of yours!"
>
> The two knights prepared to throw Baba Yaga into the fiery brook.
>
> But she begged for mercy as before, and swore she wouldn't deceive them again. "Honestly, I'll show you the right water!"
>
> The two knights got ready once more to travel, and Baba Yaga took them to another well. Katoma broke off a dry twig from the tree and threw it into the well. The twig had hardly fallen into the water before it sprouted up and became green and blue.
>
> "This water is the right one," Katoma said.
>
> The blind man washed his eyes and could see immediately. And he put the cripple into the water, and his legs grew back.[16]

Although Baba Yaga may be the keeper of these waters, you won't ever see her voluntarily using them to restore anyone. The hero will force or trick her into doing this or providing him with the waters so he can perform the healing himself.

Demonized Nature

Slavs often considered natural occurrences to be demons. However, this concept is not like the Devil or a servant of Satan. It has no religious connotation. These demons were spirits that personified nature. They were neither good nor evil, although they could bring abundance or destruction, changing from one to the other in a moment—just like Baba Yaga.

> You cannot label a thunderstorm as good or evil: for someone hit by lightning it is likely to be evil, but for the one whose fields it saturates with rain, it is good. In a similar vein, you cannot judge the sun, the moon, the wind, the day and the night, the earth and the sky, fire and water, field and forest. Essentially, every element and every part of creation, in its purest form, is by default hostile to humans. We get burned by the fire, we drown in the water, we cannot stay aloft in the air and while the earth is our mother, she is not

Baba Yaga. Viktor Mikhailovich Vasnetsov, 1917.
Public domain, via Wikimedia Commons.

9

the kindest of mothers. But man knows how to deal with each element to benefit from the interaction and not get harmed by it. Every element has a dark and a light side, as does every deity, and even those Slavic Gods that are now considered Dark never exclusively take the dark or evil side of the cosmos. Without darkness there is no light, without death there is no life, and destruction is as important as creation – everything is a boon for the world in one way or another.[17]

In the same way, Baba Yaga represents both sides of these natural occurrences.

Winter Storms

Early interpretations of Baba Yaga's character in fairy tales compared her to a raging storm. She makes the winds howl as she urges on her fiery mortar, with squealing spirits flying by her side. Her whistle causes the trees to groan and quake. Thunderstorms rage when her magical, fire-breathing horses race through the sky.

Not only is she the storm, but she is the mother of winds and summons them to obey her every command: "The old woman came out onto the porch, shouted in a loud voice, whistled with a valiant whistle; suddenly violent winds blew, arising from all sides, making the hut shake!"[18] A common folk belief was that when strong winds bent corn stalks that Baba Yaga was around, searching for children she could grind in her iron mortar.[19]

Winds were thought of as demons who lived in dark places: forests, caves, old wells, and more. Baba Yaga alone didn't hold this title. She split the seasons with the dragon Hala. While Hala dominated the warmer months, causing crop destruction, Baba Yaga brought winter storms.

Her boniness, barrenness of old age, a pestle that petrifies, raging winds that can sweep away all traces of her presence, all point to her destructive power. Some fairy tales interpret her as being an evil spirit, a "fiend of darkness," who fights against the sun.[20] When she abducts a person, it represents death—not only of the person, but also of the land. Like the Gorgon Medusa, Baba Yaga can turn her victims to stone by striking them with her pestle. With one blow, "No hero can live in the world."[21]

In one story, Baba Yaga turns men to stone in a different way. She plucks one of her hairs and tells Ivan Dévich to tie it into three knots and blow on it.

> He does so, and both he and his horse turn into stone. The Baba Yaga places them in her mortar, pounds them to bits, and buries their remains under a stone. A little later comes Ivan Dévich's comrade, Prince Ivan. Him also the Yaga attempts to destroy, but he feigns ignorance, and persuades her to show him how to tie knots and to blow. The result is that she becomes petrified herself. Prince Ivan puts her in her own mortar, and proceeds to pound her therein, until she tells him where the fragments of his comrade are, and what he must do to restore them to life.[22]

Spring rituals are performed to drive out the old hag. The popular story about Vasilisa the Beautiful is compared to "a battle between sunlight (Vasilisa) and storm (the stepmother) and other dark clouds (the stepsisters)."[23] More often, though, in fairy tales, the hero Ivan is depicted as the sun and Baba Yaga the storm. Baba Yaga's death loosens her power over her prisoners, and springtime triumphs over winter. Nature can once again revive: "at the first sounds of the spring thunders, the sleeping, as it were petrified, realm of nature awakes from its winter slumbers."[24]

In a religious sense, these types of stories also depict the banishment of paganism. Baba Yaga and other goddesses were deities of the Moon season, the autumn and winter months. These types of deities existed in older, shamanistic cultures dominated by women: the mothers and grandmothers. But when

Baba Yaga in her mortar. Alexander Petkov, 2022.

Dionysian Sun Cults arose, these male-dominated groups "spread like wildfire into every pagan culture around the world, pushing out the older Shamanic cultures."[25]

The religion and society that grew up around the Sun Cult domesticated the wild grandmother type by having her turn against the most innocent in the family—the children—and becoming a hag who fattened them up to eat them. The new religion replaced priestesses with priests and wrote laws pertaining to what women could and could not do.

They eventually broke the power of the Triple Goddess (that circle that bound grandmothers, mothers, and maidens) by focusing on the maiden, implying that only the young are desirable and trustworthy. The male powers lured maidens "into these alcohol, drug, and sex orgies until they became unstable. And when they became unstable through these festivals, they eventually left the circle. And that's how the great circle was broken from the grandmothers." The wisdom of the grandmother type that Baba Yaga exemplified was replaced with the worship of the virgin, who had no power in the patriarchal structure of leadership: "When the grandmothers fell, the goddesses rose. And when the goddesses fell, the pagan men and the religious men fought for power," and so summer prevailed over winter.[26]

Illness

From the earlier etymology, you can see that various interpretations of Baba Yaga's name connect her with being a demon of illness. One such case is the word язва, *yazva*, which means "ulcer." The modern meaning can also be "harm" or "evil," and a woman who causes harm is called this name. In ancient Russia, the word was written as яза, *yaza* and the word indicated a plague, and could also mean "wound," "trouble," or "sadness." So, how did the з (z) change to a г (g) to become яга, *yaga*? It's been suggested this was due to "linguistic changes in the Proto-Slavic language," a process called the second palatalization, in which "back-lingual consonants" became "soft whistling ones."[27]

These types of demons of illness roamed the world, trying to access villages to torment people and make them sick, before moving on to the next village. Like other demons, Baba Yaga was believed to press down on people while they slept, suffocating them and causing nightmares. However, the personified diseases couldn't directly enter any inhabited place. They either had to be called into the village by someone who performed evil witchcraft or pronounced a curse, or they were forced to wait until a peasant allowed them to come in with him.

Once the disease made a foothold in a village or home, the inhabitants would try to appease it or bargain with it to lessen the effects of the illness. They also brought the sick person into the bathhouse to steam away the illness from his pores. If none of those things worked, they resorted to magical charms and rituals to expel the demon and send it back to the "unclean" liminal places, such as forests and swamps.

Goddess

Long before Baba Yaga was called a witch, it's believed people considered her a goddess. It has been suggested that she is a child of Rod and Rodanitsa, the progenitors of the lesser gods, whose names mean "god" and "goddess." Rodanitsa represents "the beginning and the end of a day, young and old, birth and death,"[28] characteristics that Baba Yaga herself exemplifies.

Many scholars say that goddess worship existed in matriarchal societies, or what some call "pre-patriarchal matrifocal societies."[29] They claim it's the oldest form of religion that dates back to the Paleolithic period or the Old Stone Age (about 2.5 million years ago until 10,000 B.C.). Even in ancient male-centered Indo-European societies, goddesses performed an important function, that of choosing the ruler of the kingdom.

Baba Yaga. Ivan Bilibin, before 1930s.
Public domain, via Wikimedia Commons.

In Indo-European cultures, these sovereignty-figures were *enablers*, women who gave access to the throne. A man with the proper heroic qualities would marry a foreign princess, live with her at her home, and inherit her father's kingdom. He could not become ruler of the kingdom without marrying the daughter of the king.[30]

As you'll learn later, Baba Yaga in fairy tales was instrumental in helping both pauper and prince acquire their princess brides. Is this perhaps indicating her role as a deity in choosing who should be the ruler, as this was a role of the goddess? Others, however, argue that "matriarchy did not precede patriarchy, that matrilineal inheritance and kinship systems are not evidence of former matriarchal societies."[31]

Baba Yaga's role as a deity took on different forms: she was a fertility goddess, the Forest Mistress, the goddess of death and the underworld, and a mother goddess. Let's look at each of these in turn.

Fertility Goddess

Often, when people think of goddess worship, it's only her fertility and nurturing aspects that come to mind. After all, figurines that have been discovered show these goddesses with large breasts and buttocks and often pregnant, which in today's society speak of sexuality more than they do fertility.

The term "fertility goddess" may be a narrow one; the goddesses so described may actually have been multi-functional…. However, the promotion of animal and vegetal fertility was indeed an important function of such goddesses, and the female principle may well have become primary as an object of worship.[32]

Baba Yaga, too, has these fertility characteristics. Her breasts are so large they hang down to her waist or lower. She tosses them over her shoulder when she rushes around. While inside, she has to hang them over a rod, wind them around a hook, or place them on a shelf. She may also stuff up the stove with her breasts.

Another aspect of a fertility goddess was her ability to give birth parthenogenetically, that is, to become "pregnant autonomously, without the fertilization of any man or god."[33] Baba Yaga, although she has no consort, has numerous offspring: dragons, magical horses, toads, and more.

As a fertility goddess, Baba Yaga was connected to the harvest. It was believed that she lived in the last sheaf of grain or corn that was tied together in agricultural festivities. So, her death (seeds under the ground) brought forth new life (harvest).

As goddess of the harvest, Baba Yaga is compared to Mokosh, Moist Mother Earth: "As Moist Mother Earth 'eats' the bodies of the dead, so Baba Yaga eats human beings."[34] In some areas, they call her *Jitnaya Baba*, "the Corn-woman," and dress her up in women's clothing.[35] It was believed that the woman who bound that sheaf would give birth before the next harvest.

People also believed Baba Yaga might take the life-giving power of grain away from them. Therefore, in rituals they drove her away into the forest or into another field. Both of these places are associated with being the borders of the lands of the living and the dead.[36]

Forest Mistress

In some tales, Baba Yaga commands all creatures, birds, fish, and forest animals, in the same way she commands the winds. However, she is not called their mother, even though she has absolute power over them.

In one of the northern Russian fairy tales, she calls the animals like this: "Where are you, gray wolves, all run, run and roll into one place and into one circle, choose between yourself, which is more, which is more daring to run after Ivan Tsarevich." Or: "The old woman came out onto the porch, shouted in a loud voice – all of a sudden, where did they come from, all kinds of animals ran in, all kinds of birds flew in."[37]

Because of this, some scholars say she is the Potnia Therōn, the mother and mistress of animals, who has complete power over them. Other sources, however, say there needs to be more than control of the animals. This title is reserved for a specific type of deity, one who is shown as holding animals in both hands or who has animals on both sides.[38]

BABA YAGA FILM

This short film will give you a different perspective of Baba Yaga (Jaga in Polish). Here she is a powerful woman whose concern is for the land. She is young and beautiful, not the old hag who eats children. It will give you more appreciation for the diversity of her character. You can watch it here: https://www.youtube.com/watch?v=9Oc1u4bhTPA.

Baba Yaga and the bird maidens. Ivan Bilibin, 1902.
Public domain, via Wikimedia Commons.

This ancient type of goddess is believed to date back to the time of the hunter-gatherers, when nature provided the means of living, prior to the advent of agriculture. This Mistress of Animals merged with the Great Mother, and so was mother of all living things, not just animals. In the same manner that the fertility goddess did not need a consort; the Mistress of Animals gave birth from the very earth, her womb. This comes from a time when "fertility was thought through women independently from men."[39]

Deity of Death

Death is a part of the cycle of life, and so, a goddess of fertility and birth is not far removed from a goddess of destruction and death. In fact, during the Neolithic period, the fertility goddess people worshiped may have had control over the lifecycle from birth through death.

> This life-and-death-bringing goddess has been called by some the "Goddess of Regeneration." In her life-giving aspect, the "Goddess of Regeneration" was creatrix, bestowing fertility upon the womb and fruitfulness upon the Earth. In her death-giving aspect, she became queen of the Underworld, withdrawing the same life which she had created, and she held responsibility for the wintry barrenness of the Earth.[40]

It's this death aspect that many scholars see as the primary function of Baba Yaga, with her connections to initiation (which you'll read about later in this book) and weather secondary. She is the gatekeeper between the worlds of the living and the dead. She is a guide and instructor to those who wish to reach the "otherworld." She is the "Master of Souls,"[41] giving people life and taking it back.

> The Slavs venerated the underworld goddess by this name [Baba Yaga], representing her as a frightening figure seated in an iron mortar, with an iron pestle in her hands; they made blood sacrifice to her, thinking that she fed it to the two granddaughters they attributed to her, and that she delighted in the shedding of blood herself.[42]

It's debated whether her role as the gatekeeper guarding the border between the worlds of the living and the dead classifies her as a "goddess" of death. Some scholars argue that to be a goddess of death, she would have to exist solely in the realm of the dead. Baba Yaga does not. She lives on the border, neither fully in either world, but part of both. It's argued that she "stands *at* the gates of death, not *behind* them....[D]eath's gatekeeper and death's master are never the same character."[43]

Mother Yoginya

Some people believe that the Great Mother Yogina or Baba Yoga the golden leg, who was the mother of all living things, was the predecessor of the Slavic Baba Yaga.[44] According to Vedical Knowledge (religious texts that originated in ancient India), Yoginya was the eternally beautiful goddess of the forest, the guardian between the worlds of the living and dead. She was kind and set people on the right path. The ancients did not fear her, but revered and loved her. She herself was especially fond of orphaned children and wandered throughout the world on her fiery chariot to gather them to her.[45]

When children were dedicated to the gods, they were dressed in white robes, adorned with flowers, and given herbs to make them sleep. At that point, they were laid in one of two niches in a sacred cave, the one farther from the entrance. Either Mother Yogina or a priest set firewood ablaze in the front niche, supposedly to burn the children, roasting them like in an oven. Some said, after this, the goddess ate them. This latter part has transferred to Baba Yaga.

However, unknown to those who witnessed the events, Mother Yogina lowered a stone wall between the niches to protect the children, her sacrifices. When they awoke, priests and priestesses raised the children as family and taught them the sacred rites. After the children became adults, they returned to the community as priests and priestesses, and no one realized they were the same orphan children left to die.[46]

Priestess

A study claims that various roles Baba Yaga plays (such as, the *benefactor*, who has secret knowledge and tests the hero with riddles before supplying him with gifts; the *kidnapper*; the *warrior*, who has unmatched strength; and the *warden* of the underworld) all point to "Yaga the Priestess, the performer of the ancient rituals."[47]

Perhaps this refers to the old Slavic spring rites of the Suida Baba, where a priestess served the goddess for a year by guarding the sacred fire. On the day when she chose a successor, she smeared herself with soot. As she looked through the village, she blessed people and marked their faces with soot from the temple.[48]

This priestess was associated with transitional rituals, the three "sacred milestones" that brought a person from one stage of life to the next: birth, marriage, and death.

> Yaga did actually play a stabilizing role – the violation of the sacred rituals could possibly shatter the World of men. Hence there appeared a great importance of educating

Baba Yaga. Ivan Bilibin, 1900.
Public domain, via Wikimedia Commons.

and examining the neophytes. Yaga was this educator (again as a mediator between the worlds), who brought harmony into this world and taught people of their social role by showing the initiates the Path of the social Force and the Path of the individual Force. She knew and saw something different from what common people could see and she passed this knowledge to her apprentices.[49]

Other sources say Baba Yaga was a priestess who performed cremation rites for the dead. Not only did she sacrifice cattle, but also concubines were added to the ritual fire.[50]

Shaman

In pre-Christian Russia, Baba Yaga was "the keeper and guardian of the clan and folk traditions."[51] The name "Yaga" in this situation is said to mean "decisive," referring to a woman who makes the decisions.[52] This concept of Baba Yaga may have been centered around the wise old "grandmothers," those women of old who led their communities as shamans or priestesses in early matriarchal societies.

It's interesting to note that sometimes Baba Yaga is depicted as having horns. The same goes for Baba Roga from eastern Slavic folklore. The possible origin of this was due to the fact that these grandmother leaders had stag or bull horns on their ceremonial headdresses. The horns demonstrated their leadership. The larger the headdress, the more power the women had.[53] These horned grandmothers eventually became demonized as dark, night goddesses or witches, with their horns becoming associated with the Devil.

Baba Yaga was often depicted with wearing a *povoinik*, which was a married woman's headdress that could be pointed or horned. This gave her "the appearance of being crowned with a bull's horns or the crescent moon."[54]

Baba Yaga, as a shaman, initiated youths into adulthood with various rites of passage. Suffering and fear were inherent in initiation rituals, which enabled the initiate to overcome his or her old self.

Unlike a goddess of death, who existed within the realm of the underworld, a shaman exists between the world of the living and that of the dead, where the real and magic intermingled. And Baba Yaga likewise resides in this in-between land, acting as a shaman or perhaps "half-goddess." She doesn't belong fully in one world or the other; instead, she is a part of both and can easily transcend from one to the other.

In other ways, Baba Yaga is caught in an in-between world. Neither deity, nor human, but both. A mother, but without a consort. A mother of beasts, but not of humans. And so, she has her feet in both worlds.

She is a male hero's guide to the underworld, the mediator between the worlds, giving him tools and knowledge to make his quest successful. For females, she is the initiator into the sacred rights; the women become her apprentices. To them, she shares her sacred knowledge.

Warrior

In a few stories, Baba Yaga appears as a warrior leading an army of soldiers who are created by tailors, shoemakers, and other artisans. This warrior Yaga was perhaps the Scythian goddess Tabiti, who had many similarities to the Russian Yaga. In appearance, she was a woman or half-woman, half snake. Some say she was the leader of the Amazons, and rode a fiery horse. In addition, she had control over animals and was mistress of the hearth and fire. It's been said that "when her people stopped riding, Tabiti went to live in a little hut deep in a Russian birch forest where she eventually emerged as Baba Yaga."[55]

Where did this warrior Yaga live at first, if not within the forest?

THE FIRST SLAVIC WITCH

The legend that follows tells how the first witch gained her powers.

A beautiful young woman was going through the woods to pick mushrooms. Shortly after, the skies above her became gloomy and it started to rain.

The woman hid beneath a tree, took all of her clothes off, and put them in her bag. The rain finally stopped and she carried on with picking mushrooms.

Suddenly, Veles, the god of the forest (a horned, grand creature) approached her. Mesmerized by her beauty, the god asked her if she knew any magic to protect herself from storms and rain in the forest.

The woman said to Veles that if he showed her the secrets to his magic, she would teach him how to keep dry during storms.

Tempted by her beauty, Veles told her all his magical secrets and then the woman told him how she removed her clothes and hid under the tree. Veles felt tricked and ran off in embarrassment and rage. This is how the first Witch was born (Nikitina).

This one lives beyond the steppe river, by the silken grass at the seaside. Pastures, livestock and herds of excellent horses are constantly mentioned in fairytales. All of this is located somewhere near the mountains with cliffs and ravines either at the seaside or overseas. Apparently, as the author [B.A. Rybakov] implicates, this is the pre-Turkic steppe realm of the Amazons of Cimmerian-Sarmatian origin.

Could well be the case that the armed conflicts between Russian bogatyrs and snake women in the "snake lands" reflect the setting of VIII BC, when male Cimmerians went on campaigns to the Middle East (722-611 BC).

The very means of fighting the bogatyrs, who reached the core of the snake lands, were different from the ones in the Cimmerian period, when there was evident aggression from the Yaga's forces infiltrating Russia; snake women here are no Amazons, no self-sufficient warriors. This is just the women left in the rear with no part in warfare. The means of fighting the bogatyrs here are purely female: snake women turn into ruddy apples, spring water and duvets in order to lure the conquerors and kill them subtly.[56]

The last sentence in the above quote is referencing a fairy tale in which the dragon daughters of Baba Yaga turn into these items in an attempt to trick and devour Ivan and his companions.

Another source connects Baba Yaga with fierce, bloodthirsty warrior tribes that were believed to be cannibals. They lived near Tuapse along the northern shore of the Black Sea and built their homes on the water, and so their dwellings resembled Baba Yaga's hut on chicken legs.[57]

Sergey Mikhaylovich Solovyov (1820-1879), in his *History of Russia from the Earliest Times*, said at one time there were people from Yaga, but they were merged into Russian tribes. These were cannibalistic people who lived in forests. Over time, they became associated with Baba Yaga.[58]

Baba Yaga also makes an appearance as a warrior in mythology. There, she was the young, beautiful daughter of Viy, the ruler of the kingdom of Navi (the underworld). She often traveled to the upper world of the living. Her father was unable to find her a husband because she vowed the only man she would marry would be one who could best her in a duel. The god Veles met her in the upper world after he betrayed Perun and was expelled from the heavens. They battled and he won, and he claimed her as his bride.[59]

Baba Yoga

A few sources say Baba Yaga originally was a yogi, who came from India. Those who believe this cite the following reasons:
- She lives a hermitic lifestyle in the forest.
- Her mortar resembles the yogi's places of worship.
- Their hair is long and shaggy.
- The Nag tribes hold rituals by bonfires and perform sacrifices (*yagya*).
- They smear their bodies with ashes, walk naked with a staff (symbolizing Baba Yaga's bony leg), and repeat mantras.
- They perform rituals with skulls.
- Nags are snakes in their mythology and can have multiple heads.[60]

Alien

One of my favorite theories (because I love bizarre, off-the-wall information) is the belief that Baba Yaga, as well as Koshchei the Deathless, was not originally from Earth. It's easy to see how this would relate to Koshchei, who is an emaciated, skeletal old man. In the controversial Slavic-Aryan Vedas, ancient texts that followers say have been handed down from generation to generation, it says Kashcheis were an extraterrestrial race from the Zen star system, from whom Koshchei gets his name.[61]

In some stories, Baba Yaga and Koshchei are connected, and Baba Yaga falls into the alien category because of her bony leg. People who adhere to this belief say her mortar was a spaceship. It was so small, with no windows or doors, just like her hut, and she had to squeeze into it for long travel.[62] The fact that the chicken hut twirls around also gives the impression of a spinning flying saucer, and the chicken feet are likened to three-pronged landing gear.[63]

Adherents to the alien belief point to a slab found in a Mayan burial chamber, in which a person controls a device that resembles a mortar.[64] The roar this flying mortar made sounded like several women crushing grain in their mortars, and Baba Yaga's sweeping away traces was the fire from the jet engine. And finally, her desire to eat people was her alien nature to understand the composition of the species, with her bubbling cauldron being her chemical laboratory.[65]

Other Suggestions

Other, less common theories exist about Baba Yaga's origins. The following are a few of these ideas.

Devil's Grandmother: The Russian saying of "Go to the devil's grandmother" (*Idi k chertovoi babushka*) had its origins in the fact that Baba Yaga was the devil's grandmother.[66]

Babai Aga: Baba Yaga comes from a Mongol-Tatar Golden Horde tax collector called Babai-Aga, with "Aga" being a rank or title of honor. He was said to have a dreadful face and squinty eyes, and he wore clothing that resembled the attire of females, making it difficult to tell if he was a man or woman. Over time, the character became associated with the feminine "baba" and subsequently, Baba Yaga.[67]

Cooked in a Devil's Cauldron: An account of Baba Yaga's origin also occurs in a collection of literary fairy tales by Vasilii Levshin [*Russian Fairy Tales, Russkie skazki*, published in 1780]. In this account, the devil created her by cooking twelve evil women in a cauldron. It's unknown whether Levshin created this story or took it from oral accounts. You can read his full tale in the "Baba Yaga Tales" section at the end of this book.

From Goddess to Witch

You may think a witch is the opposite of a goddess. She is, after all, a demon, isn't she, or at least one who calls on her satanic powers? Actually, no. As you'll discover later, those who were called witches among the Slavs had no dealings with the Devil, although the evil ones might use dark arts. Instead, a witch and a goddess may be "inseparably integrated," with the witch being the crone aspect of the goddess. At least that is a theory supported by proponents of modern-day goddess worshipers, who reconnect the goddess and witch and claim the power of both.

So, how did a goddess become a witch?

As myths of the old deities collided with the advent of Christianity, the old and new intermingled, at least within the Orthodox church. The church attempted to eliminate them, but they were too ingrained in the beliefs and customs of the people. It was easier to transform the main gods and goddesses into saints instead.

But what could they do with the crone and all those secondary deities, in particular those of a chthonic nature, who represented "life events"?[68] The church leaders could not put a positive spin on any being that dealt with death and the underworld. That would be glorifying Satan and his hordes. The solution was to demonize the crone and others like her.

Baba Yaga. Сергей Панасенко-Михалкин, 1990. CC BY-SA 3.0 <https://creativecommons.org/licenses/by-sa/3.0>, via Wikimedia Commons.

The witch, although in a sense a mortal follower of the chthonic goddess, was also herself a transmutation of the more ancient goddess. Whereas the powers over both life and death were natural to the prehistoric goddess, her powers over death were feared by many of the assimilating historical male-centered cultures. Her vast powers were detrited into negative magic that a clever hero, or anyone who knew the proper apotropaic chant, might hope to avoid. The witch was generally a woman, and always a person with connections to the Underworld. She could be old or young, ugly or beautiful.[69]

Another factor that contributed to the crone becoming a witch was the fact she would not willingly submit to a male-centric world. She had power over death and life, and she meant to keep it.

What made some goddesses assimilate into saints while others were demoted to witches?

A HISTORICAL NOTE

Folklore reflects the society that created it. And their cultural norms dictate what is good or bad. Baba Yaga didn't escape these judgments. The system of dvoeverie (double faith), the acceptance of Christianity on top of pagan beliefs, helped keep beings like Baba Yaga alive, while male deities fell into obscurity. But being kept alive did not mean remaining the same. This once-upon-a-time goddess fell all the way to wicked witch as Christian patrilineal societies replaced pagan or matrilineal ones.

Baba Yaga has been politicized as well. Stories in which she appears make frequent references to tsars of Russia. Men were bogatyrs, valiant warriors, of a type reserved for nobility. In these stories, however, a clever peasant could climb the social ladder and find himself a prince or tsar himself if he possessed the same heroic skills. Women, too, had their social roles—being the good wife, and they could obtain a title of royalty, that of the tsar's wife, if they played the game right. Baba Yaga did her best to give both men and women the tools they needed to achieve their goals.

Because of the fairy tales' connection to the tsardom, in the late-1920s through 1930s, the Soviet government attempted to eradicate traditional folktales. They would not tolerate having Imperial Russia glorified (Johnson, 11). Baba Yaga in particular was vilified and removed from acceptable stories as folklore was redefined (Johnson, 49).

Folklorists themselves did not escape the Soviet scrutiny. Some sources say Vladimir Propp, leading Russian folklorist, "yielded to communist pressure and abandoned his 'genuine' commitment to true scholarship" and that his studies were "considered heretical in the Soviet Union." Others say he was "never censored by the Soviet academy or government" (Propp, ix, x).

In any event, it wasn't until World War II that Baba Yaga once again gained popularity, when she went from being used for anti-Soviet propaganda to anti-German propaganda (Johnson, 11). And now she is becoming more well-known to the Western world in all her folklore glory.

[T]hey all possessed one characteristic in common: they were autonomous; they possessed powers which were not controlled by men. They were thus, in one way, a projection of men's fears, fears of energies which they did not control. Whereas virgins and matrons have been tied to the patriarchal culture, and have given energy in some form to man, the witch, whether old, depleted woman or simply woman who has reserved her powers for herself, has not been possessed by the patriarchy. Patriarchal men have always feared powerful women.[70]

And so, the crone became the powerful, but evil, Baba Yaga, who had a morbid taste for children.

Appearance

The most common description of Baba Yaga is that of a hideous, hunchbacked, scrawny old woman. Her white or gray hair is disheveled and matted, and it hangs loose. Sometimes she covers her hair with a black headscarf or a horned *povoinik*, a married woman's headdress. Her clothing is in tatters, and she wears only an unbelted long garment.

She has bony, clawed hands. On the rest of her body, her bones poke out in places, perhaps like an exoskeleton. Her most prominent features are her long hooked nose (sometimes said to be blue), which may be made of iron; her sharp iron tooth or teeth that can devour anything; and one ordinary leg and one bony one. In some stories, she's described as having one leg and hops around. Her bony leg is completely devoid of flesh. It may be made of clay, wood, iron, gold, silver, tin, steel, or the polished thighbone of a young boy.

Her eyes glow and flash red, and some people say she is blind. Her face has been described as clay, furry, or mangy. In addition, her giant breasts, which may be made of iron, hang down to her waist or lower. When she's lying in her hut, she tosses them over a rod or onto shelves, or she may throw them over her shoulders when she rushes about.

A narrative poem, "Baba Yaga and the Bony Leg," written by Nikolai Nekrasov in 1840, describes her as wearing a toadskin cap and a snake coat. She has fangs, huge ears, horns on her forehead, holes where her eyes should be, and nostril hairs that hang down to her breasts.[71] In another tale, her appearance resembles magic horses, with smoke billowing from her nostrils, flames shooting from her mouth, and sparks flying from her ears.[72]

Some people claim she is a giant or grossly misshapen, due to the fact she takes up the entirety of her hut, stretched from one corner to the next, with her nose literally grown into the ceiling, raking coals, or closing up the chimney. She's able to sweep her tongue into her oven and cleans the floor with one lip. Others claim she is ordinary size, or quite tall or large, but because her hut is small, it's confining. When the hero enters her hut, he finds "an old woman, large and very scary."[73]

There is never any mention that a hero feels confined or crowded in Baba Yaga's hut, so it's likely she was oversized. Regardless, she's large enough that her hut shakes as Baba Yaga snores and farts in her sleep.

Baba Yaga is also a shapeshifter, changing into enormous sizes: a cat as big as a haystack, a pig that drags one tusk into the ground and the other in the sky, a dragon. It's this latter image of her that traces back to earlier forms. Here, she's so large she can have one lip on the ground and the other reaching into the heavens.

> ## Did you know?
>
> A version of Baba Yaga known as the "Iron Tooth" carries live coals in a pitcher and burns distaffs of lazy spinners (Ralston, *The Songs of the Russian People*, 164).

Lubok of Baba-Yaga dancing with old man. Unknown author, mid-18th century.
Public domain, via Wikimedia Commons.

An evocative description of her, that takes into account her zoomorphic features, follows:

> A toad-like creature with gnarled arms like tree trunks clutches a massive pestle and a spindly broom in dark brown claws. Protruding from the top of a wooden mortar, the old crone squats, her thin lips as downcast as her dark eyes. Wild strings of mangy hair fly out behind her. Around her, toadstools rise up, red and plump in contrast to her jerky-dry skin.[74]

She can also shift into inanimate objects. And, in stories from Poland and Ukraine, she may appear as a beautiful young woman who is a seductress. In any event, Baba Yaga is certainly someone you'd remember if you saw her. There's more to her looks, however, than meets the eye. Scholars and folklorists have written much about the significance of her appearance.

Bony Leg

You may wonder: Was Baba Yaga's leg really just a bone? Perhaps the word was simply used to complete a rhyme, in the same way that many other traditional fairy-tale phrases about the witch rhyme:

Baba Yaga Bony Leg, which in Russian is *Baba iaga kostianaia noga*. Another thought is that her bony leg was a way to designate her as being extremely skinny, like the saying that someone is all skin and bones. It's also quite possible her leg literally had no flesh.

If indeed one leg had flesh and the other lacked it, this difference between them is another aspect that connects her to both the land of the living and that of the dead. In addition, her bony leg (as well as one-leggedness, which indicates lameness) also connects her with snakes, and, ultimately, the land of the dead.

> K.D. Laushkin derives the following rule: "if there's something wrong with the mythical creature's legs, there's a snake at the bottom of it" or "if the mythical creature bears relation to snakes, there's something amiss with his legs."[75]

For this latter observation, it's important to go back to prototypes of Baba Yaga (and other such deities). Many mythological creatures sported animal legs. Since Baba Yaga was connected with death, the animal legs transformed into a bone one, a dead man's leg.

Her snakelike form is also especially relevant to this bony leg analysis. Over time, the appearance of snake deities transformed. First, they were completely snakes, eventually evolving into part human with a snake tail. From there, the pseudo-human with a slithering snake tail became a hobbling person with a single or deformed foot or leg. As time progressed further, that deity could transform into a being with two functional legs.[76] This lame creature is called a *tsmok*, snake, in Belarusian tales. In some stories, Baba Yaga turns back into a snake before she dies.

Did you know?

In folk belief, a Nav bone has an association with Baba Yaga. This is a bone "that appears in a person's body because of some transgression and becomes the cause of their death" (Nikolskaya).

Blindness

Although it's never stated in fairy tales, some scholars believe that Baba Yaga is blind or visually impaired because of the emphasis on her keen sense of smell. They believe that "blindness represents her inability to see the living (the hero), just as the living are unable to see the dead."[77]

However, in many tales, she must be able to see. How else would she know if the heroes and heroines accomplished their tasks? And the hero definitely can see her, even before Baba Yaga performs any initiation rites (more on this later). Not only that, but in some tales, the hero is hiding inside her hut, or Baba Yaga's daughter has changed him into an inanimate object, thus masking his smell, and so Baba Yaga would neither see nor smell him.

Sense of Smell

In many of the tales about Baba Yaga, you'll find her familiar statement about a Russian scent: "Fu, fu! It smells of this Russian scent" (*Fu, fu, russkim dukhom pakhnet*). The word "dush" can also mean "spirit" or "breath." In some instances, "Russian scent" becomes "Russian bone." This reminds the reader of the witch's connection to death from her association with bones. This sense of smell is another attribute that is ascribed to the dead. With Baba Yaga having such a long nose, it's no wonder she could smell an uninvited guest.

In a second part of Baba Yaga's statement, she mentions she hasn't seen the Russian scent in this place (*slykhom ne slykhat', vidom ne vidat'*). But *slykh* can also refer to hearing, making the meaning of the phrase possibly "not heard with the hearing," instead of "not smelled with the scent."[78]

However, the mention of Russian scent is mostly absent in stories from Ukraine, Belarus, and other nationalities. Perhaps this is because, as one source has suggested, "it may be the exclamation in question occurred in a land invaded by the Russians, and was afterwards inserted in Russian tales."[79] Her hostility to visitors who reek of Russian scent has also given rise to the belief that Baba Yaga was integrated with a Samoyed deity of Death (Nga).[80]

Another thought is that Baba Yaga's sense of Russian smell or spirit indicates she can sniff out whether a hero or heroine has good moral qualities.[81]

This sense of smell also points back to her animal origins. Like an animal, she can detect intruders by their scent.

An additional thought about what the Russian scent or spirit refers to comes from the nomadic Ob Ugrians.

> The tar, which was widely used by the Russians for preservation treatment of leather shoes, harnessing, and ship tackles, irritated the sensitive sense of smell of the taiga dwellers, which used goose and fish oils to treat their shoes. A guest wearing boots who entered the yurta was smeared with smell of tar and left behind a persistent odor of the "Russian spirit."[82]

Most sources, however, believe the Russian scent Baba Yaga speaks about is the odor of the living, which offends or even frightens the dead.

Appetite

Baba Yaga has an insatiable appetite that goes beyond her cannibalism or her threat to eat visitors. She has an abundance of grain, meat, and drinks that she has her female visitors prepare for her. Even though Baba Yaga gorges down her meals, she forever remains skin and bones.

She perhaps gets more nourishment from the souls of the dead, which Death itself brings to her. This is supposed to make her and other witches become as light as the spirits she consumes.

Having a voracious appetite is also symbolic of sexual desire, enslavement, or empowerment.[83] In addition to this, the eating of someone's flesh and the subsequent rolling in his bones was a way to gain the victim's vitality, since Slavs believed the soul resided in the bones. Contact with bones was a way to gain great power.

> The goal of such use is defined in two ways: when they serve as a means for the conquering of powers or features of someone or something outside themselves, the bones are an intermediary between this and the other world, an agent freeing the chthonic forces, channeling them and securing their controlled effect; when, however, the activities with bones are aimed at the bones themselves, the used means have different origin, and the expected goal is to activate the vital force which they carry in themselves, namely – the resurrection. In the fairy tales – and, of course, in folklore at large – it is possible to find both examples.[84]

Baba Yaga had to eat away the perishable flesh in order to get down to the essence of her victim. The bones were the only "true connection with the eternal world of ancestors and, therefore, the only valid instrument for acquiring and transmitting knowledge from one world into the other."[85] In the eyes of the world, this taking of the energies of others made her an evil witch.[86] The ritual of rolling in bones was also often accompanied by her uttering a formulaic text like the following: "Let me rock, let me roll over Žiharko's bones!"

It's uncertain what, if any, original ritual this may have been derived from. In the Slavic culture, the act of rolling, not in bones, but in dew, signifies "a ritualistic communication with earth aimed at providing good crop and survival," as well as health, fertility, and prosperity.[87] These celebrations also occur during holidays in which families communicate with the souls of the ancestors, so "direct contact with the earth (rolling), is not only chthonic (which by definition it is), but also communication with the dead."[88]

Iron Features

Baba Yaga's claws, teeth, leg, nose, and breasts all can be made of iron. In Slavic stories, iron is an attribute of the world of the dead, the otherworld, because it is cold, immovable, and doesn't grow. In

Baba-Yaga. H J Ford, 1890.
Public domain, via Wikimedia Commons.

addition, it relates to the dead because it is retrieved from under the ground and from swamps, both places that are hostile to humans. Iron body parts not only indicate a being is not from the living world, but also that these features are "a privilege of 'high-ranking' magical creatures" and therefore signal that the being has an "elevated sacral status."[89] This is in contrast to iron being used to ward off other malicious creatures like water spirits and vampires, the unclean dead, who did not have a sacred position.

Loose-Flowing Hair

In ancient beliefs, and perhaps even today, loose, unbound hair held magical powers and made the strongest charms. It was also believed that fertility resided in one's hair, so long, thick hair was a desirable attribute for a woman. "Proper" Slavic women braided their hair—unmarried women with one braid and married with two.

The hair of the bride was left loose only on two occasions. First, on her wedding day, her hair was unbraided and left that way until after she was married, when it was braided in two strands and wrapped around her head. In addition, a married woman covered her hair with a head scarf—to cover that fertility, which was meant solely for her husband to see. The other time a woman's hair was unfastened was for her burial. Rituals and the funeral procession mimicked that of the wedding. These were both considered "liminal" times in a woman's life, a time of transition, an "in-between" world.

So, what does that say about Baba Yaga? Fairy tales hint at her hair being unfastened.[90] Is it merely a sign that she is a witch? Or is her hair loose because of her connection with death?

Getting to Know Baba Yaga

Before diving deeper into the character of Baba Yaga, it's necessary to define what the words "Baba Yaga" mean in the fairy tales in the first place. This is not about the etymology, as that has already been discussed. This is about whether Baba Yaga was a unique person or a general classification to describe a scary old woman.

A few facts point to the latter. First, her name is not capitalized in stories. Second, Russian, Ukrainian, and Belarusian, lack the articles "a" and "the," so it is uncertain whether the story is talking about "Baba Yaga," "*a* Baba Yaga," or "*the* Baba Yaga."[91] And third, at times the fairy tales contain three Baba Yagas, who are sisters, all with the same name.

The series of three is common in Indo-European folklore. The hero meets each character in turn, but never all at the same time. What distinguishes one Baba Yaga from the next is age, strength, knowledge, or some other attribute. It may even be a physical characteristic: "the first Baba Yaga has 'a wooden leg, a pewter eye'; the second, 'a bone leg, a silver eye'; the third has a 'steel leg, golden eye.' "[92] When they appear in threes, these Baba Yagas in general are good characters, who willingly help the hero along in his journey by providing advice or magical gifts. But that is not always the case. One of the sisters, the last visited, may try to hinder or kill him.

The name "Baba Yaga" may also be a euphemism for a being whose name was either too evil or too sacred to be spoken, thereby pointing to her original demonic or godly nature.

Habitat

If you dare venture into Baba Yaga's territory and can overcome your fear, you'll discover her residence is fraught with symbolism. Not only the location, but also her abode, her transportation, and the beings that are her helpers.

Forest

Traditionally, Baba Yaga lives in the deep forest, a place filled with treasures and mystery that many believe holds secret knowledge. Her residence is always at the entrance to the lands of the dead, and no one can pass without Baba Yaga's permission or some magic object that lets them escape her.

One fact that points to her goddess status rather than that of a witch is that it was more common for ancient Slavic people to worship in the woods rather than at shrines. In Proto-Slavic, these woods were called *gaje*. A fence might encircle the sacred area, and it could also contain a cemetery as well.[93]

The deep forest as Baba Yaga's home is especially true in stories where she helps the hero and heroine. Many tales, however, do not specify where she lives. On occasion, you'll find her dwelling in other locations: the underworld, the sky, the edge of the thrice-ninth kingdom within the castle with her daughter, near the fiery Smorodina River, or perhaps even in a swamp, open field, or seashore. In one story, Ivan travels for three months until "he came to a place where his horse was in water up to the knees, and in grass up to the breast," at which place he found Baba Yaga's miserable hut.[94] All of these places were borderlands, liminal locations where evil spirits roamed free. These are places of "mystery, magical beliefs, and life-threatening experiences. Or the pit, the most somber part of the human soul."[95]

Forests for the early Slavs were an important source of provisions: wood, herbs, food, honey, furs, and more. As agriculture began to take root, however, forests and the religion associated with them became something evil.[96] The forest became a place of terror for anyone who didn't know how to survive within it. It was vastly different from their familiar world. A child's entrance into the forest often led to his death if he became lost or injured or drowned in a swamp. Other dangers were being attacked by an animal or eating poisonous berries or mushrooms.

Scientists have suggested that eastern Slavic tribes encountered forests as they traveled north and east from their homeland. As they had never seen them before, the dense wooded areas were considered hostile places.[97] Stories about wicked wood spirits and the dreaded witch Baba Yaga grew from their fears and anxiety.

Symbolically, a forest is the world of the subconscious, and entering the woods represents "a journey into one's soul."[98] It's the unknown, the dark side of life, and contains the shadows of death. Baba Yaga lives alone, far away from any community, which is symbolic of her being on the border of consciousness, as you'll discover if you look more closely at the meaning of the words "deep forest."

> The witch's hut is always found deep in the forest, which in the original is "les dremúchyi" or its plural, "lesá dremúchiye." The first word translates rather conveniently as woods or the more preferable "forest." The word "dremúchiye" in modern Russian means "dense" or "thick," but coming from the root of such words as "dremóta" or "dremát'," it means drowsiness or slumber and lends itself to interpretation as a dream world or realm of the unconscious.[99]

In addition to being considered the border of consciousness, deep forests also have an association with women called witches. It's a place where they lived, far from others. They gathered roots and herbs to use for healing. Although these women were not bent on evil, they were often feared, because the community believed the women communicated with evil spirits.

Chicken Hut

If there's one thing about Baba Yaga that's easily recognizable, it's her iconic hut (*izba*), a traditional peasant house built of wood.

> The *izbá*, or hut, always has a *dvor* or courtyard, access to which is gained through double gates as well as through a postern. Often the hut is raised by a flight of steps from the level of the courtyard.[100]

What distinguishes Baba Yaga's hut from traditional ones is that hers stands on between one and four chicken legs (*izbushka na kur'ikh nozhkakh*). Less common, goat legs, ram horns, rooster heads, a dog's shin or paws, or spindle heels may hold up the hut. A proverb indicates her hut is covered with pancakes (*bliny*) and propped up with pies (*pirogi*), which are symbols of death, because they are funeral foods. Not quite as pleasant, in the story about the Tsar Maiden, the hut stands in fresh manure.

Like Baba Yaga and the forest location, the hut does not belong to either the world of the living or the dead, but is a mix of both. It's position high above the ground sets it apart from normal huts: the living reside on the ground, and the dead beneath it, but the hut is in neither location.

Additionally, although it's a wooden structure and should be inanimate; instead, it is alive and mobile, turning and spinning. Sometimes, the hut is described as having no door or windows. At other times, these portals appear suddenly, blinking and glowing like a feral beast. The windows are eyes through which the hut can see, and its doorway is a mouth through which it can speak.

It's possible the hut can even think as it understands words and always obeys when it's commanded to turn. It does so seemingly reluctantly, emitting blood-curdling screeches as it turns and spins. Or perhaps this reaction shows how old the hut is, and moving is painful. It may even indicate that Baba Yaga doesn't take care of the hut the way she should.[101]

Looking for prey. Nelinda, 2022.

Other parts of Baba Yaga's residence are also alive. In some stories, she commands the gate to prevent her captives from escaping. However, when a heroine pours oil on the gate's hinges and ties a ribbon around a tree, they both disobey their mistress and make their own decisions. The gate and tree also speak to Baba Yaga when the witch scolds them.

> The gate wanted to slam on her [the escaping girl]; she poured some oil under the hinges, and it let her pass. The birch tree wanted to lash her eyes out; she tied it back with a ribbon, and it let her pass. …
>
> Baba Yaga threw herself … on the gates, on the birch tree, … [and] started scolding each one and pounding them. …
>
> The gate said, "I've been serving you for so long, and you've never even poured water under my hinges, but she poured some oil."
>
> The birch tree said, "I've been serving you so long, and you've never tied me up with a thread, but she tied me up with a ribbon."[102]

Does this chicken hut signify anything, or is it created from the imagination of a story-teller long ago? It's uncertain, but one possible meaning is that it is a remnant of past nomadic life, where dwellings were made of constructions that were light and easy to move.[103]

The fence that surrounds Baba Yaga's hut is unique as well. It's constructed of human bones, topped with skulls with glowing eye sockets. Is this the aftereffects of a macabre slaughter and feast by a cannibalistic witch? Or could it be something that aligns Baba Yaga with her role as the one who guides souls to the otherworld?

When a family member died, it was a common practice to light a candle in the home in order to enable the soul of the deceased to find his way back. Perhaps this was how Baba Yaga guided souls to herself. The bone fence and gate are also symbolic of death to oneself, requiring any who enter to "leave all humanly/earthly attachments behind."[104]

Often a story states there are twelve of these skull-topped posts, with only one that is lacking a head. That one, according to Baba Yaga, is waiting for the newest hero to fail in his assigned task. The gate to her hut is just as gruesome. Human legs make up the gate posts, arms and hands are the bolts, and a jaw with sharp teeth serves as the lock.

One source relates these skulls on the fence as having a Celtic origin and point to a time when stories of Baba Yaga may have originated.

> Skulls on stakes around the temple provides us with the exact dating of the tale. The cult of decollated heads has Celtic origin. It did not gain popularity among the Slavs and was almost forgotten. For example, Lucice people, having killed the Mecklenburg Bishop John, cut off his head, put it on a spear, and this way dedicated it to Radigost. The Celts attributed special vital and magical qualities to the head. In the fairy tale, the skulls not only glow with fire, but also talk like severed heads talk in Celtic legends. The only period of Slavic history when the Celtic culture was prevalent among the Slavs was the age of Przeworsk archaeological culture (second century BC – fourth to fifth century AD).[105]

You already know that Baba Yaga lives on the borderland, but you may not realize that it is her hut that is the portal through which heroes must pass in order to traverse the land of the dead. When people arrive, the hut faces the forest, that is, the land of the dead. The hero or heroine cannot walk around and enter from that side. Beyond the hut is only pitch darkness. As the visitors are not dead, they must enter from the side where living creatures reside. It is essential to utter a traditional phrase to turn the hut

House of death. Nicholas Roerich, 1905.
Public domain, via Wikimedia Commons.

around, so that the visitor may enter. It's interesting to note that everyone who arrives knows what to say to achieve this.

> In the mythical vocabulary there are not only names but also phrases that may look common on the surface yet imply sacred or magical references to the power of gods and other supernatural beings.[106]

The charms to turn the house possibly at one time had more magical meaning. One charm is "Hut, hut! Stand with your back to the forest, your front to me" (*Izbushka, izbushka! Stan' k lesu zadom, a ko mne peredom*). On occasion, the hero Ivan may blow on the hut as he recites the magical words. The approaching hero may also say to the hut, "Hut, hut, turn your eyes to the forest, and the gate to me: I do not live forever, but spend one night. Let the passerby go."[107] An alternate phrase is to tell the hut to "Stand the old way, the way mother put you" (*Stan' po staromu, kak mat' postavila*). The word "mother" here may have an association with the Mother Goddess or Forest Mother, with whom Baba Yaga has connections.

The hut may also be spinning. In a Belorussian version, the hut is told to *stand still*, keep its eyes toward the forest and its gate toward the visitor: *Ostoisia, izbusbetska, k lesu glazami, k mene vorotami.*

How has this spinning been interpreted?

It suggests a connection to the world tree, which unites heaven, earth, and the underworld.[108] The hut's ability to move around can also exemplify the "weirdness and instability of her [Baba Yaga's] nature." The rotating hut can look in every direction, symbolizing the vast knowledge Baba Yaga has access to.[109] Also, the spinning of the hut may be connected to the phases of the moon, with Baba Yaga being a moon goddess.

> When the moon is full, the opening points to the west, and the charnel hut is accessible to the living. The Yaga who sits in the house is like the full moon, pregnant and healthy. But when the night skies show only a crescent like the horns of a headless sacrificed bull, Yaga no longer lives in the hut. It is as empty as her barren belly.[110]

Vladimir Propp, however, says that the spinning of the hut is a contamination of the tale. The hut's purpose was to act as a sentry to guard access to the land of the dead. When Ivan or another visitor tells the hut to turn, it does so. Propp says, "This 'turned' has become 'keeps turning around,' and the expression, 'When it has to, it turns this way and that' has become 'It turns all the time,' which even if vivid is meaningless."[111]

Let's look now at the significance of the chicken legs.

Baba Yaga's hut has a possible connection with the burial practices of ancient Slavic, Finno-Ugric, and other ethnicities. In these rituals, the ashes of the deceased were placed in small wooden structures, *domovynas*, which means "coffins," which were shaped like huts.[112] These structures stood on short poles to protect them from flooding[113] and had circular fences around them.[114] The word "chicken legs" (*kur'i nozhki*) possibly came from the word for "smoke-stained" (*kurnyye*), that is, fumigated with smoke. This refers to the pillars on which the hut stood,[115] since they were smoked with incense to keep them from rotting and to deter insects.[116]

Did you know?

A crossroad or a fork in the road was called a "chicken leg." This was an unclean place where evil spirits liked to gather (Ulasevich).

Other sources say it was not the ashes, but the deceased himself who was buried in the hut. The feet were located near a hole in the floor, which was the only access point to the hut. The body was left in the hut until it dried out, leaving only bones.[117] Therefore, anyone looking up would see only the bony leg.[118]

Some ancients believed that the soul of the departed did not proceed to the afterlife until the body had decomposed.[119] And so they built a similar, but smaller ceremonial cabin on top of a tree stump as a place to hold a wooden or bone-carved doll that represented their gods. The dolls were dressed in national fur clothing, and took up the entire cabin.

The dolls "served as a container for the soul of the departed until it was reborn in a child."[120] The dolls remained in the houses for one to two years. They were thought of as family members and had to be fed and put to bed. If the person was revered or a shaman, the dolls may have been left at home or brought to a sacred place in the forest.[121]

The doll filling the entire cabin brings to mind Baba Yaga stretched out inside her small hut.[122] Another interpretation of Baba Yaga's restricted mobility in her hut is that it represents a child in the

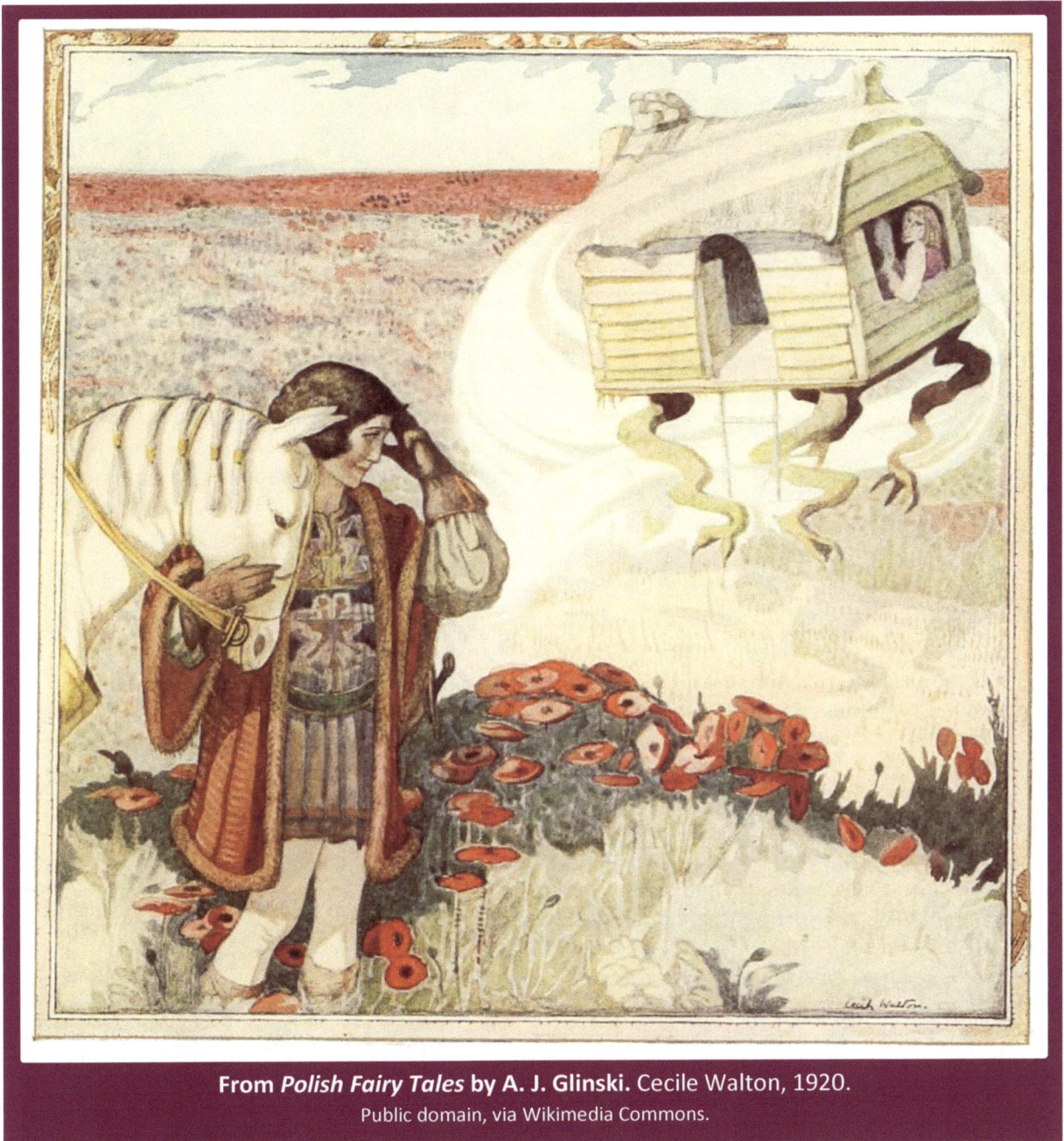

From *Polish Fairy Tales* by A. J. Glinski. Cecile Walton, 1920.
Public domain, via Wikimedia Commons.

womb. Or possibly a "reflection of infantile experience," such as a swaddled child who is constrained.[123] On the other spectrum, it can also reflect death, with Baba Yaga confined in a coffin.

On a more practical nature, the hut on chicken legs resembles Sami storehouses built on stilts made from tree stumps. Nomadic hunter-gatherers from Siberia used a similar log-cabin construction for storing gear and supplies to keep them safe from animals during times the people were away. They built it to a height of eight to ten feet from the ground, supporting the structure on the stumps of two or three trees that grew close together. The roots gave it the appearance of having chicken legs. This cabin lacked doors and windows, with access to the inside available from a trapdoor in the floor.[124] In addition, "[t]hese tree stands are always positioned 'with the back turned to the forest and the front turned to the traveler' so that the entrance can be approached from a river or a wood trail."[125]

Mortar and Pestle

Whenever the wind rages and the trees moan, look to the sky. What do you see? It could be Baba Yaga flying through the air in her wooden or iron mortar (*stupa*), rowing it with her pestle (*pestik*), and brushing away all traces of her activity with a fiery or silver birch broom (*pomelo*): *v stupe edet, pestom pogoniaet, pomelom sled zametaet.* She may also ride on an oven fork, a shovel, or a broom. Such an odd sight. If you're thinking this scene must have some symbolism, you're right.

These peasant mortars were tall, narrow, and deep. Although they were capable of holding much grain, they weren't large enough for an adult to sit in. Folklore scholars have suggested that Baba Yaga did not originally fly through the air on her mortar.[126] Instead, according to folk tradition, she used it as a horse.[127] In this way, she would use the broom to wipe away actual traces along the ground, so that her path couldn't be traced.

> **Did you know?**
>
> Baba Yaga flies on her mortar through her chimney to gain access to her house (Mythoslavic).

The mortar, pestle, and broom were common tools women used in the household. These, along with other instruments used with the hearth and cooking—poker, baking shovel—also played a role in Baba Yaga stories. Although basic tools in everyday life, they took on magical qualities in fairy tales. Connected to both life and death, they could be used as instruments to either nurture or destroy.

Stupa is related to the word "stomp" and refers to the grinding action of a pestle in a mortar. The traditional use of mortars was not to fly in, but rather to crush grains or flax, to combine herbs and roots for cooking, and to create medicine or concoctions to ward off evil or perform other magical spells for good. This latter concept connects Baba Yaga to being a healer or *znahar*. (More about this topic later.)

The pestle may have been a tool Baba Yaga used well before the mortar became her iconic image. In some instances, she uses her pestle as a staff to beat people, such as in the stories where she turns men to stone. In folklore, a pestle is a tool of transformation. This sacred, magical item beat down diseases, pounding sickness into health.[128] In much the same way, Baba Yaga "transforms" the hero, although not directly with those implements.

Pomelo, Baba Yaga's broom, was originally an old word for a tool bakers used to sweep out ovens.[129] Is this what Baba Yaga uses after she cooks her supposed victims?

> **Did you know?**
>
> According to folk tradition, if you eat chicken legs, you cannot remain silent; you must tell the truth (Petrova, 440).

When she's flying and wiping away the traces of her flight, however, it possibly has a deeper meaning. Although she may not be dead, Baba Yaga is a part of the world of the deceased. And in that world, it is common for whirlwinds and storms to wipe away footprints of spirits. When Baba Yaga sweeps away traces of her journey, she removes the ability of the living to follow in her path. If they wish to find her, they must do so at her hut, not on her travels, where she scours the world for souls or victims.

Also, the broom may symbolize that a connection with and direct contact to the spirits of the decease are no longer possible.[130] This is based on a burial custom. When Slavic people accompanied the dead to their resting place, they covered up tracks the wheels of the cart made in the dirt to hide the route back.[131] This was a way to prevent the deceased from returning to torment those they knew in life.

Old Woman with mortar. Alexey Fedorovich Protopopov, 1878.
Public domain, via Wikimedia Commons.

These household instruments have additional meanings. Sometimes, Baba Yaga's mortar is made from wood. In this case, the mortar, like other wooden objects, including at times her leg, is a symbol of "prosperity, knowledge, health, happiness and life." The reason for this is that trees themselves have these qualities, and so objects made from them retain these attributes.[132]

When the mortar is made from iron, however, it is symbolic of a storm cloud. The pestle striking it is thunder. As Baba Yaga gathers with other witches on their favorite haunt, Bald Mountain, they boil rain water in their mortar-kettles under raging fires, and lightning flashes.[133]

Some say the mortar is symbolic of her coffin, and Baba Yaga can only travel this way, because she herself is a corpse that cannot move on her own.[134] The mortar-coffin refers to a Slavic burial custom from the tenth century where the deceased were wrapped in birch bark. Around the twelfth century, people began to bury the dead in oak logs that were hollowed out and called "stupas." These types of coffins existed until the beginning of the eighteenth century, when Peter I prohibited oak trees from being cut down on penalty of death.[135]

Did you know?

Baba Yaga may fly in her mortar, but the dead fly on coffins (Ustinova, 5).

The mortar and pestle also have sexual connotations, representing the womb and phallus. In this way, they connect Baba Yaga to fertility, like ancient goddesses. In folk rites, a woman sat on a mortar so she would conceive a daughter, and on a pestle for a son.[136] Also, marriage customs have a connection to the mortar and pestle.

> During the wedding ritual, the midwife threshed water in a mortar, and this was a symbol of the penetration of the masculine into the feminine. And water was chosen because any new life is born in it.[137]

In fairy tales, Baba Yaga has a role of initiating youths into adulthood, and so her instruments symbolize "the confrontation to the Baba Yaga, the arising power of reproduction. The 'erasing' broom can in this case symbolize the cleansing, after the act."[138]

Helpers

Baba Yaga has various types of helpers, living and inanimate (which really aren't that inanimate after all, because they can talk and move). One of their main functions is to prevent her victims from escaping or to chase after them when they do. Often, this backfires when her so-called helpers fail to assist. All it takes is a small amount of compassion from the victim for Baba Yaga's helpers to turn face and let the children go, such as giving a handkerchief to a servant, tying a ribbon around a birch tree, oiling gate hinges, and giving rolls to dogs and bacon to a cat.

Baba Yaga's helper may even conspire against her and be an accomplice in the victim's escape, such as the cat in "The Baba Yaga" who gives the girl a magic comb and towel with instructions on how to use them, and then the cat pretends to be the girl weaving so she can sneak away. (You can read the full story at the end of this book.)

Other animals, in particular birds, are truer to their mistress. Geese and swan carry away children and bring them to Baba Yaga, such as in the story of "The Geese and Swans" where a girl is left in charge of her younger brother, but she forgets and he's kidnapped.

> She caught sight of the geese and swans far away, and then they disappeared beyond the dark forest. These geese and swans had had a bad reputation for a long time; they did a lot of harm and would steal little children. The girl guessed that they were the ones who had taken away her brother, and she ran off after them.[139]

Even after the girl rescues her brother, the birds chase her, trying to return the boy to Baba Yaga.

But did the swans truly have a bad reputation? Geese most certainly do, but most often, swans are portrayed as divine creatures, good and proud. Would such pure animals serve an evil woman? The argument has been made that the fact that swans are Baba Yaga's helpers means she isn't such a bad old crone.[140]

Swan-Geese. Franz Teichel, 19th century.
Public domain, via Wikimedia Commons.

At other times, the animals at Baba Yaga's command willingly help the hero with her blessing. Birds, like the eagle, raven, and crow, which are connected to shamans, point to her mystical side, her wisdom of the ages. In the story "The Three Kingdoms—Copper, Silver, and Gold," she tells the hero stranded in the underworld how to approach an eagle so he can return home.

Then Ivashko said, "Here's why, granny. The powerful Idol told me to come and ask you for a mighty eagle-bird, so it could carry me out to Rus'."

"You go along into the garden," said the Yega Baba. "There's a guard standing beside the doors, and you take the keys from him and go through seven doors. When you open the last door, then the eagle will start to beat its wings, and if you aren't frightened, you climb up on it and fly. Only take some beef with you, and every time it starts to look back you give it a piece of meat."[141]

Baba Yaga, the three Yaga sisters, or sometimes an unnamed old woman have at their command all the animals. Each woman merely needs to call, and the creatures will swarm toward her, ready to obey her command. The Baba Yagas summon the animals of the earth, the birds of the air, and the fish of the sea, as in the story "Go I Don't Know Where, Bring I Don't Know What."

> The old woman went out onto the porch, called in a loud voice, and suddenly—where did they come from?—all kinds of beasts ran up, and all kinds of birds came flying. "Greetings, forest beasts and birds of the air! You beasts search everywhere, you birds fly everywhere: have you heard how to get I don't know where and to bring back I don't know what?"
> …
> The old woman called with a loud voice, and all the monsters and fish of the sea swam to her: they were just teeming! Their bodies hid the blue sea! "Hail, monsters and fish of the sea! You swim everywhere, you visit all the islands. Have you heard how to go to I don't know where, and to bring back I don't know what?"[142]

Baba Yaga's numerous animal helpers give insight into her goddess role, her connection to the Mistress of the Forest, which has already been discussed.

In some stories, Baba Yaga breeds fantastic horses. Koshchei the Deathless, as well as Ivan, served her to acquire one. The mares may even be her daughters. When a hero comes to the old woman seeking one of her mares (not the daughters, but a scrawny one that's actually more powerful), Baba Yaga tasks him with taking care of the animals for three straight days. The mares are magical creatures who can shape-shift into other types of animals: wolves, hares, fish. They do so at the command of the witch, in an effort to make sure the hero fails in his task. If the mares aren't safe and sound back where they belong in the morning, off with his head. Baba Yaga has a new ornament for the final fence post.

The fact that swans and mares obey Baba Yaga may suggest she is a goddess of sexuality, love, cycles of time, destiny, death, and new life, since these animals symbolize such a goddess.[143]

Let's look at swans first. They are creatures that have access to all three realms and the areas they represent: air (the heavens and deities), water (the earth and the living), and earth (the underground and the dead).[144] In ancient times people viewed the constellation Cygnus, the Swan, as "both a guide for the living and a psychopomp for the dead due to its position in the skies," since it "lies in the middle of the Milky Way, the river of stars, that has long been seen as both the source of life and the eternal residence of the dead."[145]

Horses are majestic creatures and have an association with deities in many mythologies, carting gods and goddesses to whatever place strikes their fancy. The winged creatures also transport heroes and heroines into battle or toward safety—often from the land of the dead to the land of the living. They appear to have the speed of the sun, moon, or stars as they streak across the sky. Their natural habitat, though, is *terra firma*, solid ground. And so, they too represent all three realms. Mares in particular are known to take charge. They lead the herd to safety, and they decide which stallion will be their mate.

In more modern thinking, Baba Yaga makes use of the animal magic at her command, not to watch over victims, but to create balance.

> There are animals dead and living, old and young, gentle and fierce, surrounding her dwelling at all times. She lives in balance with them all using their skills and senses. She uses them to do her Elemental work, commune with the land and to create companionship in order to maintain balance. She is the creature of the forest, lakes and sky, in charge of all the Elements and in complete alignment with their qualities.[146]

40

Not least of all, we shouldn't forget her cat. One animal that every "witch" needs is a cat, especially a black one. Baba Yaga's feline makes a good creature to have around (except when he helps her victims escape) because cats are known to be guides to the underworld.[147] You've already read how goddesses were demoted to witches. The same may have happened to cats.

> The witch's cat, one suspects, is the descendant of the ancient lions which flanked the "Great"-Goddess and accompanied prehistoric female figures in "Sacred Display," just as the "wicked" witch is a descendant of the Goddess herself.[148]

Baba Yaga's cat can help out when she is off doing whatever task she may be doing at the time a soul arrives at her hut for its final journey. As mentioned earlier, other creatures subservient to her, such as the geese, swans, and eagles, also behave in this manner—bringing the dead on their soul's journey or helping the living return to their own world.[149] But there's something special about a cat's association with this activity.

Most often the cat is nameless, but during the Soviet era he earned himself the name of Kot Bayun ("cat storyteller"). He's her companion only on occasion. Most of the time, he's off on his own adventures. Legends claim that Veles, Slavic god of the underworld, created Kot Bayun. The god had stopped to spend an evening by a haystack. That night, mice crept into a bag in which Veles had bread, and the rodents ate it all. Frustrated, the god threw his glove at the mice, and it turned into a cat.[150]

Koshchei the Deathless. Ivan Bilibin, 1901.
Public domain, via Wikimedia Commons.

Now this cat is not your ordinary looking feline. He's much larger than a regular cat and is an ancestor of a lynx or Siberian wild cat, which were common in the land five to seven thousand years before the Russians arrived.[151] Some say the cat is as large as a horse, while others claim he can be seen from 7 versts (4.6 miles) away. But, on the other hand, he's small enough that a hero can carry him in a cage.

Kot Bayun has fangs and claws, and he's covered with iron armor. He's also been described as connected to Gamayun, a prophetic bird with a magical voice. The bird knows everything past, present, and future. Because of this relationship, Kot Bayun may possess a birdlike face with a cat's body. In addition, his body is folded like an accordion. As he steps forward, his body stretches while his hind legs remain firm until he can determine that the location he is going to is safe. If it is, he'll pull his back legs and tail forward, making sounds like an accordion as he does so.[152]

He gets his name from the Russian *bayat'*, to talk or to tell. This is related to the word *bayukat'*, to lull someone to sleep.[153] That is his claim to fame: he puts travelers to sleep. There is more to the creature than that, though.

Before he came to live with Baba Yaga, he lived in a dead forest with no birds or animals. High on top of an iron post he sat, singing and telling made-up tales to travelers who crossed his path until they became drowsy. He didn't do it to offer rest to a weary traveler. No. It was so he could eat them! Many refer to Kot Bayun as a "cannibal cat," but the designation is inaccurate. He didn't eat his own kind; he ate people.

Few can resist the cat's power. His mesmerizing voice fills the air from 7 versts (4.6 miles) away, and once they reach a distance of 3 versts (2 miles), the cat's purring lulls travelers into a sleep that verges on death. Die they will if they come within the sound of his voice and can't resist the urge to fall asleep. For then, Kot Bayun will creep up on them, slash them with his iron claws, and devour them.

His voice has been described in terms of the spectrum of frequencies, some of which can adversely affect hearing. Animals can hear these frequencies and get to safety beyond the sounds, but humans can't hear them. This would account for the fact no animals exist in the vicinity of where Kot Bayun resides. When a human happens upon these frequencies, first his head will hurt, then his health worsens, and finally he loses consciousness before he dies.[154]

A hero may purposely seek out the feline or be commanded to do so. If he can catch the cat and not fall victim to his charms, Kot Bayun will do whatever the hero asks. Not only that, but the cat's tales have healing powers, able to soothe an anxious heart or cure any disease.

Before the hero can even think about accomplishing this, though, he'll have to equip himself with special items: iron gloves, three iron caps, and three metal rods, one each of iron, copper, and lead. To overcome falling asleep, the hero must put on the three caps and gloves, set one hand over the other, shuffle his feet, and roll like a roller in some places.

Once the man reaches Kot Bayun's pillar, the cat will jump down onto his head and easily scratch through the iron caps, because the feline has the strength of an army. The hero must grab the cat before he makes it through the third one, toss the animal to the ground, and beat him with one rod after the other. By the time the third rod is bent, Kot Bayun will begin to tell his stories. If the hero doesn't succumb, the cat gives up and agrees to do whatever the hero asks. (You can read a tale with Kot Bayun in it at the end of this book.)

Roles in Fairy Tales

The types of stories in which Baba Yaga appears are called *skazki* in Russian. Although we call them fairy tales, they are called "wondertales" by those who study and analyze them. These Baba Yaga *skazki* have fragments of the old myths of gods and goddesses and are possibly quite ancient. However, since

Kot Bayun. K. Kuznetsov, 1985.
Public domain, via Wikimedia Commons.

the tales lack religious significance, they themselves are not myths.[155] What these stories mean has long been debated by scholars.

Some folklorists believe the fairy tales are remnants of past rituals, with only the stories remaining.[156] Lacking any formal text about the Slavic mythology, the fairy tales and folklore become the sacred books that "contain information on the mythological structure of the world, the magical creatures and the magical places connected to them, on where the transitional spaces from the human world to the Otherworld are located, the rules for communicating with the supernatural."[157] Although fairy tales are fictitious, they reflect the life of those who tell the stories. They "fulfill both the need to understand life as it is and to dream of life as it ought to be."[158]

In the western world, fairy tales are simple, charming stories with a moral, told to entertain children. Much of the original horrors within them have been watered down so as not to terrify today's children. For example, in the original story of Little Red Riding Hood (or Little Red-Cap), the wolf eats her and her grandmother, and they are not saved by the woodsman. In addition, the wolf tells the girl to take off her clothes and burn them before getting into bed with him. This was a story to warn young ladies about the danger of talking to strange men and what could result from it. And that charming Ariel in *The Little Mermaid* was an unnamed mermaid in the original tale. She was tempted to murder the prince, especially after she had her tongue ripped out, lost her voice, and felt excruciating pain whenever she walked, all for the sake of being with him and hoping to make him love her enough to marry her.

Slavic fairy tales told to children today are still terrifying, especially those about Baba Yaga. For me, Baba Yaga has always been the old, ugly, scary woman from fairy tales who likes to eat children. I was raised in Eastern Europe with tales of the wicked witch who bakes children in the oven and likes to bargain to get something in return for giving life. As a child, I always imagined that she lived in the dark under my bed. Even today, for this reason, I don't like beds with an opening, because the witch's bony hands might grab my bare feet, and she will take me into the woods and keep me captive in her hut on chicken legs. As with many other children, I was told these tales not only to make me behave, but also as a warning about the dangers in the world and perhaps even to help me overcome fears.

Fairy tales are more than simply stories told to children. The rhymed opening and ending of many Slavic stories contain mysterious, humorous sentences, such as "I was there and I drank beer; I drank the beer, and it flowed up to my moustache, but none of it reached my mouth."[159] Other rhymes may be statements that are the equivalent of "And they lived happily ever after." They return the reader or listeners to the real world after the fantasy is over.[160] But these sayings might once have been magical charms that hunters told while searching for game in the forest. Spirits abounded, and it was wise to appease and entertain them, so the spirits rewarded the hunters.[161] It may also mean the storyteller was saying the story is much more powerful than any of the listeners will ever understand.

> But the story merely grazed his mind, like the liquid on his moustache. Nothing really penetrated, like often is the case with the reader of the skaski, who does not really understand it, who does not think so much about it, who does not so much use it in his life. Like with the parables of the Bible, the text remains far for us, the message is too powerful to be really heard and internalized. Unless we prefer a more Slavic and romantic interpretation of the idea: the order of the universe, this world and even more the other world, is far too mysterious to be grasped by a weak and frail human mind. But whatever is the explanation, we still heard and felt the story: our moustaches got a whiff of it.[162]

In these Slavic fairy tales, various roles have been identified for Baba Yaga: villain (the bad witch) and donor (the good witch) being the most common. The evil cannibal witch is the one most people recognize. Even in stories where Baba Yaga assists the hero or heroine, she may threaten to eat them.

It's part of her normal greeting to strangers, but it has its purpose, as you'll learn later. So, it's best not to base whether or not she is evil on that factor alone. It's better to look at the interpretation of her role and actions to understand her, rather than defining her as either good or evil.

Healer

Stories in which Baba Yaga is classified as the villain or "Yaga the Kidnapper" may be the "first genuine folktale about Baba Yaga to be published."[163] However, like Dorothy in *The Wizard of Oz* movie, Baba Yaga might reply to the question of whether she is a good witch or a bad witch with the answer, "I'm not a witch at all." At least she's not a witch in the sense that the western world perceives witches.

In the kidnapper types of stories, Baba Yaga is out on the prowl for children—boys, in fact, those who are younger than marriageable age. Having waited long enough for someone to come to her hut, she's now starving. She tries different approaches to seize the child: imitating words his mother has spoken, offering him food, waiting until the child gives away his hiding place, or outright grabbing him when no one is looking. She may also enlist her daughters or helpers, such as swans, geese, or an eagle to assist her. Normally, she fails in her first couple of attempts, but that doesn't deter her. Eventually she succeeds—even if it means having her voice reforged by the blacksmith until she sounds like the boy's mother.

Cast iron pot being slid into oven. VladimirZhV, 2010.
Public domain, via Wikimedia Commons.

A WITCHY POTION

Harry Potter had a cloak of invisibility, but there's a way to create a bone of invisibility. This is not for the faint of heart, as you have to kill a black cat to acquire the bone. This cat has to be completely black; not a single hair can be another color. After murdering the poor feline, you'll have to tear it into pieces and boil it in a cauldron until the meat falls away from the bones. Scoop out the bones and lay them in front of you. One by one, place each bone onto your head while you look in a mirror. When you turn invisible, you've found the magic bone (Live Journal).

Once she has the boy in her clutches, she prepares to cook and eat him. She may have her daughters do the deed, getting the child to sit on a bread spatula (a utensil used to slide bread into an oven). The daughters always fail, because the boy sits on it with his arms and legs askew, so he won't slide into the oven. She tells him he's doing it all wrong and has to show him how to sit properly. Into the oven she goes instead, and Baba Yaga ends up eating her own daughters. Eventually, Baba Yaga herself tries to get him into the oven, and she, too, gets pushed inside, much like the witch in the story of Hansel and Gretel. The boy may let her out, or she may end up being cooked and possibly eaten by the boy.

Baking Children

What is the meaning behind Baba Yaga's desire to bake children? On the surface, she comes across as a villain in these stories. Numerous folklorists, however, believe that placing children into an oven has a deeper connection with a Slavic ritual for healing ailing infants. This ritual was called *perepekanie, perepechen'e, zepekanie,* or *dopekanie.*[164] In many Slavic customs, it's believed that fire has healing powers, which may originate from ancient Slavic worship of fire.[165] The fire was believed to burn the disease and expel it from the home through the chimney, along with the smoke.[166]

This ritual may date back to the matriarchal period, since it was performed by an older woman in the community, one who held the knowledge and secrets of healing and the mysteries of birth and death. She had a strong connection with nature and drew from its magical powers. The woman was revered, although sometimes also feared.

In Bulgaria, this healer is called a *znahar.* Although the word can mean "sorcery," it's not used in the way you might think. Sorcery was the practice of using herbs with spells or charms for physical, mental, or emotional healing. It was practiced for protective actions, and the women often called on the saints and angels for assistance. "Witchcraft," on the other hand, had more of a tendency to refer to bad spells, hexes, those meant to do harm. Those who practiced this were wont to conjure demons and unclean spirits.

The word *znahar* comes from *znat',* for "know." It referred to women and men (although mainly women) who had knowledge of herbs and their uses in charms and potions. Witchcraft, on the other hand, comes from *vedat',* also for "know," but this knowledge was more mystical and performed through "invisible means."[167] At one time, however, even the *ved'ma* was a wise old woman, knowledgeable in herbal arts, but she had become a fiend by the time these Slavic fairy tales were written down.[168]

To understand the ritual cooking of a child better, let's first start with the Slavic stove (*pech'*). This large structure built from bricks and plaster dominated the room, often extending the length of the hut, and was an essential part of a traditional peasant home. Its warmth kept the family alive during the harsh winter months, and a large raised platform (*polaty*) above served as sleeping quarters for the entire

Stove. State museum of folk architecture and life, Belarus. Hanna Zelenko, 2007.
CC BY-SA 4.0 <https://creativecommons.org/licenses/by-sa/4.0>, via Wikimedia Commons.

extended family. It was here that Baba Yaga could sometimes be found "lying on the stove, on nine bricks, and grinding her teeth."[169]

> Inside the hut is that essential and central feature of Russian peasant life, the stove, which occupies one side of a wall. In front against it three long implements stand, the poker, broom and shovel. The oven rests on a brick or tile foundation, about eighteen inches high, with a semicircular hollow space below. The top of the stove is used for a sleeping bench (*poláty*) for the old folk or the honoured guest. In larger houses there may be a *lezhán'ka* or heating stove, used as a sleeping sofa.[170]

The stove was considered female and was symbolic of the womb. It was a device through which Baba Yaga taught her female initiates about "the secret of fertility and generation."[171] The stove was a place of transformation, connected with death and rebirth. People believed that the souls of the ancestors lived in the stove and fed on the smell of baking bread.[172] Bread itself is symbolic; it represents the earth in which bodies are buried in order to be reborn.[173]

This brings us to the ritual of baking children, a practice once done to cure a premature, weak, or ill infant, one suffering from atrophy and rickets (called "dog's old age"). People believed that the child had not "ripened" in his mother's womb, and so he needed to "bake" a while longer. Therefore, he was placed into a symbolic womb, the stove. This was considered a temporary death, as he entered the domain of the ancestors in the otherworld, only to be returned to the land of the living with his second birth once he had "baked" fully.[174]

> It is interesting that Baba Yaga invites her guests to clean up and eat before eating them, as though preparing them for their final journey, for entering the death, which will result in a new clean rebirth.[175]

To perform the ritual, at dawn the village znahar collected water from three different fountains. She used this to knead a batter of rye dough, which she smeared over the infant, leaving only his mouth and nostrils uncovered, so he wouldn't suffocate. Either a midwife, the mother, or the oldest woman in the village would then tie the baby to a bread spatula. While she placed him into a warm oven with no flame, she might chant, "Bake, bake, doggy old age." This would happen three times, with the infant being left in the oven for only a brief moment.[176] Afterwards, the dough was removed and thrown to the dogs to eat.

Sometimes, while the baking occurred, a longer dialog took place between two women, one, possibly the mother, operating the baking shovel, and the other, the mother-in-law, standing near the entrance.

> The mother-in-law asked while entering the house, "What are you doing?" The daughter-in-law answered, "I'm baking bread." While saying these words, she moved the shovel into the oven. The mother-in-law said, "Well, bake, bake, but don't overbake" and went out the door. And the mother took the shovel out of the heating stove.[177]

A similar, but longer, conversation could take place in a more elaborate ritual. The znahar would walk around the house three times in the direction of the sun, then come and stand by the window, while the mother would place the baby inside the oven. The role could also be reversed, and the znahar would attend to the infant.

In a ritual where the infant suffered from tabes, a wasting disease, when the znahar cautions the mother not to bake the baby too long with the disease, the mother says what can she do, she has to get rid of the sickness. To this the znahar replies to bake the child, then sell it to her. She gives the mother

Inside an izba. Dmitry Yakhovsky, 2018.

three coins, and the mother passes the child outside on the baking shovel. The znahar takes the child and runs around the outside of the house with him, returning him to the mother saying he is too heavy, meaning he needs to be baked more to become lighter. The two women do this three times. Then the znahar takes the child home for the night and returns him to his mother the next day.[178]

A variation of the ritual follows:

> If a child has *sushets* (i.e. the child becomes thin) they heal it in this manner: After kneading dough in the evening, they put a stopped bottle of water into the dough and leave it there until loaves of bread are made and put in the oven in the morning. Then they tie the child to the bread spatula the bread was put on, and they hold it in the oven for several moments, over the loaves. Then they pour water over the sick child from the bottle that was left in the dough overnight.[179]

It is these ancient wise women who were eventually turned into the cannibalistic witch Baba Yaga of folklore. Midwives were particularly susceptible to this kind of vilification, because of their knowledge of herbs and medicine and their ability to assist women with contraceptives, labor, and other feminine concerns. And her ability to kill a child through abortion added to her evil qualities. These tasks "denoted the loosening of the power over female sexuality and put the midwives with their inexplicable powers in a suspicious position."[180] And in a patriarchal society, this "power" had to be suppressed instead of glorified. Therefore, Baba Yaga "the priestess saving babies" becomes "Yaga having the urge to 'eat the baked child.' "[181]

These types of stories about baking children also served another purpose. With infant mortality high among the peasants, these folkloric customs were "designed to help families cope with their fears of infant and child mortality." They were "a way to destabilize fear of mortality in a culture where poverty, hunger, and untimely death have been a way of life for the underclass and working class for centuries."[182] Yeshe Matthews, in a blog post, sums up nicely an imaginary conversation with Baba Yaga about this subject:

> That whole, 'I eat children,' thing? Actually, I eat ALL OF YOU, young, old, etc. The stories about me eating children actually point to the fact that I am the Great Dark Earth that will one day consume your very bones. From the moment a child is born, his or her days are numbered till we meet in consumptive decay. It's not like I want to eat children more than anyone else, but the metaphor is designed to help people cope with infant mortality and their own mortality.[183]

Initiator

Perhaps the most popular interpretation of Baba Yaga's role in many fairy tales is that of an initiator of young people. This type is called the donor or "Yaga the Giver," as she tests the hero or heroine and gives them gifts or her wisdom—but only if they prove themselves to be worthy. In these stories, she is preparing them for adulthood and marriage. Here, she is a teacher, but her ways are not straightforward, since Baba Yaga is known to be a trickster. As Madame Pamita says in her book *Baba Yaga's Book of Witchcraft*, "Like all the best teachers, she is indirect in her approach, offering the student puzzles that seem mysterious in the moment but elicit the most profound flashes of brilliance in the end."

The best teachers never reveal all the answers, and neither does Baba Yaga; she'll provide a hint, a clue, a magical object, but she expects her pupils to analyze the situation so they can discover answers on their own. Ultimately, she teaches them how to think, so they can survive in the world.

In his examination of folktales, well-known folklorist Vladimir Propp tried to reconstruct ancient initiation rites from these tales. Controversy exists about his methods and assumptions, but fundamental ideas about initiations remain popular. It's believed that deep in the forests was a place where many of these initiations took place. It was here, that the initiates experienced their own symbolic ritual death, enabling them to enter the otherworld, the land of the dead, to acquire new knowledge. This brought about the death to their old, childish ways, in order to be reborn as an adult, one who has a new social status in the community, and more importantly, one who was ready to partake in marriage.

It was a shaman who taught the youths, who assisted them with their transformation, answered their questions, and instructed them in the secret traditions. In the fairy tales, Baba Yaga plays this role of shaman. She provides the heroes and heroines with the tools and knowledge they'll need not only to prepare them for their new life, but also to make the world a better place for themselves when they return from their journey.[184]

Those to be initiated were taken out of their society, outside of their established world. This idea is reflected in fairy tales by the children often becoming lost in the forest and not being able to return home, symbolizing "the initiatory process of leaving the secure nest and stepping out into the wilderness."[185] Initiations occurred in locations that represented the womb, such as a cave. Another place was deep within a forest in a special initiation hut shaped like an animal, with the door being the animal's mouth.[186] Entering the hut represented being devoured by an animal, which was symbolic of the initiate's

Baba Yaga's hut. Ivan Bilibin, circa 1900.
Public domain, via Wikimedia Commons.

temporary death. In the Baba Yaga stories, the animal is gone, and the only animal aspect that remains is the hut's chicken legs.

Before the initiate can even begin his journey, he must know the rules. The first obstacle or test to overcome is entering the hut, and that means knowing the secret words. Once the hut turns to the uninvited guest, he must climb up the steep steps. This is said to be symbolic of the initiate's test, to determine if he is worthy of receiving Baba Yaga's help.[187] The turning of the hut symbolizes opening the doors to the otherworld, the place where the initiate is bound.[188]

Baba Yaga is a wise old woman with knowledge and secrets of the ages. She may not always willingly help the visitor further his development or continue his quest, for she tires of people always expecting—demanding—something from her. She lives alone in the deep woods because she wishes to be alone, with only her pets and forest animals for company. But assist them she does, in her own way.

When Vasilisa wants to ask questions, Baba Yaga replies, "Ask me. Only not every question leads to good. If you know too much, you'll soon get old!"[189] Or perhaps what Baba Yaga really meant was that she herself would grow old. Because with each question someone asks, the old crone ages a year. In order to recover, she must brew a special tea made from blue roses, her "elixir of immortality," to restore that year of her life.[190] So, to prevent too many questions, it's wise for Baba Yaga to tack on a comment that she'll eat people who are overly inquisitive. Then she can save her special tea for when she really needs it.

But, Baba Yaga *does* want to instruct those she considers worthy of her knowledge. Caution is advised, though. Natalia Clarke, in *Pagan Portals: Baba Yaga Slavic Earth Goddess*, says, "Baba Yaga's teachings are to be explorative, daring, creative, and curious and yes, one might be scared, but when one is willing to look for things beyond that fear something new and different happens."[191] It's only by confronting fear that her pupils can grow courageous to confront the challenges Baba Yaga sets before them. Like Slavic people, she values the traits of courage and honor, and desires to instill them in those she teaches.

Her students must be on guard, however. Baba Yaga says whatever she thinks, and her first response to her visitors is her desire to eat them. This is the beginning of their initiation. They must be swallowed up and hidden in the womb before they can begin their journey. Even though she doesn't physically eat them, the desire is there to start them on their journey of rebirth into adulthood.

Next, she spouts off, asking her visitor why he or she is there. Before Baba Yaga will even think about imparting her knowledge, she wants to know if a person has come willingly or unwillingly. She may outright ask, "Have you come of your own will or not?" or "Why have you come? Is it of your own accord or by compulsion?" although often her question is not that direct.

"Are you looking for business or running away from business?"
"Are you walking under your own volition or under duress?"
"Have you come to rest, or are you in quest?"
"Have you come to do deeds, young men, or to flee from deeds?"
"Is it work on your way, or for sloth do you stray?"
"Do you come gladly or does sorrow drive you?"

If they come willingly, they come out of despair in response to a crisis. Under the surface, that crisis will be a situation that requires a young person to transform from adolescence to adulthood. For who would approach the witch otherwise, knowing her penchant for young flesh? And so, if they come willingly, Baba Yaga knows they are ready to learn from her. Her teaching and gifts will be valuable to those who are honest with themselves.

If the beseecher comes begrudgingly, then there is no hope. Baba Yaga can't waste her time teaching a deceiver, someone who doesn't want to learn. She smacks her lips and sniffs the air—a ready-made meal has arrived.

She eats naive people who think life should bring them only happiness. She gobbles up the uninitiated, to whom suffering is unacceptable. She devours those who see life in terms of dualistic categories such as white or black, good or evil, life or death.[192]

The next test the potential initiate must endure before the serious teaching can begin is that of politeness. She expects her visitors to be polite despite how crass she may be. The Russian *vezhlivyy* for "polite" comes from the old Russian *vezha*, which refers to "a knowledgeable, well-versed person, one who knows how to do things the correct way."[193]

Baba Yaga is certainly not kind in her teachings. She practices tough love. She offers no pity in a world devoid of pity. In order for the youths to survive in their harsh world, Baba Yaga has to ensure they become tough, even if it means she is cruel at times.

The kind of help Baba Yaga provides, however, differs depending on whether a young man or a young woman has approached her, for they both had different roles to play in their community.

The Hero's Journey

When a young man arrives at Baba Yaga's hut, he's in search of something or someone. This may be living water or apples of youth, or he may be seeking a kidnapped maiden: a princess or his mother, sister, or bride.

Baba Yaga and Ivan. Ivan Bilibin, 1911.
Public domain, via Wikimedia Commons.

Before Baba Yaga will assist him and send him on his quest, she prepares him for entering the otherworld. For the Slavs, the otherworld or underworld (*Koshnoe tsarstvo*) had two layers. The ancestors lived in the uppermost layer. It was the entrance to this level that Baba Yaga guarded. Well below this level lived the demon spirits. It was here that Baba Yaga prepared her initiates to travel.[194]

The living cannot go there without affronting the dead. Baba Yaga must make the living man appear the same as those who are dead—that is, a spirit. Only she has the ability to send someone to the otherworld, whether it's by killing them or preparing them to cross over with the ability to return.

> [T]he hero and heroine's journeys to and from the "other realm" are a denial of the irreversibility of real time and the inevitability of death. The passage of time is expressed in spatial terms as a journey to a symbolic "other world" or land of death. Unlike human beings, whose life journey proceeds in one direction only, the fairy tale heroine or hero can return from the other realm, reflecting the human desire to control time. This denial of time and death is the essential latent mythic context of the fairy tale.[195]

One way or the other, the hero will end up in the land of the dead. Either he passes Baba Yaga's tests and is prepared to go there as a living being. Or he fails the tests and dies, Baba Yaga eats him, and his spirit remains forever entrenched in the otherworld.

One of Baba Yaga's first tests is that of respect. The male initiate sometimes shows her the respect she demands, but other times he ignores her demands and is as rude to her as she is to him. He may even threaten to kill her the way she threatens him. Instead of her flying off in a rage, she accepts this action.

Perhaps this is her real test for the hero. The youth's journey when he leaves her hut will be filled with dangers, where torture and injury are possible. In the ancient initiation rituals, a youth was "symbolically burned, boiled, fried, chopped into pieces and resurrected again" to represent his temporary death, actions which were achieved by making him suffer hunger, thirst, darkness, and other horrors.[196]

And so, the youth must prove to Baba Yaga that he is brave. By standing up to her, he implies that he is not afraid of what she might do to him, and that he has the necessary skills to survive in the otherworld. He must be a true warrior—strong, resilient, able to endure difficulties and pain, because the trials ahead of him will prepare him to grow up and become the protector society expects of him. Baba Yaga herself "represents the challenges of growing up, since she incarnates the fearful and angry side of the human soul, the dark forces that have to be surmounted."[197] It is these fears the initiate must conquer.

In addition, he gets away with his rudeness by reminding Baba Yaga that she is forgetting the rules of hospitality. She must act in the proper manner and offer him refreshments and rest before she questions him. If he was ignorant of the proper etiquette and failed to remind Baba Yaga of the rules, he most likely would be eaten by her.

What is this proper etiquette? She must feed him, allow him to bathe in the *banya* (like a sauna), and give him a place to sleep. When reminded of this, Baba Yaga does what he demands without hesitation, possibly either chuckling that her guest knew the answer, or grumbling because she missed out on a good meal.

Knowing her initiate now has a chance to survive and contribute meaningfully to his community, Baba Yaga prepares him for entering the otherworld, where his initiation challenges will begin. First, she must feed him the food of the dead. Next, she must prepare a steam bath to wash away his "Russian scent," the smell of the living, so he can enter the land of the dead unnoticed. And finally, she must allow him to sleep one last time. In order for a living person to enter the land of the dead, "he must simulate death: he is not supposed to sleep, speak, see, or laugh."[198]

The food Baba Yaga feeds him is "magical." One thought is that she fed mushrooms to heroes to give them the ability to unlock "the keys to eternity."[199] But this food is taboo and intended only for the

Baba Yaga. Каразин Н, Nikolai Nikolayevich Karazin, 19th century.
Public domain, via Wikimedia Commons.

TOO OLD, IVAN

On occasion, jokes with a sexual context may appear in the stories about Baba Yaga, such as the following:

Ivan the Fool was once lost in the woods. He went round and round until he arrived at a house that stood on chicken's feet. He knocked on the door and Baba Yaga opened it.

"Baba Yaga," Ivan said, "can I spend the night at your place?"

"You really are a fool, Ivan!" Baba Yaga replied. "I'm far too old for such things. Too old!" (Järv, 18).

dead. What she feeds him could possibly be toadstools, which allow him to become part of the world of the dead, to speak and see there in the same manner as the dead.[200]

> Mushrooms often act as a classifier of binary oppositions in mythology: plant kingdom – animal kingdom, profane – sacral, "food for the Gods" – "food for the dead", food – antifood. Exuberance of mushrooms is coupled with the fact that toadstools serve as the main ingredient of hallucinogenic drinks commonly used by shamans in their journeys into the underworld. Mushrooms are also included in the "life – death – fertility" triad, thus resembling the functions of the world tree (journeying to upper and lower realms from the center of the world).[201]

Fairy tales that explicitly connect Baba Yaga to mushrooms are difficult to find, however, so the association is implied. Most often, the references to the fungi are those in which someone enters the forest to collect them, which was a common pastime among the peasants. This is considered the same as saying, "Once upon a time."[202] Although there is no definitive proof that mushrooms played an integral role in the Baba Yaga stories, fly agaric, *Amanita muscaria*, the white-spotted, red-topped mushroom that appears in certain illustrations with Baba Yaga, may have a deeper connection to her. It's possible that artists took into account folk traditions as they created their illustrations.

Considering Baba Yaga might have Baltic, Ugric, or other non-Slavic origins, the following ideas have been suggested about her connection to mushrooms:

> Baba Yaga is also strongly associated with water birds and bird-maidens (*rusalki*). Khanty myth references a water bird assisting creation of Earth from a red-capped mushroom. Baltic myth contains a "Mother of Mushrooms." Pre-Slavic Balkan (Vinča) artifacts include figurines of bird-women, and mushrooms sculpted from rock crystal. Relationships of Balkan, Baltic, Ugric, and other mythic figures to Baba Yaga and to mushrooms are conjectured here and in other literature.[203]

Regardless of what Baba Yaga fed the hero, her next task is to prepare a bath for him. She alone has the knowledge of how to properly perform a spiritual cleansing of the hero in her magical banya and steam away his living scent, which will force "his soul out of his body" in the same way the bathhouse was used as a way to force diseases out of one's body. Her means of cleansing the hero leaves him "ritually dead."[204]

Inside a banya. Dmitry Yakhovsky, 2018.

And finally, once the hero is fed and bathed, he needs to sleep before he continues his journey. This may be in order to "gain emotional distance from the problem" he is facing, such as the almost impossible task of finding living water or searching for his kidnapped sister, mother, or bride. Or sleep may be needed to give him strength to overcome all the obstacles he will face along the way.[205] But more importantly, he must be fully rested before he ventures out, because sleeping in the land of the dead would give away the fact that he is a living being, for the dead need no sleep. When he goes to sleep in the in-between world of Baba Yaga's hut, he enters a state of unconsciousness, like being buried in a tomb,[206] because sleep was seen as a temporary death.[207]

In the same way that spirits do not sleep in the land of the dead, neither do they laugh or joke. If the hero does any of these things, he "will provoke the wrath of its inhabitants as a transgressor who has crossed the forbidden threshold."[208] Even before he reaches the land of the dead, he cannot laugh in the presence of Baba Yaga, for she knows that if he laughs there, he is doomed.

> This motif is further elaborated in a Komi folktale. "At the entrance to the hut a girl says to her brother, 'Let's go in, but don't dare laugh. Don't be a fool. If you want to laugh, bite your lower lip. And if you should laugh, Baba Jaga will catch us both, and that will be the end of us.' "[209]

Even so, Ivan sometimes responds flippantly to Baba Yaga about the dangers she warns him about. In one tale, she explains how he'll never reach his destination because "there are three ferries; at the first they'll cut off thy right hand, at the second thy left, and at the third thy head." To which Ivan replies, "Well, Granny, one single head is not such a great matter. I'll go—and God's will be done!"[210] In another story, she warns him that his sister's husband, the Forest Monster, will devour him. Unconcerned, Ivan says, "Well, little Granny, perhaps it will choke him. A Russian man is a bony morsel, and God will not give him over to be eaten by a swine like that!"[211]

In the world outside of fairy tales, these feeding, bathing, and sleeping rituals mimic funeral rites performed for the dead to allow them safe passage to the otherworld. And so, the hero too must complete these rites, so he is able to exist in both worlds, the same as Baba Yaga. He will be alive in spirit, and yet dead in appearance.

Finally, Baba Yaga lets her initiate know that without her help, he will fail in his quest. She offers him advice to achieve his goal, such as the following from "The Tale of the Daring Young Man and the Apples of Youth."

> The Baba Yaga gave him food, gave him something to drink, asked him for his news, and gave him a horse better than the first two. "Go with God! There's a kingdom not far away. Don't you ride in at the gates. There are lions on guard at the gates, but give my horse a good lashing and jump right over the fence. Watch out, don't snag on the strings. If you do, the whole kingdom will rise up, and then you won't remain alive! And once you jump over the fence, open the door softly, and you'll see the Tsar-Maiden sleeping. She has a vial with the water of youth hidden under her pillow. You take the vial and hurry back. Don't look too long upon her beauty."[212]

Even if his initial quest is something other than finding a bride (such as when he's searching for living water as in the above excerpt), the all-knowing witch understands that the ultimate result of his journey will be to secure himself a bride. The hero doesn't always listen to her wise counsel, and as a result, he may need her help to fix the problem he caused.

> The prince did everything as the Baba Yaga had told him. There was only one thing he could not resist—he looked too long at the maiden's beauty . . . He mounted the horse, and the horse's legs were shaky. He went to jump over the fence, and he hit one of the strings. In a moment the whole kingdom awoke; the Tsar-Maiden got up and ordered her horse saddled. But the Baba Yaga already knew what was happening to the young man, and she was preparing for the response. She barely had time to let the prince come in, when the Tsar-Maiden flew up and found the Baba Yaga all disheveled.
>
> The Tsar-Maiden said to her, "How dare you allow such a rascal into my kingdom? He lay with me, he drank some kvass and didn't cover up the pitcher."
>
> "My lady, Tsar-Maiden! You must see how my hair is messed up. I fought with him for a long time, but I couldn't overcome him." The other two Baba Yagas said the same thing.[213]

In a variation of the story, the three Baba Yaga sisters aid the hero by changing out his exhausted horse. When the Tsar Maiden arrives, the sisters detain her so the hero can escape.

Baba Yaga provides him not only with knowledge, but also bestows upon him his goddess-given right to marry the princess and become ruler of his people. As with ancient initiation practices, her actual words remain secret, and are known only through the hero's actions after he departs her company.

Baba Yaga also provides the hero with magical gifts so he can be successful in his quest. In ancient rites, initiates were given "sacred bundles," amulets for luck, without which the initiate would fail in his tasks. As part of the ritual of receiving the amulets, the initiate learned the tale about the origins of their magic. This is a verbal charm, endowing the initiate with the knowledge of how the amulets led to the

THE THREE BROTHERS

In many fairy tales, three brothers set off on an adventure, together or separately, to rescue their mother, sister, or a princess, or perhaps they're looking for the water of life for their father. Whatever the situation, it's always only the youngest brother who succeeds, despite his brothers' attempt to kill or hinder him.

This and other fairy tales have their origins in ancient myths and rituals. The three brothers originally represented winter, spring, and summer, with summer being the youngest brother, who was symbolic of the sun overcoming winter. This type of story is believed to originate from the creation myth of the Proto-Indo-European mythology.

> The prototypes of the three fabulous heroes were the mythological heroes of the age of foundation – *Manu 'man', *Yemo 'twin' and *Trito 'third'. Each of the heroes served as a mythological model for one of the three main social groups (people, warriors, priests) (Koptev, 131).

The three kingdoms the brothers came across (copper, silver, and gold) represented the heavens, the earth, and the underground. In the mythology above, *Manu sacrificed his brother *Yemo to create the world and humans. *Trito was the first warrior. So *Manu can be seen as belonging to the celestial world, *Yemo to the underworld, and *Trito to the earthly world.

> This ['ndugu'] rule was formed during the transition from the social (group) relationship to an individual kinship and implied the transfer of inherited value not to all sons of the father, but only to three of them (in fact, there was an inheritance from one triad to another). If there were fewer than three sons, they were supplemented by nephews (cousins). Initially, the title of ruler was given to its holder for a limited time, after which he conceded it to his next brother. In historical times, when the inheritance became lifelong, the preeminent right usually had the youngest of three brothers, while his two older 'ndugu' played the role of his attendants (Koptev, 146).

Fairy tales and folklore show a reversal of these statuses, with the older brothers becoming ordinary men, while the youngest outshines them in the end, even though initially he is perceived as dim-witted. At one time in Russia, a system of a triad of rulers over the management of the land existed. And so, the youngest brother's distinctive position over his brothers may have come about because in pre-Christian times, it was the youngest prince who succeeded to the throne.

original owner becoming the ruler of his people.[214] In much the same way, Baba Yaga supplies her initiate with this secret knowledge, so he, too, may become a ruler.

Some of the gifts Baba Yaga gives him are things a warrior needs: a self-cutting sword or a fire-breathing flying horse. At other times, the gifts are objects from a woman's world. These hold the most power, as they enable the hero to travel from one world to the next: a mirror, ball of yarn, scarf, or towel. By giving him these gifts, Baba Yaga is initiating men into the ways of women, into "the mysteries of the female world of fertility,"[215] for that is the ultimate goal—to teach him not to fear women or the process of becoming a husband.

But what does he have to fear about women? Aren't they all docile like Vasilisa? The answer is no. In some stories, women are warriors, like the Tsar Maiden. A strong woman like this instills a fear into men about women's sexual powers: he fears figurative castration.[216]

> The greatest threat to a man's masculinity is a threat to his penis, and a "strong" woman in the bedroom is precisely such a threat. The trouble with the typical Russian male, however, is that even outside of the bedroom he often cannot handle a "strong" woman, or even just an "equal" one. He behaves as though a woman were a sexual threat even when the interaction is not sexual (e.g., at the workplace, in the kitchen).[217]

The hero may associate Baba Yaga's phallic characteristics (her bony leg, large nose, iron tooth, deep voice) with all women. Not only because of these features, but also her pestle (another phallic symbol) can be dangerous to a man, as it can crush seeds in the mortar.[218] On the other hand, Baba Yaga's phallic features might alleviate his fears of women, with Baba Yaga not only being sexually unappealing, but also representing everything that women should not be according to him: dominant, aggressive, assertive, masculine.[219]

In the fairy tales, women are presented according to their relationship to men: daughters, mothers, wives, and any who fall outside of the accepted norm, such as those who were ambitious or warriors, are portrayed as evil—at least until they "came to their senses" and behaved the way society deemed they should behave. Among those is Baba Yaga. It's possible that at one time "strong women were acceptable in Russian folklore since they existed in real life, but that 'later storytellers were uncomfortable with the strong woman character, so reduced her to someone less threatening.' "[220] But the feminine power that Baba Yaga personifies was feared, and so it had to be vilified.

When the hero finally overcomes his fear of the female sex, only then can he learn to cohabitate with his future bride. When he finally returns to his community (or becomes its ruler) after his initiation, he will have acquired not only the ability to lead, but also magical powers and wealth. Whether he is of noble blood or destined to become nobility, he will become a true hero—filled with integrity, strength, goodness, kindness, and gentleness. He will have learned obedience by following Baba Yaga's advice. And he will have learned how to love his family, care for the weak, and never be rash or cruel.

The Young Boy's Journey

A young boy's initiation with Baba Yaga varies from that of a youth who is ready for marriage. You've already learned about the healing interpretation of stories in which Baba Yaga attempts to cook a young boy in her oven, but these stories also have another meaning.

Why does Baba Yaga have a fascination with putting boys, and rarely girls, into her oven? She threatens to eat girls, of course, as well as most people who come to her hut, but the oven scenes are ones which predominantly involve young boys.

This relates to a male child's relationship to his mother. You may not think of Baba Yaga as a mother figure, at least not a positive one. Her role here is one of pseudo-mother; with her wisdom of the ages, she teaches her charges all they need to know to succeed in life. That's on a good day. On a bad day she's more like the step-mother (who's always wicked in fairy tales, isn't she?), and is considered a "false mother."

Children's first sense of identity is one that is merged with their mother. In the peasant society in which these stories were told, a male child needed to develop an identity different from his mother's, so he could turn into the fairy-tale hero who came to Baba Yaga for advice later in his life.

Among the Russian peasants, a woman was basically a slave to or the property of a man for most of her life, whether this was her father or her husband after she married. The only time she was likely to have any freedom was when she became the old crone. In the meantime, she and her children often endured much abuse from the male head of the family. A male child, in turn, often displayed this same hostility toward his mother as he began to assert his independence. In their society, he desired to "repress the 'mother's boy' inside [himself] in favor of 'rugged, swaggering, "masculine" behavior.' "[221] At the same time, he was torn and identified with her victim status. The mother, in turn, wanted to keep her child close to her as long as possible, to protect him from the dangers of the world around them.

In the oven-scene stories, Baba Yaga is like that kind of mother figure, one who strangles her child with love. The cooking of the boy represents "the danger a mother presents if she is too attached to a male child." She is trying to put him back into her womb, so he doesn't become independent from her. To overcome this male anxiety over separation from his mother, the boy must project a negative attitude toward women and femininity.[222]

Portraying females such as Baba Yaga as "evil" is a way to suppress women. Among the women who fall into this evil category are bad mothers, those who are barren or childless, and midwives (who murder children).

Baba Yaga. Koki B-wa, 10 years old, 1916.
Public domain, via Wikimedia Commons.

The idea of the female evil works in two ways: either the perceived harmful supernatural and magical forces or beings are presented as female, or the actions of women can be associated with harmful magic and sorcery. Therefore, the female evil can be a woman embedded in a discourse which sees evil as an innate characteristic of women – the dark side of the feminine, or it can be an evil force or being, represented as female, or appearing in the form of a woman.[223]

All of this is what Baba Yaga represents from the male perspective. She has escaped from the demands that society places on women, on mothers, and therefore is to be feared and vilified. She becomes the illegitimate or false mother, one who is evil, and so a boy can break away from this type of mother and assert his independence without feelings of guilt.

The Heroine's Journey

During the time these stories were being told, a peasant woman's traditional role was that of a homemaker. Therefore, the heroine's tales primarily focus on teaching a young woman how to become a good wife. To be judged worthy by Baba Yaga, the female initiate must excel at women's domestic and farming tasks: preparing and cooking food, spinning and weaving, washing, and maintaining the stove and bathhouse fires. She must learn not only about household chores, but also about motherhood and taking proper care of children. She has to be able to work long hours and perform strenuous tasks. Lacking these essential skills lessened her chance of survival and that of her family.

On top of that, she must be docile, faithful, kind, patient, generous, and uncomplaining. When she married, the young woman moved into her husband's household, which included multiple generations. So, perhaps the most important lesson she had to learn in order to be a good wife was obedience, not only to her husband's demands, but also to her mother-in law's.

Along with this, the girl must pass the test of politeness. A female visitor will not get away with behaving the way a male visitor does. The young woman must show the witch the respect due her age and wisdom, in the same way she will have to show this respect to older women in her new household.

In some fairy tales, Baba Yaga takes on this role of mother-in-law, forcing the girl to perform numerous tasks to perfection or be eaten if she fails. These types of stories usually start with the girl being driven from her home by a malicious older woman, most often her stepmother, who sends the girl to Baba Yaga to retrieve such things as fire or a needle and thread to sew a shirt.

For example, on the first day Vasilisa the Beautiful arrived at Baba Yaga's hut, the witch ordered the girl to: "Clean up the yard, sweep out the house make dinner, get the laundry ready, and go into the granary, take a quarter measure of wheat and clean the wild peas out of it."[224] And on the second day, Baba Yaga told her, "Tomorrow do the same things you did today, and besides that take the poppy-seed from the granary and clean the dirt out of it, grain by grain."[225]

All Vasilisa actually had to do was cook the meal, because her doll did the rest. In other stories, however, the girl does the required tasks herself: weaving is a popular activity Baba Yaga sets before her initiate, as well as bathing the witch's children, which you may recall from an earlier discussion were worms, frogs, insects, and more. Once the girl gains the necessary skills, her initiation into adulthood is complete, and she returns home.

A similar type of story shows a contrast between a "good" girl and a "bad" girl. It demonstrates the proper behavior for girls.

The significant stable elements in this tale type are a wicked stepmother, a supernatural figure who tests the kind stepdaughter and the unkind stepmother's daughter, the rewarding of the kind girl and the punishment of the unkind one.[226]

Vasilisa the Beautiful. Ivan Bilibin, 1899.
Public domain, via Wikimedia Commons.

First, the step-daughter performs tasks for Baba Yaga. The girl does everything she is told to do without complaining and is awarded for home-making skills and obedience. She is "good" because she possesses the qualities a young woman was praised for in a traditional Slavic culture and what a prospective bride should possess. When the stepmother sees this, she sends out her own daughter, expecting she will receive rewards, too, but the girl is rude and doesn't do anything she is expected to do or she does the tasks poorly. She is "bad," and Baba Yaga punishes her for her slovenliness, gives her a terrible gift that kills her, or gives her nothing at all. In extreme cases, Baba Yaga eats the girl.

These types of stories demonstrate the beginning of a power struggle and concealed aggression between the girl and her mother or her mother-in-law that is likely to endure throughout her lifetime until she becomes that older, married woman herself. Unlike the stories of young boys who must try to create an identity different from his mother's, a girl is taught to mimic the female traits. In a sense, as she gets older, she is considered to be in competition with her mother.

Stories that contrast the good and bad girls "reflect a young woman's own love and hate, for herself and her mother" and "symbolize her adjustment to her proper role."[227] Furthermore, "[t]he 'bad' actions of the stepmother's daughter express sibling rivalry, but also allow the heroine's own latent hostility to be acted out. The stepsister does what the heroine would like to do; she 'violates' the mother by not carrying out the tasks."[228]

Some sources attribute a Freudian, incestuous view to the relationship of children with their parents. As a girl matures, she looks for a love interest, a husband in the old peasant society. The closest male in her world is her father, and she "unwittingly tries her feminine charm" on him. She and her mother become rivals for his attention, and the mother "helps the growing daughter to overcome the oedipal difficulties of a romantic relationship with her father."[229]

So, how does Baba Yaga fit into this situation? She herself doesn't have a husband, so she shouldn't be afraid her female initiates would try to take away his affection. Baba Yaga's role as a mother is one that is not encumbered by jealousy or threat. She must direct the girl's attention to the desired path: making herself "desirable" for a suitor of her own.

Baba Yaga plays a similar role with a young man of marriageable age who has begun to untangle himself from his mother's apron strings. At this point, Baba Yaga must prevent him from developing sexual desires for his mother. The peasant society he lived in placed a high value on masculinity, but the boy still had ties to his mother. And, as he grew older, unlike young females, he did not leave his home when he got married. By the time he matured, he could develop an Oedipal affection toward his mother. Baba Yaga becomes the mother who helps arrange a suitable marriage for the young man. Her sexually unappealing appearance ensures he doesn't foster any amiable feelings toward her.

And so, the kind mother must become a "Baba Yaga" and distance her children from herself to ensure they pursue an acceptable and traditional relationship. They must become adults and find their own spouse. And the story of Vasilisa the Beautiful is a perfect example of this:

> But sooner or later the moment comes when the light goes out in the cozy parental home, and you have to go and get fire from Baba Yaga, go through trials, defeat monsters and learn to weave a fabric of your own life because only by yourself you can weave the thread of your fate.[230]

In the same way that Baba Yaga prepares a young man for a leadership role, the successful woman who comes to the witch is one who has the potential to "become leaders in the society of matriarchy (wives of princes or those women who claim the role of a ruler)."[231]

In other stories, where a girl rescues her brother from Baba Yaga, a different type of initiation occurs. This is not one that Baba Yaga teaches directly, but one that the girl has to learn on her own. She is learning about how to prepare for motherhood, how to properly care for young children. As she escapes

Hiding from Baba Yaga. Nelinda, 2022.

from the witch's hut, the girl finds refuge in various places as Baba Yaga's servants look for her. For example, a stove, an apple tree, and a birch tree hide her.

> She left with her brother. She came to the stove and said, "Stove, stove! Hide me!"
>
> "Sit down, fair maiden!" Right away the stove spread out, it got much wider. She sat down in it.
>
> …
>
> The sister and brother came to the apple tree. "Apple tree, apple tree! Hide me!"
>
> "Sit down, fair maiden!"
>
> The apple tree made itself fluffy, curly.
>
> She sat right down in a crevice in the trunk. Then the gray eagle came flying again and flew to the apple tree. "Apple tree, apple tree! Did you happen to see, did a girl happen to pass here with a little boy?"

MAGICAL ESCAPE ROUTE

In fairy tales, household items may have magical powers, especially if they have any kind of connection to Baba Yaga. For example, as mentioned earlier, a ball of yarn leads the hero where he wants to go—whether it is to Baba Yaga's hut or to the kidnapped maiden.

At other times, the hero and heroine steal the witch's possessions or are given items that enable them to escape her clutches. As the intended victims flee, they hurl objects behind them. Mountains, forests, and bodies of water arise, thwarting Baba Yaga's advancement.

It may seem strange that these common items produce the results that they do. However, these magical objects have command over the elements, and like produces like. The following are a few examples of the significance of the magical objects.

Mirror: Becomes a deep sea. Its surface, like water, reflects images. Many superstitions are associated with mirrors, which are "a corridor to the other world." Through it, a person can both see and communicate with spirits (Naumovska, 550).

Kerchief or towel: Creates a vast lake or a river of water or fire that cannot be crossed. The river that is created represents emotions (anger, pity, jealousy) that a girl must learn to control. It separates the two worlds she can no longer reconcile: her childhood and adulthood (Bouthillette, 44).

Brush: Turns into a dense forest. The bristles, all packed closely together, bring to mind dense woods, and the handle itself is made of wood. Once the person throws it behind him, it returns to its natural state (Forrester, xxxi). The dense, impenetrable forest itself is symbolic of the darkness of the womb. It is a dangerous place where the initiation occurs. As with the river, which separates her old self from her new, mature one, the initiate must learn to establish a boundary between these two worlds (Bouthillette, 44).

Comb: Causes a mountain range to rise. The outline of the comb's teeth resembles a mountain range. A comb, as well as a towel, represents beauty and utility. When thrown behind her, the girl is "abandoning the domestic considerations and possessions" in order to "gain access to the "outside" world, and obtain power and maturity through this change of attitude and new behavior" (Bouthillette, 44).

Vasilisa the Beautiful. Alexander Petkov, 2022.

It answered, "No."

"Why have you, apple tree, gotten so curly, lowered your branches right down to the ground?"

"The time has come," it said. "I'm standing here all curly."

…

And the girl came to the birch tree. "Birch tree, birch tree! Hide me!"

"Sit down, my dear!" it said. It made itself fluffy, curly, like the apple tree.[232]

The concept of the stove being symbolic of a woman's womb has already been discussed, and its being "wider" suggests pregnancy, as does the "curly" tree with its branches to the ground.

The wording, as well as the position of the girl and baby concealed beneath the lowered branches, suggests that the tree is pregnant, that its "time has come."[233]

Now the girl has passed her initiation. During this time, she has learned "to imitate in the most exacting manner the tasks which will be her lot when she assumes the role of mother and old woman herself."[234] Note that this includes all stages of her life, not just her initial subserviate role.

The role of the old woman is one that many studies overlook when discussing a girl's initiation. This latter stage of her life is a role that holds the same power Baba Yaga wields. The power she once had to obey is now the power she herself can exercise.[235] The young woman is empowered to carry on Baba Yaga's teachings, either by being made a priestess to the goddess Yaga or by becoming a new, powerful sorceress like Baba Yaga. Failure to pass these initiation tests will result in the girl's literal death; according to Baba Yaga, a girl who cannot take on this power is not worthy to enter the phase of adulthood.

This tells us there's more to Baba Yaga's instructions, secrets that lie subtly beneath the surface. Consider the fact that among the peasants, older women told these stories to children. These elders of the community could transmit secret knowledge that their female listeners would understand, while the males would not.

What does this hidden knowledge entail? More modern stories talk about female empowerment and intuition, rather than servitude. Baba Yaga teaches her female initiate the ability to develop her individuality, enabling her to come to terms with her feelings about adulthood, define her identity as a woman, and understand her desires and fears.[236] So the woman's story becomes one "of handing down the blessing on women's power of intuition from mother to daughter,"[237] with Baba Yaga taking on the role of mother.

Perhaps these were the underlying themes in the story of Vasilisa the Beautiful as well. Is it possible the tellers of the story understood this? That the story held some hidden meaning for them that they transmitted to the younger generation? Although the stories were written by men, they were told by women, who could put their own twist onto the tale.

To recap the highlights of that story if you are unfamiliar with it: Vasilisa was told to go to Baba Yaga's hut to get fire, because the light in her home went out. While there, Vasilisa performed chores impossible for a human to complete in the timeframe given. The girl, however, had a doll that did all the tasks. In the end, Baba Yaga reluctantly gave Vasilisa a skull torch to take home. When she arrived, the skull burned her stepmother and stepsisters to ash.

What is the "self-realization" Vasilisa came to? Perhaps it was that she didn't have to live being tormented by her stepfamily. Baba Yaga had taught Vasilisa many things and given her a magic skull torch. The witch empowered Vasilisa to discover her own path, one which "stands for the transformative, dynamic power of creativity, which both destroys and gives life."[238]

Some people say that it was Baba Yaga's power from the torch that killed Vasilisa's stepfamily. But consider this. While Vasilisa was on her way home, the skull torch went out as daylight approached. Is it possible that Vasilisa herself re-ignited the light when she reached her home? Her only hope of a better life was one where she was beyond the control of her stepmother.

It crossed my mind when reading about the power of bones that if coming in contact with them transferred their power to the one who touched them, did Vasilisa embrace her darker side? Was it her wish to burn up her stepfamily? Did Baba Yaga transfer the knowledge of how to do this to the girl when the witch gave her the skull torch? Passing on knowledge like a mother did to a daughter? Because Baba Yaga did not have to give Vasilisa that kind of fire. She could have given her non-magical fire. Although Vasilisa asked her doll advice in all other matters, she did not ask her doll (embodiment of good) what to do with the torch.

The fire-burning skull gave Vasilisa knowledge of the ancestors, which told her that she would be rewarded if she listened to her intuition. When the skull spoke to her, perhaps it was Vasilisa's intuition speaking. By refusing to allow anyone to repress her any longer, she strengthened a connection to her intuition.[239]

Vasilisa then went to live with an older woman in town and wove a beautiful cloth, which she later sewed into shirts for the tsar. When the old woman told her the tsar wanted her to make the shirts,

MAGICAL DOLLS

In the story of "Vasilisa the Beautiful," her doll is a marvelous gift. It not only listens to the girl's complaints and gives her advice, but it also does her chores, all for just a little food. This doll is at times described as a miniature version of Vasilisa herself. It's like cloning herself into something that never tires. It has been described as "a little piece of the soul that carries all the knowledge of the larger soul-Self," representing "the inner spirit, … the voice of inner reason, inner knowing, and inner consciousness" (Cagnolati, 32).

The doll has also been explained in other ways. It's symbolic of the girl's deceased mother. It protects Vasilisa the way a mother would. In addition, there's role reversal here, since Vasilisa is the one who needs to nurture and care for the doll. Now that her mother has died, Vasilisa is becoming her mother and learning to accept and internalize her legacy. This is her first step into gaining insight into who she really is. Without an over-protective mother, Vasilisa can face new challenges and mature as a woman (Popławska, 17).

Another purpose of the doll, and one that I find most interesting, is as a talisman. The doll "represents religion, or rather the outward embodiment of some object of devotion" (Kraus Reprint, 38). Vasilisa's doll may be the literary equivalent of ancient female figures archaeologists have dug up from Neolithic sites and perhaps "provide clues about how ancient Europeans might have interacted with their goddess figurines: about what they did with them – and when, and why, and how" (Studebaker).

The small, palm-sized Neolithic figures may represent goddesses. It's possible women carried these dolls with them during initiation rites at a time when societies worshiped a female deity, so the goddess would help them succeed. The fact that Vasilisa was instructed not to let anyone know about her doll may possibly refer to a period when goddess worship was forbidden in the patriarchal society. During this time, women may have carried the dolls in secret, hidden in pockets or sewn into clothing.

Vasilisa's response was, "I knew this work would not pass by my hands." He ultimately married her, and Vasilisa, the old woman, and the doll lived happily ever after.

She worked her "artistic" magic (taught to her by Baba Yaga perhaps?) by weaving this marvelous cloth. The story does not say where she learned to weave a cloth "so fine that it could be put through a needle's eye in place of thread," but she didn't have this ability before going to the witch's hut.

Weaving is a characteristic of someone who defines fate (more about this later), and it was her weaving ability that led to her improvement in her station in life. I can visualize Vasilisa turning toward the forest and giving Baba Yaga a thumbs up, and the witch winking back at her.

After all, Baba Yaga, by awakening Vasilisa to her true self, made her "free to make independent choices, strong enough to fight obstacles and ready to develop as well as to bear the consequences of [her] own behaviours."[240]

Warrior

The tales in which you find "Yaga the Warrior" are perhaps the most unusual. In the story of "Ivan Tsarevich and Bailoi Polyanin" (which you can read at the end of this book), she is called Baba-Yaga Golden Leg (*zolotaia noga*), while she is Ježibaba in similar tales. The hero has been waging war with Baba Yaga for a long time. In the case of Bailoi Polyanin, it's because he wants to marry her daughter.

Unlike Baba Yaga's daughters in other stories, this one is a beautiful human, not a creature. Nothing is said about why Baba Yaga doesn't want to let her daughter marry, but from what's been written about the old woman, it's likely this "daughter" was some young girl Baba Yaga had stolen away and kept as a servant, and now she's unwilling to part with her ready-made slave. Why else would the woman in the end allow her "mother" to be killed, unless she had been kidnapped or mistreated?

The heroes meet the warrior-witch on the battlefield and trample thousands of her soldiers with the hooves of their horses, but more and more soldiers appear. Even when the hero strikes them with his saber, the men magically regenerate and also continue to increase: "And as the sabre starts to hew the heads were falling one after another, but the more enemies they slayed the more were around them."[241]

In the story of Ježibaba, the hero cuts the witch to pieces and ends the war, while in the tale with Baba Yaga, she escapes to the underworld when the heroes overwhelm her and her army. The hero Ivan follows her and discovers how her unending army is made: by magic blacksmiths, tailors, weavers, and shoemakers. With each strike of his sledgehammer, the blacksmith produces a soldier. A tailor pricks a needle toward himself, then away, and a soldier on a horse is created. Each time a girl moves her shuttle on a loom, a soldier jumps out. When a shoemaker pricks an awl, out comes a mounted soldier with a gun.[242]

> Worth attention is also the image of soldier-producing artisans under the command of a hag. Perhaps there is more about this motif than only a picturesque fairy tale way to express the unlimited amount of the hag's human resources. Perhaps it refers to another common aspect of witch-war theme identified above, to the witch's tendency to dominate the baseborn and marginalised groups within the population.[243]

Ivan knows he has to put a stop to this soldier manufacturing. He tricks the artisans and cuts off the heads of all the workers. He then continues until he comes to the place where Baba Yaga lives. A woman close to the warrior-witch, often her daughter, helps Ivan deceive Baba Yaga. In some stories, the witch has waters of strength and weakness, which the maiden tells the hero to switch so he can defeat Baba Yaga in battle. In other stories, her daughter leads him to the sleeping witch. He cuts off her head, but the head speaks to him, telling him to hit her again. He refuses, because he knows that striking her again would resurrect the witch.

Ježibaba. Painting by Xénia Hoffmeisterová, 2000.
CC BY-SA 4.0 <https://creativecommons.org/licenses/by-sa/4.0>, via Wikimedia Commons.

This Baba Yaga is quite different from the witch who appears in other stories, and tales such as this are rare. She is an immensely strong, fierce warrior, leading an army and fighting on a horse the way Russian bogatyrs did. In one version of the story, she perceives the blows the hero gives her as nothing more than "Russian mosquito bites." The story itself suggests a more mythological origin than folk belief, due to its epic heroic scenes,[244] and it is believed to have "evolved outside the fairy tale tradition and only secondarily entered the genre."[245]

Certain aspects of this warlord-witch theme, with "the central moment [being] a war or battle of masculine elite against the army led by a demonic female being,"[246] set it apart from typical fairy-tale traditions. The first is that the conflict arises within an aristocratic and political context, with the hero's companion being a foreign king or old family friend. The second is that in some versions of the tale, the pursuit of the villain to the underworld is "substituted by the motif of a royal escort." Even the battle scenes are atypical of the fairy tale, displaying a "kind of berserker scene; the hero's exceptional martial performance during the battle expressed through the scene of mowing the hostile warriors." All of these components are said to have resemblances to the Beowulf epos.[247]

All these moments support the assumption, that the Slavic hag-war theme, and especially its western variants, can be considered a relic of different and more archaic folklore genre. Coexistence of several factors, i.e. non-fairy tale heroic content and rare but territorially extensive occurrence combined with textual stability, suggest that 1) by its nature it is alien to European as well as Slavic fairy tale and 2) probably it originated in a tradition of extensively disposed and complexly developed militaristic narratives. Thus the certain layers of the archaic IE (Slavic) epos seem to be the most likely candidate for its original environment.[248]

In other stories in which Baba Yaga is classified as a warrior, she doesn't appear on the battlefield, but she's vicious to strangers who enter her home while she's away. With animal-like instinct, she "views any presence from the outside as a threat," as an "unforgiveable crime."[249]

In addition to entering her property without permission, the hero takes the liberty of eating her food or worse, slaughtering her livestock for his meal. She flies in with her tongue lolling out of her mouth, or she appears unexpectedly from under the ground. Baba Yaga beats all but one of the men half to death or carves a strip off of their backs. Only the last to encounter her is able to defeat the witch, because he is the cleverest of the bunch.

> She enters the hut and, after some short parley, seizes her pestle, and begins beating the hero with it until he falls prostrate. Then she cuts a strip out of his back, eats up the whole of the viands he has prepared for his companions, and disappears. After a time the beaten hero recovers his senses, 'ties up his head with a handkerchief,' and sits groaning until his comrades return. Then he makes some excuse for not having got any supper ready for them, but says nothing about what has really happened to him.
>
> On the next day the second hero is treated in the same manner by the Baba Yaga, and on the day after that the third undergoes a similar humiliation. But on the fourth day it falls to the lot of the young Ivan to stay in the hut alone. The Baba Yaga appears as usual, and begins thumping him with her pestle; but he snatches it from her, beats her almost to death with it, cuts three strips out of her back, and then locks her up in a closet. When his comrades return, they are surprised to find him unhurt, and a meal prepared for them, but they ask no questions. After supper they all take a bath, and then Ivan remarks that each of his companions has had a strip cut out of his back. This leads to a full confession, on hearing which Ivan 'runs to the closet, takes those strips out of the Baba Yaga, and applies them to their backs,' which immediately become cured. He then hangs up the Baba Yaga by a cord tied to one foot, at which cord all the party shoot. At length it is severed, and she drops. As soon as she touches the ground, she runs to the stone from under which she had appeared, lifts it, and disappears.[250]

You can read a variation of this tale ("The Story of Yvashka with the Bear's Ear") at the end of this book.

Seductress

Among the Polish and Ukrainian stories are those in which Baba Yaga is not an old hag. She is young and beautiful, and she uses those characteristics to her advantage. Here, she plays the role of "Yaga the

Baba Yaga the seductress. Alexander Petkov, 2022.

Seductress." She lures a man to her and takes wild flights at night, using him as her vehicle. That sounds like a euphemism to me for uninhibited sex.

She does that as well, seducing men and making them remain with her forever—which might not be that long. She "drinks" their youth, causing them to wither and die, in order to prolong her own life. One poor soul won't do; she must seduce numerous young men if she desires to keep her youth and beauty.

After her latest lover has gone to sleep, Baba Yaga gazes in the mirror to see how much his life has restored her own vitality. She determines how many more lovers she'll need to achieve her goal of being beautiful and not looking like a shrew.

If the men don't come to her, this Baba Yaga is not beyond kidnapping youths who have completed coming-of-age ceremonies. She can fake her beauty long enough to enchant an unsuspecting youth, until she has trapped him in her lair. Other deceitful methods include giving her guest a potion that makes him stay. If no young men are nearby, she'll kidnap an engaged girl and wait for her fiancée to come rescue her. The brave, honorable young man would be too much in love to fall for Baba Yaga's charms, so instead, she takes on the appearance of the kidnapped girl and seduces the youth that way.

If, by chance, any man can survive her amorous advances and perform all the tasks she demands of him, only then will she let him leave. She has done her duty, the part of initiation rarely spoken about: teaching a man not only how to accomplish tasks in life, but also how to flirt and behave in the game of love, and not least of all, what to do with his wife in the marriage bed.

If, after all of this, he thinks he's fallen in love with Baba Yaga, she will either disappear, forcing him to return home, or she'll change her appearance into that ugly old crone she tries so hard not to be.[251]

Mistress of Fate

Those arriving at Baba Yaga's home may find the old woman spinning. All the while she's plotting her trickery, like a spider, devising tasks for her visitors to perform that will trap them in her web of deceit.

Whenever you read about a woman spinning thread or weaving in fairy tales, you can be sure that she's a supernatural being, likely a goddess of birth and death, and has a connection to fate. This is someone who resides in a liminal space, that is, an in-between location, one that borders the land of the living and the land of the dead, as these deities weave a person's life and death, connecting them to both places. Baba Yaga is no stranger to these tasks. This is especially true when three Baba Yagas appear in the story. The three sisters of fate are a common theme in the mythologies of other cultures as well.

Other folklore beings prohibit these domestic chores such as spinning and weaving on certain days of the week, in particular on Friday. Any woman caught weaving on this day is guaranteed to be visited by the avenging creature—be it a deity or a demon—and pay the price. Is the cost of having her skin torn off and her fingers bent and deformed worth it to not take a break one day a week? No, I didn't think so.

Unlike these other deities, however, Baba Yaga doesn't prohibit spinning or weaving on any day. In fact, she demands it, regardless of the day a girl visits. Baba Yaga finds it to be a necessary task to determine a girl's worth. When one arrives, Baba Yaga asks her to spin, spin, spin. Whether she succeeds in the assigned task depends on the girl's character. Is the girl kind or unkind? If the girl is good, she'll get a reward, or at least not lose her life. If she's bad, Baba Yaga has a feast.

At least that's how it looks on the surface. If you dig deeper, you may discover another intent to Baba Yaga's frantic spinning. It's not only the act itself that is associated with fate. The materials have special meanings for one's birth, fate, and eventual death.

- **Wool basket**: Represents the womb or the otherworld.
- **Unspun wool**: A child's "before-birth" state in the otherworld.
- **Spun thread**: The child's existence in the world of the living.[252]

Prediction. Sergey Solomko, before 1928.
Public domain, via Wikimedia Commons.

When Baba Yaga completes a ball of thread or spun yarn, she creates a link between the world of the living and that of the dead. It's a ball of yarn like this that enables heroes such as Ivan to traverse between the worlds.

Let's look at this in more detail. Baba Yaga has a golden spindle and spins golden or silver thread.

> In a fairytale published by Nikolai Onchukov in 1908, we read: *A hut stands on a chicken's leg, on a spindle heel, it spins in circles and you can't see the door [...] in the hut sits a woman, spinning silk, spinning long threads, the spindle spins and the threads fall beneath the floor.*[253]

It's said her thread is made from the bones and guts of victims as her chicken hut continually spins around, this time on spindle heels rather than chicken legs.[254]

Did you know?

Bridges to the otherworld were often depicted as a thread or a hair. Only the righteous were light enough to cross this narrow passage. Heavy sinners fell into the pit of Hell (Mencej, 63).

The act of spinning was more than simply a means to determine the child's fate; it's compared to "(pro)creation," moving from the otherworld into the land of the living. "All life comes from death, and every death foreshadows renewal" is a traditional European worldview, "understood as an eternal circulation of souls between this world and the other."[255]

So, what is Baba Yaga making with this thread? One possibility is new life. This goes along with a belief that "the dead rejuvenate from tomb to womb, afterwards to reincarnate so as to progress from womb to tomb."[256]

Baba Yaga is at the center of it all. She destroys life and she creates new life. Perhaps she is remaking those who fell prey to her cannibalism, those who were not worthy to be initiated. From their remains she is creating a new life, one that no longer holds the faults of the previous one, a child she can be proud of.

Spinning thread may also represent integrating a child into society, such as Baba Yaga does through her initiation tasks. It removes the wild, untamed nature from her initiate and develops a sense of culture. Raw flax or unspun yarn represents unharnessed potential or wild nature, while when it's made into clothing, it's refined, and like the initiates, cultured.

> The technique of "turning human" therefore shows that, of the basic working processes of human culture, it is mainly spinning and weaving that "play a vital role in taming or ennobling the demonic world of nature and the initially demonic aspects of human nature and in protecting human culture."[257]

In all, Baba Yaga is not only creating new life, she is doing her best to ensure that her creations are worthy of her scrutiny, that they will be outstanding citizens in their communities, and that they will continue the cycle of goodwill for the betterment of mankind.

Weaving Time

Another aspect of weaving is to weave time itself. Baba Yaga has faithful servants who make time move forward: three riders on white, red, and black horses. These horsemen pass Vasilisa on her way to Baba Yaga's house.

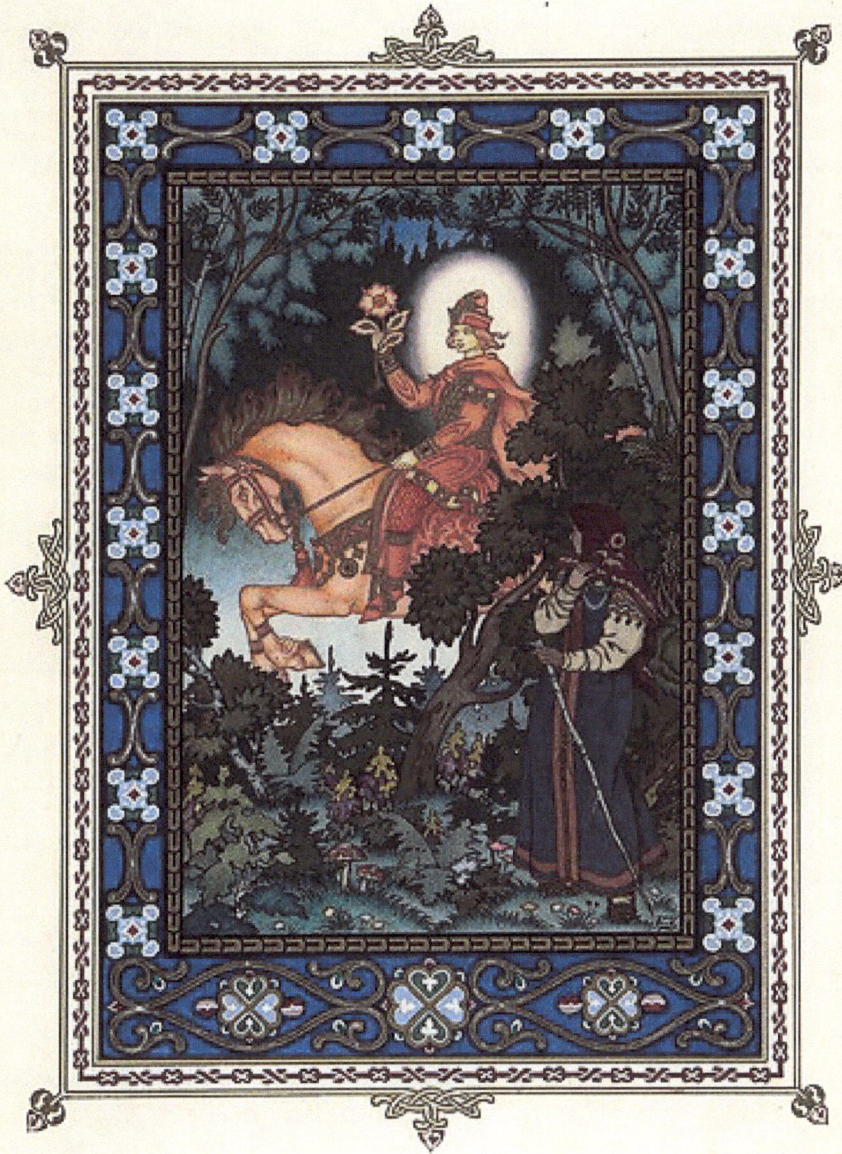

Vasilisa the Fair. Boris Zvorykin.
Public domain, via Wikimedia Commons.

Suddenly a knight on horseback galloped past her all in white. His cloak was white, and his horse and the reins: and it became light. She went further, and suddenly another horseman passed by, who was all in red, and his horse was red, and his clothes: and the sun rose. Vasilisa went on through the night and the next day. Next evening she came to the mead where Baba Yaga's hut stood.... Suddenly another horseman pranced by on his way. He was all in black, on a jet-black horse, with a jet-black cloak. He sprang to the door and vanished as though the earth had swallowed him up: and it was night.[258]

The old woman explains that these men mark the time of day: white is dawn, "the bright day," red is midday, "the red sun," and black is twilight, "the dark night." Baba Yaga controls time. It may also indicate that Baba Yaga lives "on the border of creation, where sky meets the earth."[259] She draws her creative powers from the very earth she lives on.

But these colors in Slavic culture have more significance than the time of day. They represent the passing of the seasons. Initially, in the herding culture, the year was thought of as two seasons: winter (black) and summer (white), with winter being the start of the year. The colors were neither good nor evil; instead, they were referred to as a time of either destruction or nurturing and creation.

Saint Demetrius on his black horse began the winter season on October 26 (or November 8). Black represented a time when the earth would rest and become fallow. Saint George, riding on his white horse, banished winter on April 23 (or May 6) and heralded in the summer. White here represented "radiance and energy," a time for creation and renewal.[260]

As agriculture began to flourish, a third season became more widespread. White still was the color that followed the harsh winter, but now it became associated with the springtime. Red took on the color of summer, while black remained for winter.

> In the indigenous religion, they saw all things as connected, so morning, noon and night were also seen as white, red and black. This also indicated the stages of a person's life: white for a pure maiden or youth, red for a man or woman in their fertile time of life and black for elders.[261]

Another theory is that the spinning of the hut represents the passage of time. It revolves around the twelve posts in the fence, which signify the twelve months of the year.[262] In stories where the hut has spindle heels, its constant spinning is said to imitate the turning of the Earth and "serves as an axis around which the heavens revolve."[263] As the hut twirls around, it passes by each stake, that is, through each month of the year.

> The word 'time' in Russian, *vremia*, comes from the same *vr-* root of turning and returning as the word for spindle, *vereteno*. A spindle holding up a rotating house where a frightening old woman tests her visitors and dispenses wisdom suggests a deep ritual past.[264]

The colors also demonstrate that Baba Yaga's control is not only over time and seasons, but also over the creation and destruction of life itself. This is demonstrated in the colors embroidered on a Bulgarian woman's shirt and their significance.

> The white and the red represent generally the male and the female principle, the sky and the earth in a holy union. Their combination (the traditional Bulgarian *martenitza*) symbolizes "the live life". They form together an opposition to the black color, which represents the destruction of the body and of earth itself, the connection with the

Baba Yaga looking through time. Alexander Petkov, 2022.

chthonic creatures. Based on this, the most general color message in the Bulgarian female costume can be brought down to the white of the male principle (heaven) as opposed to the red and the black of the female principle (earthly or chthonic). A combination expressing the idea of stimulating fertility and its protection.[265]

The three horsemen are also thought of as "the sacred masculine, in service to the sacred feminine/The Earth." They portray "the importance of chance, impermanence and balance." White is "pure, new, spring, young energy"; red represents "energetic peak, the burning time, inspiration and passion, summer time"; and black is for "the womb of darkness, black night, winter, rest, dream time."[266]

The horsemen are the passing of time, the seasons, the cycle of life, the male counterpart or consort to the feminine, which Baba Yaga represents. They are neither good nor evil. Together they create and destroy life, only to repeat the cycle of rebirth from death.

Triple Goddess

The image of Baba Yaga that best represents this passage of time and cycle of life is the Triple Goddess—maiden, mother, crone. Although mostly Baba Yaga is perceived as the crone, "[i]n her the cycles of feminine life are brought to completion, and yet she contains them all."[267] She embodies experiences from each phase of the goddess.

The Triple Goddess does not only "valorize fertility" and maternal qualities. It also embraces "the warrior, the virgin, the destructive crone, or any other of the Goddess's 'thousand faces', all of which are as valid as the nurturing mother."[268]

In Indo-European beliefs, a goddess expended energy, "a life-force which both motivates and characterizes all people." The manner in which she achieved this varied depending on her life phase within the Triple Goddess—either distributing or dissipating energy.[269]

Maiden

The Maiden, the first phase of the Triple Goddess, has no consort. This time of her life was one in which her powers were being stored for later use, for when she reached the Mother stage.[270]

> She is spring, the fresh beginning of all things. The Maiden is the continuation of all life, the repeating of endless cycles of birth and rebirth, both of the body and of the spirit. She is the dawn, eternal youth and vigor, enchantment and seduction, the waxing Moon. Traditionally, Her color is white, denoting innocence and newness.[271]

As maiden, she is independent, responsible to no one except herself. She must only adhere to the laws of nature, the Mother. She "dreams of the potential for what She can become."[272]

The Maiden is the Forest Mistress, the Huntress, not only of the animals, but also of the mind. She symbolizes growth in every aspect of life, to prepare the way for the one she is responsible for. She prepares him to face the truth about himself and his need for change. He cannot hide the truth from her, because she is the Prophetess, who will help him see himself for who he truly is and what he can become.[273]

Mother

The Mother stage of the Triple Goddess is one of fertility. She releases her powers to her male counterpart. This may be her husband or lover. A more independent woman can determine whom she

Baba Yaga with herbs. Alexander Petkov, 2022.

will transmit her powers to, and do so in a manner that will not deplete herself.[274] She is the bearer of children.

Baba Yaga, has offspring of various forms, the creatures of nature. In addition, she possesses features that denote her fertility: breasts so enormous she can toss them over her shoulders or must leave them outside her hut, because they don't fit inside. When she dies, the soil beneath her becomes a swamp, a place noted both for its dangers as well as its tremendous fertility.[275]

> The Mother aspect of the Goddess is summer, the ripening of all things. She is the re-creation of life, both plant and animal; She is also the creation of universal bodies. She is the high point in all cycles, whether of living or creating, for the Mother blesses and gives with open hands. She is the Great Teacher of the Mysteries. Symbolically, the Mother aspect is the boiling or churning cauldron, the re-creative pot, and the ripeness of womanhood (or adulthood in general). The day, lustiness, reproduction, creation in any form and of anything—these are all within Her realm. Traditionally, Her color is red, the color of blood and the life force.[276]

The role of the Mother is one of the initiator. Her color red is that of blood. With it, she prepares men for the fears and hardships of war, and women for the fears and hardships of giving birth.[277] She knows who she is and teaches her pupils to understand themselves and how to accept responsibility for their own actions. She instructs them in the ways of self-discipline and patience, and provides for them the means to obtain balance in their lives. She provides guidance on any spiritual journey and enables those in her care to discover their potential.[278]

The Mother has many aspects, some of which blend with her other incarnations. She is a creator, nurturer, judge. She is the keeper of the secret knowledge. She assists in removing the negativity in life and transforming it into the positive. She teaches those she has embraced how to use their intuition, in exchange for accepting responsibility for their actions. For those who refuse to listen, she will refine their souls until they are willing to learn.[279]

Crone

In the final stage of the Triple Goddess, the Crone is perceived in two ways: the wise, nurturing grandmother, who is venerated for her knowledge, or the evil, fearsome witch, who sucks the energy and life from all she comes in contact with to replace her own depleted energies.[280] It's the latter image that persevered over time; Baba Yaga became the crone who devoured children to restore her vitality. However, the Crone is much more than either of these ideas. She is simultaneously "ageless, timeless, exquisite and terrible, frightening and awesome."[281]

> Because She deals with death and the end of cycles, most people tend to avoid this face of the Goddess. Black is Her color, and sometimes dark blue and the deepest of purples. Black is the absorber of all light, the color of darkness where all life rests before rebirth. The Crone is winter, night, outer space, the abyss, menopause, advancement of age, wisdom, counsel, the gateway to death and reincarnation, and the Initiator into the deepest of Mysteries and prophecies. The waning Moon is Her monthly time of power.[282]

The Crone is the most feared aspect of the Triple Goddess, because she brings illness and death. She knows "that she has been and will be."[283] And so, she has command over opposites: birth and death, youth and old age, hope and despair. She prepares all who come to her for the transitions in their life by

Baba Yaga. Bogatov Nikolai Alekseevich, 1894.
Public domain, via Wikimedia Commons.

teaching them about "insight and self-reflection, facing the truth, childlike naturalness, acceptance of 'the conditions of [their] existence.' "[284]

One must seek out the Crone; she will not come to you. She teaches that life continues on the other side. She breaks everything down in order to rebuild it. She holds the key to life's deepest mysteries.[285] Although she represents death, it is death as a beginning, not an ending.[286]

The Crone is the female shaman in the matriarchal society, the leader who made the moral and legal decisions. She represented the powerful feminine and understood the mysteries of life and death. When women reached menopause, "it was because the 'wise blood' had backed up to be held in the womb where it would create a new way of being, …wisdom birthing from an aging psyche."[287]

How to Appease

There's not much you can do to please Baba Yaga. She's lived a good long life and is set in her ways. The best way to get on her good side is to show her respect, be willing to learn, and do everything she tells you to do without complaining. She rewards a hard worker, and she'll impart whatever wisdom she decides you need to know. Don't ask too many questions. They are likely to get you eaten by her. Mostly, however, she'd much prefer it if you left her alone and solved your own problems.

How to Defeat

If you're in combat with Baba Yaga the warrior, you'll need magic objects before you can overcome her. Either that, or you'll have to make sure she can't access her own magical items, such as strengthening water. Switching her magical potions around will work: she'll get the weakening water, while you grab the one she thought she was drinking. If that doesn't work, it's likely you'll have to resort to the same kind of brutality that she herself inflicts upon others: carving her body with iron rods, cutting off her head, chopping her body into little pieces, or throwing her into a fiery river.

In less hostile situations, your best chance of survival is to stand up to her—at least if you're a male. Rebuke her when the first thing out of her mouth is that she wants to eat you. Remind her of the rules of hospitality. If you're female, pay close attention to everything she tells you. She truly wants you to become a better person, knowledgeable in everything that Baba Yaga herself understands. She wants to make you into a newer version of herself.

At other times, you may have done all of this, and Baba Yaga is still bent on eating you. If this happens, you'll have to resort to trickery to escape from her. Being kind to the witch's companions is a good way to start, because they are unfamiliar with this gesture. It won't take much to get them on your side, and they'll tell you how you can escape, give you special objects to aid you, and even pretend they are you to make sure you have enough time to slip away.

Another form of trickery is to pretend to be clueless about what she expects. She wants you to climb into the oven? Pretend it's the most difficult thing you have ever been asked to do. She'll have to show you the proper way, and then all you have to do is push her in the way she had intended to do to you.

Fact or Fiction?

You've now learned what the Baba Yaga of fairy tales is all about. But another side of her is just as fascinating: the one where she interacts with the lives of people today. She has a devote following, who think of her as a mother figure. While others wish they could have avoided their meeting. As in the fairy tales, she behaves differently with people: some she mentors, while others she terrifies. Does it depend on how she is approached or a person's preconceived perception of her? Or is there some other method to her madness? We present to you some of the encounters we have discovered and let you be the judge of her intentions.

Baba Yaga. Elena Polenova, 1906.
Public domain, via Wikimedia Commons.

Baba Yaga Within

In our interview with shaman Baba Phoenix, she spoke about dream walking. We asked if she had ever seen or felt Baba Yaga while in that state. Her response was that it was more of a feeling, not a physical presence. Baba Yaga was within her, a part of her soul and dreams, but that part of her didn't express itself fully until she reached the age of 50. In our interview, she said:

> I feel like a representation of that archetype [the dark night goddesses]. Because it's inward and not outward, I'm not going to see it outside myself. I've never attracted dark women [goddesses]. I've never attracted bad witches. I've never attracted any of that in my path, and I was even on a very intense journey that got darker and darker and darker in my own karma. … I am going back to the core of myself, which is a Baba Yaga archetype and type of woman. Now, it just happened to be my destiny, so everything I understand about her, it's already incorporated in what I do with my apprentices, what I do as a shaman, and what I do as a bone mother, mystic, and all of those things are actually enacted out.[288]

Phoenix says that Baba Yaga washes away obstacles hidden in the unconscious mind. She awakens a desire for life and reconnects generations as a living ancestor incarnate. Baba Yaga feels the entirety of life and fills people with great changes and challenges. You call to her during stressful times when you need healing, but you must do the tasks she demands of you.

Baba Yaga's Apprentice

Another person who has experienced a positive side of Baba Yaga is Natalia Clarke. In her book *Pagan Portals: Baba Yaga Slavic Earth Goddess*, she talks about meeting Baba Yaga.

> She came on the morning of the Full Moon in February and took possession of my awareness. She held on tight and I could not ignore the feeling or shake the energy off. … I woke up with the sense of her in my skin, her words on my lips and her face close to mine. Her breath was cold, indescribable, terrifying, but I tried to hold my nerve and bow in reverence. [289]

If Baba Yaga comes to you and accepts you, Clarke says, she'll take you under her wing and slowly initiate you.

> During the last level of the apprenticeship into Baba Yaga's magic you will be invited inside the house, which is both a cauldron of wisdom, a resting place/coffin, and a burning fire oven of transformation. To have reached this stage you must be born again, so to speak and on the way to understanding yourself, others and the world to a degree that brings you complete peace, trust and acceptance. There is a big "but" here, however. Let us not forget that an important side to this Goddess is her trickster character. She tends to disrupt proceedings if she sees it fit. There might be an ultimate test that comes your way here. One never knows what is to come when it comes to Baba Yaga. That is for certain. When we knock on the door of her hut, we never know what we are going to get and if we are going to come out the other side. We won't know until we are ready to do it.[290]

A Cook's Heart

Are you looking to make some special recipe? Ask Baba Yaga for her guidance because as one person says on a forum post, she is known for her cooking and baking skills—even beyond that of placing children in her oven. This Baba Yaga is the one who is skilled with herbs and can assist you with traditional recipes that call for berries, roots, herbs, and spices. The poster says, "When I make something in the kitchen that I don't have or know a recipe for, I ask for her guidance. And she whispers in my ear what to do. And I must be honest, she once shouted at me to stop while putting in too much spice. Some of my best meals have come from her."[291]

Hair Turned Gray

Another person's encounter with Baba Yaga was not quite so pleasant. The day started out normal for a twenty-five-year-old man as he and friends went into a dense forest to pick berries. They got lost on their way back and ended up by a swamp, where they discovered an abandoned hut. Since it was evening, they decided to spend the night and look for the way back in the morning.

This one man woke up around 3 a.m. and went outside. The forest was unusually quiet, until the moment when a rumbling began. The stars disappeared into complete blackness. Thunder, lightning, and hail followed. Then a light moved quickly in the man's direction. He thought it might be a UFO. He couldn't move. When it got close enough, he saw a woman with loose-flowing hair. She was sitting in a cylinder-shaped object that emitted a blue glow from behind. She shook her finger at the man, and a current passed through his body. She disappeared as rapidly as she had appeared, until only a glowing point remained in the sky. The man could move again, and he returned to the hut. In the morning, he discovered that the hair on his head had all turned gray.[292]

Baba Yaga Will Eat Me

Imagine being a six-year-old boy lying in the dark in his grandfather's room. The corridor outside the room is lit, and a soft orange glow seeps in from a window behind the bed. Suddenly, he felt someone stroking the hair on his head. He lifted his eyes to see a little old woman with gray hair sitting at the head of the bed. He recognized her as Baba Yaga from the fairy tales his mother told him. She started combing his hair with a wooden comb.

The boy became frightened. He asked, "Are you Baba Yaga?" To which she answered in a low voice, "Yes." He had to ask the obvious question weighing on his mind: "Will you eat me?" and then "Will you eat my mom and dad?" Baba Yaga replied in the affirmative to both questions, but her words came out as if she didn't understand what he was asking. Instead, she continued to comb his hair and admire her work.

Years later, the boy, now an adult, described the tension in the room as "electrifying," with smells of ozone. He fell asleep to her still combing his hair.[293]

The Scourge We Know

Slavs love their Baba Yaga, whether the fairy-tale version or the one who yet wanders their minds. In Ireland, St. Patrick drove out the snakes and evil, but the same is not true for Slavic nations. Superstitions abound, and crossing one's self is often a natural response to anything troublesome.

When walking through a dense forest, a glade may suddenly open, and Baba Yaga can appear at any moment. She's accepted by the masses "without comment or criticism," and people have no need to explain "the true significance of her mysterious rides across the country." She is what she is and always has been so.

I agree with the writer who said: "I, therefore, should regard it almost in the light of a national calamity if some Russian St. Patrick were to make it his life work to drive every Baba Yaga from the country; it is so much easier to get rid of your scourge than to get him back again."[294]

Baba Yaga Tales

Baba Yaga is most often a minor character in the tales in which she appears. This is especially true for tales in which a hero seeks a bride and those stories in which she is a "donor." She plays a larger role in tales in which she is the villain. Within the stories that follow, you'll see her in all her glory, performing many roles that you've learned about earlier in this book. She's kind, vicious, helpful, hindering, and even humorous at times. In all, she is BABA YAGA!

Baba Yaga and the Strawberries

In a land far, far away, near an ancient river, near a large village, there was a dense forest. Mushrooms and berries were found there in immense quantities. But local people were not happy about this at all, because an old witch Baba Yaga lived in the depth of those woods. She was greedy beyond measure and did not allow anyone to step into the forest: some of the visitors she would lead into boggy grounds, and others she would completely exterminate.

One day, in summer, at the time when the berries were a-plenty, she decided to feast on wild strawberries, but that was tough luck: berries didn't want to go into the old Yaga's basket. They hid under the leaves and in the grass. Baba Yaga grumbled, got angry, but she couldn't look under every leaf and bow to every bush.

At the same hour, a little girl walked around the forest. It was still dark when she went out of the house to gather a basket of berries and eat a few. Berries were happy to show up for her. "Here we are. Take us quickly!"

Baba Yaga took away the basket from the girl and went to her hut, rejoicing at the unexpected prey. And the girl sat down on a stump and wept bitterly from disappointment.

Baba Yaga was walking, shaking her basket, and the berries jumped from there onto the grass, jumped and jumped, so all berries jumped out and rolled back to the forest meadow.

The girl was sitting, sobbing pathetically, and suddenly heard from the grass, "Get your handkerchief ready, dear!"

She took off her headscarf, spread it out in front of herself, and the berries rolled onto it. The girl tied them into a bundle and joyfully ran home.

And Baba Yaga came to her hut, had a look—but there were no berries! Only their smell remained. She threw the basket angrily, trembled, stamped her feet. "Ah-ah-ah! I wish bad luck to you!"

She cursed and cursed, and broke apart out of anger, and it was such a crash and roar that her hut crumbled along with her. And a swamp appeared in this place, and many berry bushes grew along its edging. And village children every year feast on ripe wild strawberries in that place.

And so, this is the end, and whoever listened—well done.

Source: Nukadeti.ru, "Баба яга и ягоды читать." This story was published by V.A. Smirnov in 1917. Translated from the Russian by Vadym Grebniev.

The Girl and the Robbers

Going with a party of friends into the forest to gather berries, a girl lost her way, but walked along until she found a small house. She cleaned and washed the house, heated the stove, baked some pies with her berries, and then hid herself beneath the stove.

This house belonged to robbers. They came and saw that it had been washed, and the oldest robber said, "Whoever has done this work will be my wife."

The girl heard, but didn't come out.

Then the robber said, "Whoever has done this work will be my sister."

The girl came out and began to live with the robbers. They fed her well and gave her drink and provided her with clothes and boots, and she was glad to live with them. They were pleased with her, for she looked after the house and kept it well.

One day the thieves departed, and Baba Yaga arrived and said to the girl, "I have come to visit you and brought you a girdle."

The girl died immediately after the witch placed the girdle on her.

The thieves returned and wept much over the girl's death and began to wash her. As soon as they untied the girdle, she revived. The thieves and the girl rejoiced.

When the thieves went away a second time, Baba Yaga appeared and threw a necklace around the girl's neck. She died, and the thieves arrived and wept over her death. They began to wash her, and when they removed the necklace, she revived.

A third time the thieves went away, and again Baba Yaga visited the girl, to whom she now gave some earrings. As soon as the girl put on the earrings, she died.

The thieves came and picked her up. They washed her, but since they didn't remove her earrings, the girl did not revive, and the thieves buried her beside their house.

Source: Coxwell, *Siberian and Other Folk-tales*, 573-574.

The Baba Yaga

There were once a man and wife who had no child, though they wished for one above all things. One day, when the husband was away, the wife laid a big stick of wood in the cradle and began to rock it and sing to it. Presently she looked and saw that the stick had arms and legs. Filled with joy, she began to rock and sing to it again. She kept it up for a long time, and when she looked again, there, instead of the stick of wood, was a fine little boy in the cradle. The woman took the child up and nursed him, and after that he was to her as her own son. She named him Peter and made a little suit of clothes and a cloth cap for him to wear.

One day Peter put on his little coat and went out in a boat to fish on the river.

At noon his mother went down to the bank of the stream and called to him, "Peter, Peter, bring your boat to shore, for I have brought a little cake for you to eat."

Then Peter said to his boat:

"Little boat, little boat, float a little nearer.

Little boat, little boat, float a little nearer."

The boat floated up to the shore. Peter took the cake and went back to his fishing again.

Now it so happened that a Baba Yaga, a terrible witch, was hiding in the bushes nearby. She heard all that passed between the woman and the child. So, after the woman had gone home, the Baba Yaga waited for a while, and then she went down to the edge of the river and hid herself there, and called out, "Peter, Peter, bring your boat to the shore, for I have brought another little cake for you."

But when Peter heard her voice, which was very coarse and loud, he knew it must be a Baba Yaga calling him, so he said:

"Little boat, little boat, float a little farther.

Little boat, little boat, float a little farther."

Then the boat floated away still farther out of the Baba Yaga's reach. The old witch soon guessed what was the matter, and she rushed off to a blacksmith, who lived over beyond the forest.

"Blacksmith, blacksmith, forge me a little fine voice as quickly as you can," she cried, "or I will put you in my mortar and grind you to pieces with my pestle."

The blacksmith was frightened. He made her a little fine voice as quickly as he could, and the Baba Yaga took it and hurried back to the river.

There she hid herself close to the shore and called in her little new voice, "Peter, Peter, bring your boat to the shore, for I have brought another little cake for you to eat."

When Peter heard the Baba Yaga calling him in her fine, small voice, he thought it was his mother, so he said to his boat:

"Little boat, little boat, float a little nearer.

Little boat, little boat, float a little nearer."

Then the little boat came to the land. Peter looked all about but saw no one. He wondered where his mother had gone and stepped out of his boat to look for her.

Immediately, the Baba Yaga seized him. Like a whirlwind, she rushed away with him through the forest and never stopped until she reached her own house. There she shut him up in a cage behind the house to keep him until he grew fat.

After she had shut him up, she went back into the house, and her little cat was there. "Mistress," said the cat, "I have cooked the dinner for you, and I am very hungry. Won't you give me something to eat?"

"All that I leave, that you can have," answered the Baba Yaga. She sat down at the table and ate up everything but one small bone. That was all the cat had.

Meanwhile, at home, the mother waited and waited for Peter to come back from the river with his fish. Then at last, she went down to look for him. There was his boat drawn up on the shore empty, and all around it were marks of the Baba Yaga's feet, and the trees and bushes were broken where she had rushed away through the forest. Then the mother knew that a witch had carried off the little boy. She went back home, weeping and wailing.

Now the woman had a faithful servant, and when this girl heard her mistress wailing, she asked her what the matter was.

The woman told her all that she had seen down at the river, and how she was sure a Baba Yaga had flown away with Peter.

"Mistress," said the girl, "there is no reason for you to despair. Just give me a little wheaten cake to keep me alive, and I'll set out and find Peter, even though I have to travel to the end of the world."

Then the woman was comforted. She gave the servant a cake, and the girl set out in search of Peter. She went on and on, and after a while, she came to the Baba Yaga's house. It stood on fowls' legs and turned whichever way the wind blew. The girl knocked at the door, and the Baba Yaga opened it.

"What do you want here?" she asked. "Are you seeking work or shunning work?"

"I'm seeking work," answered the girl. "Can you give me anything to do?"

The witch scowled at her terribly. "You may come in," she said, "and set my house in order, but do not go peeping and prying about, or it will be the worse for you."

The girl went in and began to set the house in order, while the Baba Yaga flew away into the forest, riding in a mortar, urging it along with a pestle, and sweeping away the traces with a broom.

After the witch had gone, the little cat said to the girl, "Give me, I beg of you, a little food, for I am starving with hunger."

"Here is a little cake. It is all I have, but I will give it to you in Heaven's name."

The little cat took the cake and ate it all up, every crumb.

"Now listen," said the cat. "I know why you are here, and that you are searching for the little boy named Peter. He is in a cage behind the house, but you can do nothing to help him. Wait until after dinner, when the Baba Yaga goes to sleep. Then rub her eyes with pitch so that she cannot get them open, and you may escape with the child through the forest."

The girl thanked the little cat and promised to do all things as it told her.

When the Baba Yaga came home, "Well, have you been peeping and prying?" she asked.

"I have not," answered the girl.

The Baba Yaga sat down, ate everything there was on the table, bones and all. Then she lay down and went to sleep. She snored terribly.

The girl took some pitch and smeared the witch's eyelids with it. Then she went out to where Peter was and let him out of the cage, and they ran away through the forest together.

The Baba Yaga slept for a long time. At last, she yawned and woke, but she could not get her eyes open. They were stuck tight with pitch. She was in a terrible rage. She stamped about and roared terribly. "I know who has done this," she cried, "and as soon as I get my eyes open, I'll go after her and tear her to pieces." Then she called to the cat to come and scratch her eyes open with its sharp little claws.

"That I will not," answered the cat. "As long as I have been with you, you have given me nothing but hard words and bones to gnaw, but she stroked my fur and gave me a cake to eat. Scratch your own eyes open, for you shall have no help from me." And then the little cat ran away into the forest.

But the faithful servant and Peter journeyed safely on through the forest, and you may guess whether or not the mother was glad to have her little Peter safe home again.

As to the old Baba Yaga, she may be shouting and stamping and rubbing the pitch from her eyes yet, for all I know.

Source: Pyle, *Wonder Tales from Many Lands*, 93-98.

You can watch a cartoon of this story (in Russian) here:
https://ru.m.wikipedia.org/wiki/Файл:1938._Ивашко_и_Баба-Яга.webm.

Baba Yaga

An old man and an old woman had a young son and daughter. When the woman died, the children said, "Father, give us a stepmother."

"If I give you one, she won't treat you well."

"She will be good to us," they replied. "Get one."

The old man married, but his wife soon said to him, "Go, fool, and kill your children. Only then can I begin to live."

The father drove the boy and girl to the forest, where he found a pretty glade and many berries. He gave the children some baskets and said, "Now, children, collect berries while I go and cut wood."

He left and tied a pole to a tree with strips of bast. The wind caused this pole to strike frequently against the tree, so that while the children collected berries, they thought their father was cutting wood. They went to look for their father when it grew dark, but couldn't find him. They saw the pole and understood that they had been abandoned. Then they wept and ran into the forest. Finally, they reached a small house. Nobody was inside.

"Let's lie down," said the sister.

"Yes," replied her brother.

They lay down, and as they looked, Baba-Yaga entered. "Children, where have you come from?"

"Out from the forest, Granny. Our father has left us."

"Well, stay with me!"

They began to live. The old woman took the boy and fed him food. She gave him grains and nuts, fed him one day, two days, three days.

The sister happened to find an awl used for making bast shoes. She gave it to her brother and told him, "Brother, when Baba-Yaga says, 'Let me taste your little finger,' you must put this awl into her mouth. Let her bite it."

The old woman came. "Son, give me your little finger," she said, "and I will see if it is fat."

"Yes, Granny!" and the boy thrust the awl into her mouth.

The old woman bit, but as the awl was hard, she soon let it go. "My boy, you have not made much progress. You must eat a little more. I feed you well."

"I eat, Granny."

"You eat, but you are not well nourished."

Baba-Yaga began again to feed him. She gave him grain and cream and, after two or three days, said, "Give me your finger, and I'll taste it."

The child again thrust the awl into her mouth. She bit the instrument and, finding it hard, left it.

She came a third time. "Come, my boy, let me taste your little finger."

The boy, in his hurry, couldn't find the awl. He turned several times and at last was forced to give her his finger.

Baba-Yaga bit and crunched. "My boy, you have grown fat! But you have deceived me. Come here!"

While Baba-Yaga heated the stove, the sister said quietly to her brother, "Listen, brother. When she puts you onto the shovel, throw yourself about, this way and that, as if you can't lie down. Then say to her, 'Granny, I can't do it. Please get on to the shovel and show me how. I'll copy you!' "

The old woman held the shovel and said, "Now, son, lie down on it."

The boy threw himself about uneasily, as if he had not enough room and couldn't lie down.

"Lie better, my son!"

"I can't, Granny. Show me the right way. Then I'll position myself properly."

The old woman said, "Hold the handle of the shovel and I'll lie down."

She lay down on the shovel and drew herself together, so that she became like a ball. The girl seized the shovel, hurling the old woman into the stove, shut the door, and pressed against it with the iron poker.

The old woman groaned and said, "Daughter, let me out. There's a little silver ring under the window. I'll give it to you."

"Old witch, the ring will be mine, whatever happens."

"Children, let me out! On the ground, under the window, I have a golden snuff box, and I'll give it to you."

"Old witch, the snuff box will be ours."

"Foster-children, let me out! At the threshold, under the door, I have a pitcher full of gold. I'll give it to you."

"The pitcher of gold will be ours without doubt."

They took the snuff box and the pitcher of gold and left, but suddenly remembered the silver ring.

The boy said, "I'll go and get it."

Having returned, he entered the house and looked. Baba-Yaga's fat was flowing from the hearth.

The boy thought, "She ate my little finger, so she should be sweet. Now I'll taste her fat."

He bent down and having licked the fat, immediately became a baby goat and frisked about. He galloped off to his sister in the forest and bleated like a kid.

The sister said, "Where did this kid come from? He is certainly pretty."

In reply, the kid wept and bleated.

Then the sister understood and cried, "This is my brother."

There was nothing for her to do but to go with him. They passed through the forest, and reaching a high road, walked without knowing where they were going.

Some merchants, going in the same direction, took the kid and the girl with them. After traveling some distance, they reached a town, where they began to sell their wares.

Baba-Yaga's daughter saw the kid. Going to her husband, she said to him, "Come and buy that kid from these merchants, and mind, pay whatever you have to buy it."

She thought to herself, "This kid destroyed my mother!"

The man bought the kid and led it home. Baba-Yaga's daughter tasted the kid's flesh. It was her mother baked. Seizing the kid spitefully, the daughter slaughtered it, and now lives like a lady.

Source: Coxwell, *Siberian and Other Folk-tales*, 570-572.

The Baba Yaga

nce upon a time there was an old couple. The husband lost his wife and married again. But he had a daughter by the first marriage, a young girl, and she found no favor in the eyes of her evil stepmother, who used to beat her, and consider how she could get her killed outright.

One day the father went away somewhere or other, so the stepmother said to the girl, "Go to your aunt, my sister, and ask her for a needle and thread to make you a shirt."

Now that aunt was a Baba Yaga. Well, the girl was no fool, so she went to a real aunt of hers first, and said, "Good morning, auntie!"

"Good morning, my dear! What have you come for?"

"Mother has sent me to her sister, to ask for a needle and thread to make me a shirt."

Then her aunt instructed her what to do. "There is a birch-tree there, niece, which would hit you in the eye—you must tie a ribbon around it. There are doors which would creak and bang—you must pour oil on their hinges. There are dogs which would tear you in pieces—you must throw them these rolls. There is a cat that would scratch your eyes out—you must give it a piece of bacon."

So the girl went away, and walked and walked, until she came to the place. There stood a hut, and in it sat weaving the Baba Yaga, the Bony-leg.

"Good morning, auntie," said the girl.

"Good morning, my dear," replied the Baba Yaga.

"Mother has sent me to ask you for a needle and thread to make me a shirt."

"Very well; sit down and weave a little in the meantime."

So the girl sat down behind the loom, and the Baba Yaga went outside, and said to her maidservant, "Go and heat the bath, and get my niece washed; and make sure you do a good job. I want to eat her for breakfast."

Well, the girl sat there so terrified that she was as much dead as alive. Presently she begged the maidservant, "Dear lady, please soak the firewood so it won't burn; and get the water for the bath in a sieve." And she gave her a handkerchief as a present.

The Baba Yaga waited awhile; then she came to the window and asked, "Are you weaving, niece? Are you weaving, my dear?"

"Oh, yes, dear aunt, I'm weaving." So the Baba Yaga went away again, and the girl gave the cat a piece of bacon, and asked, "Is there any way to escape from here?"

"Here's a comb for you and a towel," said the cat. "Take them and get away. The Baba Yaga will chase you. Place your ear on the ground. When you hear that she is close, throw down the towel first. It will become a wide, wide river. If the Baba Yaga gets across the river and tries to catch you, then place your ear on the ground again. When you hear that she is close, throw down the comb. It will become a dense, dense forest. She won't be able to force her way through it."

The girl took the towel and the comb and fled. The dogs would have torn her apart, but she threw them the rolls, and they let her go by. The doors would have begun to bang, but she poured oil on their hinges, and they let her pass through. The birch-tree would have poked out her eyes, but she tied the ribbon around it, and it let her go past. And the cat sat down at the loom and worked away. He tangled everything more than he did any weaving.

Up came the Baba Yaga to the window and asked, "Are you weaving, niece? Are you weaving, my dear?"

"I'm weaving, dear aunt. I'm weaving," the cat replied gruffly.

The Baba Yaga rushed into the hut, saw that the girl was gone, and started beating the cat and abusing it because it didn't scratch out the girl's eyes.

"As long as I've served you," said the cat, "you've never given me even a bone, but she gave me bacon."

Then the Baba Yaga pounced on the dogs, on the doors, on the birch-tree, and on the maidservant. She abused them all and hit them around.

The dogs said to her, "As long as we've served you, you've never tossed us a burnt crust, but she gave us rolls to eat."

The doors said, "As long as we've served you, you've never poured even a drop of water on our hinges, but she poured oil on us."

The birch-tree said, "As long as I've served you, you've never tied a single thread on me, but she fastened a ribbon around me."

And the maidservant said, "As long as I've served you, you've never given me a rag, but she gave me a handkerchief."

The Baba Yaga, the bony-leg, quickly jumped into her mortar, sent it flying along with the pestle, sweeping away all traces of its flight with a broom, and set off in pursuit of the girl.

Then the girl put her ear to the ground. When she heard that the Baba Yaga was chasing her and was getting close, she flung down the towel. And it became a wide, such a wide river!

The Baba Yaga came up to the river and gnashed her teeth with spite. She went home for her oxen and drove them to the river. The oxen drank up every drop of the river. Then the Baba Yaga began the pursuit again.

The girl put her ear to the ground again. When she heard that the Baba Yaga was near, she threw down the comb. Instantly, a forest sprang up, such an awfully thick one! The Baba Yaga began gnawing away at it, but however hard she worked, she couldn't gnaw her way through it, so she had to go back again.

But by this time the girl's father had returned home, and he asked, "Where's my daughter?"

"She's gone to her aunt's," replied her stepmother.

Soon afterward the girl herself came running home.

"Where have you been?" asked her father.

"Oh, father!" she said, "mother sent me to aunt's to ask for a needle and thread to make me a shirt. But aunt's a Baba Yaga, and she wanted to eat me!"

"And how did you get away, daughter?"

"Why like this," said the girl, and explained the whole matter.

As soon as her father had heard all about it, he became angry with his wife and shot her. But he and his daughter lived on and thrived, and everything went well with them.

Source: Ralston, *Russian Folk-tales*, 139-142.

Baba Yaga (in Verse)

Peasants twain, a man and woman,
Lived and loved a son and daughter.

But the wife by death was taken
And the father deeply grieving,
After battling, grew despondent,
For he saw that all was spoiling
In the home, where none was ready
To assist his little orphans;
So he asked himself the question,
"Were't not better if I married?"

Soon he mated, and the union
Brought him duly other children.
But his wife was prone to anger,
Struck each stepchild, son and daughter;
Cheated them of food, and muttered,
"It would be a great advantage
If these children were not living."

Next she planned, with joy malicious,
To destroy the hateful orphans
By dispatching them, unaided,
Straightway unto Baba-Yaga,
In a forest dense and gloomy.

These were her precise directions:
"Go now, children, to my mother
Who resides within the forest,
In a hut that stands on fowls' legs.
If you offer to assist her,
She will show you she is grateful

And reward you for your goodness,
Heap upon you luscious sweetmeats."

Then, as bid, the children started,
But the girl, with simple wisdom,
To their father's sister wandered,
Spoke a little of their mission.
"Oh, you poor and wretched orphans,"
Said to them their father's sister,
"Much I grieve for your misfortunes,
But, alas, I cannot help you.
Truly stepmother is sending
You to wicked Baba-Yaga.
Children! mind that you are friendly,
If you try to speak politely,
And are honest in each trifle,
Help will be perhaps forthcoming."

Then she gave them for the journey
Both of ham and milk a portion,
And some pancakes for the pocket;
Thus dispatched them to the forest.

Going through the trees, they noticed
In a clearing, a lone cottage,
Standing strangely upon fowls' legs,
And revolving on a cock's head.

Rose the children's silvery voices,
"Cottage! we would have you face us!
Turn your back upon the forest!"

They perceived within the cottage,
After it had done revolving,
Baba-Yaga lying lonely
With her head upon the threshold
And her feet in either corner,
And her knees against the garret.

Loudly screamed she to the orphans,
"Whence has come this Russian odor?"
Now, behind each other hiding,
And, despite their fear, the children
Whispered, "Granny! please, good morning,
Stepmother has sent us to you,
We're to help you." "Very well, then,
Come in, children! If you're useful,
I'll reward you: if you're idle,
I will throw you on the shovel
In the furnace. Do not whimper!"
Now she set the girl to spinning,
Gave the boy a sieve, and told him
To get water for the bath-house.

While the maiden used the spindle,
Thus some little mice addressed her:
"Tell us, maiden, why you're tearful,
Give us cake and we'll befriend you."

So she gave the mice a pancake
And they told her of a secret:
"Baba-Yaga has a tabby;
Give her ham if you have any,
Then she'll show you, when we're working
At the distaff, how to leave us."
Forth the maiden set to happen
On the cat and, next moreover,
Find her brother near the bath-house;
He had proved the sieve was useless.

Chirping sparrows now flew hither,
Saying, "Dearest, only give us
Crumbs, we hope to tell you something."
Down the orphans threw some cake crumbs
And the birds began to twitter,
"Clay and water! clay and water!"

Thus the sister and her brother
Learned to make the sieve assistful,

Smearing it with clay well watered,
They could fill the tub completely.

In the hut, they met the tabby,
Gave her ham and stroked her, saying,
"Pussy, tell us how to issue
Out of Baba-Yaga's cottage."

"Take this towel," was the answer,
"And this comb; perhaps the witch's
Purpose will continue evil.
If you clearly hear her footsteps,
Throw the towel down behind you;
Then a swiftly running river
Will prevent her from pursuing.
Should she yet attempt to follow,
You must drop the comb! Behind you
Will arise a gloomy forest
Into which she cannot enter."

Baba-Yaga found, returning,
That the work was done, but muttered,
"Though you have today succeeded,
For tomorrow, I will set you
Harder tasks; be still, don't whimper!"

Scarcely slept at night the orphans,
Feared that they might breathe too loudly,
As on straw they lay and trembled,
If not dead, yet scarcely living.

When they rose, upon the morrow,
Savage Baba-Yaga gave them
Linen threads to weave together
And some logs to hew asunder,
While she visited the forest.

Grasping tight the comb and towel,
Then the children bravely started.
First the dogs would tear them piecemeal;
Each was quieted with pancakes.
When the gates gave signs of creaking,
Oil was lavished on the hinges.
As a birch tree's branches threatened
Peril to the sister's eyesight,
She encircled it with ribbon
And escaped the snare, uninjured.

So the orphans left the forest
Passed to treeless smooth expanses.

But the energetic tabby
Ever at the loom kept working
And producing dire confusion.
Baba-Yaga, from the courtyard,
Coming to the window, shouted,
"Are you weaving, tell me, grandchild?"
"I am busy, granny darling,"
Mewed the cunning tabby loudly.

Baba-Yaga quickly entered,
But nor saw nor heard the orphans.
She the tabby thus upbraided,
As she struck her with the poker:
"Why did you allow the children
Freedom and not scratch their eyes out?"

Tabby answered, "I have served you
Many years and never feasted,
But they gave me ham in plenty."

Then the dogs excused their actions,
Said, "Despite our trusty service,
We have ne'er a bread-crust tasted."

So the gates, explaining rudely,
Said, "You never gave us water,
But the children eased our hinges,
Using oil both pure and copious."

Too, the birch-tree was defiant,
Cried, "You gave me in requital
Nothing for my toil continued,
But they bound me round with ribbon!"

Baba-Yaga feared disaster,
Ever in pursuit, advancing,
Quickly hastened; flying strongly,
With a broom destroyed her traces.

Bending low to earth, the children

Listened well and heard her coming.
Down they threw, at once, the towel;
And, behind, up welled a river
Deep and wide and swiftly flowing.

Baba-Yaga battling, traversed
All along the bank and, searching,
Found at last, a ford and crossing,
Started a pursuit revengeful.
She is nearer, she is near them!

But the anxious sister listened,
With her ear detected danger,
Therefore dropped the comb beside her.
Where it fell, up sprang a forest
Dense and awful! There were woven
Roots with roots, and creepers twining
Branches in the closest network;
Tree-tops huge were bending downward.

Baba-Yaga into thickets:
Vainly tried to force a passage.
And, on failing altogether,
Sought her hut in fearful anger.

When the orphans met their father
They described the reign of terror
And, in touching manner, asked him,
Would he prove himself hard-hearted
And, in any way, forsake them
To new misery and sorry?

Unforgiving, deeply wrathful,
Then the father drove his wife out,
Chased her from his home forever;
And he never, from that moment,
Ceased to keep the children by him,
Never more forsook the orphans.

I have visited the cottage,
Seen the life of all within it,
Been the father's guest and always
Had from him the kindest treatment.

Source: Coxwell, *Siberian and Other Folk-tales*, 695-700.

Chufil-Filyushka

nce upon a time, there were three brothers in a family. The eldest was called the Ram, the second the Goat, and the third and youngest Chufil-Filyushka. One day all three went into the forest, where the watchman lived, who was their real grandfather. Ram and Goat left their brother Chufil-Filyushka with him and went into the forest to hunt. Filyushka had a mind of his own and considered his grandfather old and stupid. Filyushka was hungry and he wanted to eat an apple. So, he eluded his grandfather, got into the garden, and climbed up the apple tree.

All of a sudden, Heaven knows where from, who should come but the Yaga-Bura, with an iron mortar and a pestle in her hand. She leapt up to the apple tree and said, "How are you, Filyushka? What have you come here for?"

"Oh, to pluck an apple!" said Filyushka.

"Well, then, dearie, have a bite of mine!"

"No, it's a rotten one," said Filyushka.

"Well, here's another one!"

"No, it's all wormy!"

"Don't be sassy. Just come up and take one out of my hand."

He stretched out his hand. Then Yaga-Bura gripped it tight, put him into the mortar, and made off, leaping over hills, and forests, and clefts, and swiftly with the pestle driving the mortar.

Then Filyushka remembered himself and began to cry out, "Goat, Ram, come along quick. Yaga has carried me away beyond the high, steep hills, the dark, lone woods, the steppes, where the geese roam."

The Ram and the Goat were just then resting. One was lying on the ground and heard a noise of somebody shouting. So he told the other one, "Come and lie down and listen!"

"Oh, it's our Filyushka crying."

Off they went and ran and ran, and ran the Yaga-Bura down, saved Filyushka, and brought him home to his grandfather, who had nearly gone out of his mind with fright! They told him to look after Filyushka better and went out again.

But Filyushka was a real boy, and the first chance he got, off he was again to the apple tree and clambered up. There was the Yaga-Bura again, offering him an apple.

"No, you won't catch me this time, you old beast!" said Filyushka.

"Don't be unkind—do just take an apple from me. I'll throw it to you!"

"Right, throw it down."

Then Yaga threw him down an apple. He stretched out his hand, and she clutched it and leapt over hills, and valleys, and dark forests, so fast that it seemed like a twinkling of an eye, got him into her home, washed him, went out and put him into the warming oven.

In the morning she got ready to go out and ordered her daughter, "Listen! heat the oven well, very hot, and roast me Chufil-Filyushka for supper." And she went out to seek further plunder.

The daughter went and got the oven thoroughly hot, took out and bound Filyushka, and put him on the shovel. She was just going to shove him into the oven, when he went and knocked his forehead with his feet.

"That's not the way, Filyushka," said the daughter of the Yaga-Bura.

"How then?" he answered. "I don't understand."

"Look here, just let go. I'll show you." She went and lay down on the shovel in the right fashion.

But, although Chufil-Filyushka was small, he was no fool! He stuffed her at once into the oven, and shut the oven-door with a bang.

About two or three hours later, Filyushka smelled good roast meat, opened the door, and took out the daughter of the Yaga-Bura well-cooked. He buttered it over, put it into the frying-pan, and covered it with a towel, and put it into the warming oven. Then he climbed up to the roof-tree and took away the business-day pestle and mortar of the Yaga-Bura.

About evening-time, the Yaga-Bura came in, went straight to the warming oven, and took the roast meat out, ate it all up, collected all the bones, laid them out on the ground in rows, and began to roll on them. But somehow, she couldn't find her daughter and thought she had gone away to another cottage to weave. But suddenly, whilst she was rolling, she said, "My dear daughter, do come to me and help me roll in Filyushka's little bones!"

Then Filyushka cried out from the rafters, "Roll away, mother, and stand on your daughter's little bones!"

"Are you there, you thief! You just wait, and I'll give it to you!"

But little Chufil was not frightened. When the Yaga-Bura, gnashing her teeth, stamping on the ground, had got up to the ceiling, he got hold of the pestle and with all his might struck her on the forehead, and down she flopped. Then Filyushka climbed up onto the roof and saw some geese flying, and called out to them, "Lend me your wings. I want wings to carry me home."

They lent him their wings, and he flew home.

But they had long, long ago been praying for the rest of his soul at home. How glad they were to see him turn up alive and sound! So, they changed the mourning into a merry festival, and lived out their lives, and lived on to receive more good yet!

Source: Afanas'ev, *Russian folk-tales*, 230-233.

Marya Moryevna

In a certain kingdom, in a certain state, there once lived Ivan Tsarevich, who had three sisters: one was called Marya Tsarevna, the second Olga Tsarevna, and the third Anna Tsarevna. Their mother and father had died: when they were dying, they told the son, "Whoever comes first as a suitor for your sisters' hands, let them take them. Don't keep them long with you."

The Tsarevich buried his parents, and, in his grief, went with his sisters to walk in a green garden. Then a dark cloud appeared in the sky, and a fearful clap of thunder was heard.

"Let's go home, sisters," Ivan Tsarevich said.

Soon they reached the palace. The thunder rattled and the ceiling fell down, and the ceiling divided into two.

A clear-eyed Hawk came into the room, struck the ground, and turned himself into a fair, brave youth. "Hello, Ivan Tsarevich! Before, I came to you as a guest. Now I'm coming to ask for your sister's hand. I wish to marry Marya Tsarevna."

"If you want my sister, I won't say no. Take her with God's blessing."

Marya Tsarevna agreed, and the Hawk married her and took her away to his own kingdom.

Then day followed day and hour followed hour. One whole year went by without event. Ivan Tsarevich stayed with his sisters in the green garden. Then a cloud came and there was thunder and lightning.

"Let's go home, sisters," the Tsarevich said.

When they came to the palace, there was a thunderclap and the roof fell in, and the ceiling was split in two.

An Eagle flew in, struck the ground and turned himself into a brave youth, and said, "Hello, Ivan Tsarevich! Formerly I came to you as a guest. Now I come to you as a suitor." And he asked for the hand of Olga.

And Ivan Tsarevich answered, "If Olga Tsarevna pleases you, she may go to you—I won't go against your will."

Olga Tsarevna was willing and married the Eagle. The Eagle took hold of her and brought her to his own kingdom.

One year further went by, and Ivan Tsarevich said to his youngest sister, "Let's go and have a walk in the green garden," and they went for a little walk. And a cloud came over the sky with thunder and lightning. "Let's turn back, sister, and go home!"

So they turned back home, and they had hardly sat down when the thunder clapped and the ceiling was divided into two, and a Crow flew in. And the Crow struck the ground and turned himself into a brave youth. The former suitors were fair enough in themselves, but he was fairer still. "Formerly I came to you as a guest, but now I come to you as a suitor. Give me your sister Anna."

"I won't go against my sister's will. If you are in love with her, she may have you."

And Anna Tsarevna went with the Crow, and he took her to his own kingdom.

Ivan Tsarevich was there alone. For one whole year he lived there without any sisters and began to feel melancholy. "I will go," he said, "and look for my sisters."

He started out on the road. He went on and on and on. And there lay on the field a great army conquered.

And Ivan asked them, "If there is any man alive here, let him speak up! Who killed this mighty army?"

And one man who was still alive replied, "All this mighty army was conquered by Marya Moryevna, the fair princess."

And Ivan Tsarevich went on yet further, and he came upon white tents, and Marya Moryevna, the fair queen, came to meet him.

"Hello," she said, "Tsarevich! Where is God taking you? Is it at your will or is it unnecessary?"

And Ivan Tsarevich answered her, "Brave youths do not go unnecessarily."

"Well, if you have no quest to accomplish, come and stay in my tents."

And Ivan Tsarevich was glad of this, and he stayed two nights in the tents, fell in love with Marya Moryevna, and married her. Marya Moryevna took him with her to her own kingdom, and they lived together for some time. They thought about getting ready for war, and so she handed all of her possessions over to Ivan, and said, "Go everywhere, look at everything, only into this storage room you must not look."

But he was impatient: as soon as Marya Moryevna's back was turned, he at once opened the storage room, opened the door, and looked in. There Koshchey the Deathless was hanging.

Koshchey asked Ivan Tsarevich, "Have pity on me. Give me something to eat. I have been tortured here for ten years. I have eaten nothing, I have drunk nothing, and my throat is all dried up."

Ivan Tsarevich gave him a whole gallon of water. Koshchey the Deathless drank it with a single gulp, and he still asked, "I'm still thirsty. Give me a gallon more."

Ivan gave Koshchey the Deathless a second gallon, and yet a third. And when he had drunk the third, he recovered all his former strength, broke his chains, shattered them, all twelve chains. "Thank you, Ivan Tsarevich," Koshchey the Deathless said. "Now you will never again see Marya Moryevna!" With a fearful flash of lightning, he flew into the country, gathered up the fair Queen, Marya Moryevna, on the road, snatched her up, and took her to himself.

Ivan Tsarevich wept bitterly, got ready, and started on the road. "Come what may, I will seek out Marya Moryevna."

And he traveled one day, and he traveled another day, and on the dawning of the third day, he saw a wonderful palace. In front of the palace, there was an oak, and on the oak there sat a clear-eyed hawk.

The Hawk flew down from the oak, struck the ground, turned into a brave youth, and cried out, "Oh, my beloved brother, how is the Lord dealing with you?"

And Marya Tsarevna came out, went to meet Ivan Tsarevich, asked him how he was, and began to tell him all her own story.

So the Tsarevich abode as their guest for three days, and then said, "I cannot stay with you any longer. I'm going to seek my wife, Marya Moryevna, the fair Queen."

"She'll be hard to find," answered the Hawk. "At least leave a silver spoon here. We can gaze upon it and think about you."

Ivan Tsarevich left his silver spoon with them and set out on his road. He traveled one day and a second day, and at the dawning of the third day, he saw a palace fairer than the first. In front of the palace there was an oak, and an eagle sat on the oak.

The Eagle flew down from the tree, struck the earth, turned into a brave youth, and cried, "Rise, Olga Tsarevna, our dear brother has arrived."

Olga Tsarevna at once came to meet him, began kissing and welcoming him, asking how he was, and they told of all they had lived and done.

Ivan Tsarevich stayed with them three little days, and then said, "I can no longer be your guest. I'm looking for my wife, Marya Moryevna, the fair Princess."

And the Eagle answered, "It will be an evil quest. Leave us your silver fork. We will look at it and think about you."

So he left his silver fork and he went on the road. And a day went by and a second, and at the dawn of the third day, he saw a palace fairer than the first two. And in front of the palace there was an oak, and on the oak there perched a crow.

And the Crow flew down from the oak, struck the earth, turned into a brave youth, and cried out, "Anna Tsarevna, come out as fast as you can. Our brother has arrived."

Then Anna Tsarevna came out, met him joyously, began to kiss and to welcome him, asking him how he was. And they spoke of all they had lived and done.

After three days, Ivan Tsarevich said, "I can stay no longer with you. I'm going to seek my wife, Marya Moryevna, the fair Queen."

"This will be a hard search for you," the Crow said. "At least leave us your silver snuff-box. We can gaze on it and think about you."

So Ivan Tsarevich left them his silver snuff-box and set out on his road. Then a day went and another day, and on the third day he at last reached Marya Moryevna.

When she saw her beloved through the window, she rushed out to him, flung herself at his neck, wept, and said, "Oh! Ivan Tsarevich, why did you not obey me? Why did you look into the storage room and let Koshchey the Deathless out?"

"Forgive me, Marya Moryevna. Let bygones be bygones. Come away with me now, while Koshchey the Deathless is away. Perhaps he won't catch up with us."

So they went away.

Now Koshchey was out hunting. Toward evening, he returned home, and his horse stumbled. "Why, you sorry jade, are you stumbling, or is it some evil that you fear?"

And the horse answered, "Ivan Tsarevich has arrived and has taken away Marya Moryevna."

"Can we catch up with them?"

"You can sow wheat, wait until it grows up, harvest it, thresh it, turn it into flour, make five stones of bread, eat the bread, and then set out on the hunt, and we shall succeed."

Koshchey leapt on the horse and caught up with Ivan Tsarevich.

"Now," he said, "this first time, I'll let you go for your bravery, as you fed me with water. A second time I'll let you go. But a third time, take care; I'll tear you to bits." And he took Marya Moryevna, took her away, and Ivan Tsarevich sat on the stone and cried.

And he cried and he cried, and again came back to Marya Moryevna when Koshchey the Deathless was not at home. "Let's go, Marya Moryevna."

"Oh, Ivan Tsarevich, he'll catch up with us."

"Well, let him. Still we shall have one or two hours together."

So they started, and off they went.

Koshchey the Deathless came back home, and his good horse stumbled under him. "Why, you sorry jade, are you stumbling, or is it some evil thing which you fear?"

And the horse answered, "Ivan Tsarevich has again arrived and has taken Marya Moryevna away."

"Can we catch up with them?"

"It would be possible to sow barley and to wait until it grows up, reap it, thresh it, brew beer, drink it until you were drunk, sleep out your sleep and then go on the hunt, and we should still succeed."

Koshchey leapt on his horse, caught up with Ivan Tsarevich, and said, "I said you were not to see anything more of Marya Moryevna!" and he took her away with him.

So Ivan Tsarevich was again left alone, and he wept bitterly. Once again, he returned to Marya Moryevna, and again this time Koshchey was not at home. "Let's go, Marya Moryevna!"

"Oh, Ivan Tsarevich, he'll catch up with us, and he'll tear you to bits."

"Let him tear me to bits. I cannot live without you."

So they got ready, and off they went. Koshchey the Deathless returned home, and under him his good horse stumbled. "Why do you stumble, you sorry jade, or is it some evil that you fear?"

"Ivan Tsarevich has arrived and has taken Marya Moryevna with him."

Koshchey leapt on his horse, caught up with Ivan Tsarevich, broke him up into tiny bits, put them into a tar chest, took this chest, locked it with iron bolts and threw it into the blue sea. And he took Marya Moryevna away with him.

At the same time the brothers-in-law of Ivan Tsarevich looked at their silver ornaments and found they had turned black.

"Oh," they said, "evidently some disaster has befallen him!"

The Eagle rushed into the blue sea, dragged out the chest to the shore, and the Hawk flew for the Water of Life, and the Crow flew for the Water of Death. Then they all three met at a single spot and broke up the chest, took out the bits of Ivan Tsarevich, washed them, laid them together as was fit. Then the Crow sprinkled him with the Water of Death, and the body grew together and was one. And the Hawk sprinkled him with the Water of Life.

Ivan Tsarevich shivered, sat up, and said, "Oh, what a long sleep I have had!"

"But your sleep would have been very much longer if we had not been there," answered the brothers-in-law. "Now you must come and be our guest!"

"No, brothers, I must go and seek Marya Moryevna."

So he came to her and said, "Go and find out from Koshchey the Deathless where he got such a fine horse!"

Then Marya Moryevna looked out for a good opportunity, and asked Koshchey the Deathless.

Koshchey answered, "Beyond thrice-nine lands, in the thrice-tenth kingdom, beyond the river of fire, lives the Baba Yaga. She has a mare on which every day she rides around the whole world. She has many splendid mares. I was there for three days as a herdsman, and she would not let me have the mare, but she gave me one of the foals."

"How can one cross the river of fire?"

"I have a kerchief. If you shake it to the right three times, a lofty bridge rises and the fires cannot reach it."

Marya Moryevna listened, told Ivan Tsarevich all about it, and he took the cloth away. Ivan Tsarevich crossed the river of fire, and he reached the Baba Yaga. But in his travels, he neither ate nor drank. A sea-bird came to meet him with her young. Ivan Tsarevich asked if he might eat one of her chicks.

"Don't eat it," the sea-bird said. "At some time, I can be of service to you, Ivan Tsarevich."

Then he went farther, and he was in a wood, and he saw a bee-hive. "Perhaps," he said, "I may take a little honey."

Then the queen-bee answered him, "Don't touch my honey, Ivan Tsarevich. At some time or other, I can be of service to you."

So he didn't touch the honey, but went farther. Then he met a lioness with her cubs. "May I eat this lion cub? I'm so hungry."

"Don't touch it, Ivan Tsarevich," the lioness said. "At some time or other, I can be of service to you."

"Very well. Let it be as you will."

So he went on hungry, and he went on and on and on, and at last he reached the house of the Baba Yaga. Around the house there were twelve poles, and on eleven of the poles there were the skulls of men: only one as yet was untenanted.

"Hello, granny!" he said.

"Hello, Ivan Tsarevich!" she replied. "What have you come for? By your own good will or in need?"

"I have come to earn a knightly horse from you."

"Very well, Ivan Tsarevich. You must serve me not one year, but only three days. If you can guard my mares, I'll give you a knightly horse. If you cannot, don't be angry, but your head must also lie on the last of the stakes."

Ivan Tsarevich agreed, and Baba Yaga gave him drink and food and set him to work. As soon as he had driven the mares into the field, they all turned their tails and ran to the meadows so far that the Tsarevich couldn't see them. Thus, they were all lost. Then he sat down and wept, and became melancholy, and sat down on a stone and went to sleep.

The sun was already setting when the sea-bird flew to him, woke him up, and said, "Get up, Ivan Tsarevich—all the mares have gone home."

The Tsarevich got up and returned home.

But Baba Yaga was angry with her mares. "Why have you all come home?"

"Why shouldn't we come home? The birds flew down from every quarter of the sky and almost clawed out our eyes."

"Well, tomorrow don't stray in the meadows, but scatter into the dark forest."

So Ivan Tsarevich passed that night; and the next day Baba Yaga said to him, "Look, Ivan Tsarevich, if you don't take care of the mares well, if you lose one, then your false head will nod up and down on the stake."

So then he drove all the mares to the field, and this time they turned their tails, and they ran into the dark woods. And once again the Tsarevich sat on the stone and wept and wept and went to sleep.

The sun began to rest on the woods when the lioness ran up and said, "Get up, Ivan Tsarevich—all the mares have been collected."

Then Ivan Tsarevich got up and went home.

And Baba Yaga was angry that the mares had come home, and she called out to her mares, "Why have you all come home?"

And they answered, "How couldn't we come home? Wild beasts from all the four quarters of the world assembled around us and almost tore us to bits."

"Well, go tomorrow into the blue sea."

Once again Ivan passed the night there, and the next day Baba Yaga sent her mares to feed. "If you don't guard them, then your bold head will hang on the pole."

He drove the mares into the field, and they at once turned tail and vanished from his eyes and ran into the blue sea and stood up to their necks in the water. So Ivan Tsarevich sat on the stone, wept, and went to sleep.

The sun was already setting on the woods when the bee flew up to him and said, "Get up, Ivan Tsarevich. All the mares have been gathered together. But, when you return home, don't appear before Baba Yaga. Go into the stable and hide behind the crib. There a mangy foal will be rolling in the dung. Steal him, and, at the deep of midnight, leave the house."

Ivan Tsarevich got up, went into the stable, and lay behind the crib.

Baba Yaga made a tremendous stir and cried out to her mares, "Why did you come back?"

"How couldn't we come back? All the bees from every part of the world, visible and invisible, flew around us, and they stung us until our blood flowed."

Baba Yaga went to sleep. That same night, Ivan Tsarevich stole the mangy horse from its stall, mounted it, and flew to the fiery river. He reached that river, waved the cloth three times to the right. At once, from some strange source, a lofty, splendid bridge hung all the way over. The Tsarevich crossed the bridge, waved the cloth to the left twice, and all that was left of the bridge was a thin thread.

In the morning, Baba Yaga woke up, and she couldn't see the mangy foal, so she set out on a hunt. With all her strength, she leapt into her iron mortar, and she pushed it with the pestle, and soon she was on their track. When she came to the river of fire, she looked across and thought, "Ah ha ha! a fine bridge!" Then she went on to the bridge; but as soon as she got onto the bridge, it snapped. Baba Yaga slipped into the river, and it was a savage death she had.

Ivan Tsarevich fed his foal on the green, and a splendid horse grew beneath him. Then the Tsarevich arrived at the palace of Marya Moryevna.

She rushed out, fell upon his neck, and said, "How has God blessed you?"

He told her how it had gone with him.

"I'm frightened, Ivan Tsarevich. If Koshchey catches up with us, you'll again be torn to atoms."

"No, he won't catch up with us now. I have a fine knightly horse that flies like a bird." So they sat on the horse and went.

Koshchey the Deathless came back home, and his horse stumbled. "Oh, you sorry jade, why do you stumble, or is it that you fear some evil?"

"Ivan Tsarevich has arrived and has taken away Marya Moryevna."

"Can we catch up with them?"

"God knows. Now Ivan Tsarevich has a knightly horse better than me."

"No, I won't stand for it," Koshchey the Deathless said. "We'll hurry up after him!"

And, sooner or later, so soon he caught up with Ivan Tsarevich. Koshchey the Deathless caught up to Ivan and was going to slice him with his curved saber, but then Ivan Tsarevich's horse kicked Koshchey the Deathless with all his might, and split his head. The Tsarevich struck him down with his club. Then the Tsarevich gathered together a mass of timber, set fire to it, burnt Koshchey the Deathless on the pile, and scattered the dust to the winds.

Marya Moryevna then sat on Koshchey's horse, and Ivan Tsarevich on his own, and the two went and stayed as guests, first of all with the Crow, then with the Eagle, and lastly with the Hawk. Wherever they went, they were joyously received.

"Oh! Ivan Tsarevich, I'm so glad to see you! We never expected to see you back. And your work has not been in vain. Such a beauty as Marya Moryevna might be sought for all over the world, and you wouldn't have found any other."

They were as guests and lived well, and arrived into their own kingdom, reached it and began to live a life of joy enduring and to drink good mead.

Source: Afanas'ev, *Russian folk-tales*, 192-203.

Prince Ivan and Princess Maria

A variation of the previous story.

There lived in a certain kingdom a tsar and a tsaritsa, who had three daughters and a son, Prince Ivan. But the father and the mother died, and the children remained alone. One morning the eldest sister went out, and a hungry beggar married her. She took him by the hand and led him home.

Her brother said, "Why have you brought home this old beggar?"

The sister answered, "It seemed to be my fate."

"Very well!"

They took the beggar and washed him until he was clean. But the next day, the middle sister went out and met an ugly beggar without hands and married him. The brother asked her why she had brought home the hungry beggar, and received the reply, "It seemed to be my fate."

Next the third sister went out early and married a hungry man with only one hand and one leg. She led him home.

Her brother said, "Why have you brought with you a handless, legless, hungry man?"

She replied, "Brother, it was apparently my fate."

"Very well!" said the brother.

They took the hungry man with one leg and one hand and washed him.

After staying with Prince Ivan some time, these beggars said, "Brother, we will go where we were living to our own homes."

They departed, leaving the prince alone. One day when he went on a walk, a storm arose. The wind tore Ivan's dog away, so that the prince remained alone. He set forth at random, and, having traveled far, came to a steep mountain. Here stood a house built of copper, at whose gates were bears and much else was disagreeable.

Ivan said to himself, "I'm not afraid."

He went on, and the gates opened. He entered several rooms, one after another, and in the last one found his sister and said to her, "Greetings, sister!"

To which she answered, "Greetings, brother! Where is God sending you?"

"To court Princess Maria."

But his sister remarked, "Brother, don't go there. Many go there, but few return! Take your place under the bed. My husband will fly here as a twenty-headed snake."

Ivan got under the bed. Now the wind arose and tore the roof from the house, and there flew up a twenty-headed snake, saying, "Phoo, Phoo, I sense a Russian odor. Truly our brother is here." The snake struck the ground and became a man even handsomer than Ivan.

Next, they took the prince, fed him, and gave him drink and put him to bed. He got up early, but his brother-in-law was sewing on him three peacock's feathers.

Prince Ivan said, "Brother, why are you sewing on me these peacock's feathers?"

"They," said the snake, "will be useful in time."

But his sister gave him a small egg and said, "Go past the gates and let this egg roll along. Wherever it goes, follow!" She further gave him a table napkin and added, "When you wish to eat and drink, this will unfold itself."

He went through the gates, and wherever the little egg rolled, he followed. It mounted a steep hill, and he did likewise. A golden house stood there, but on the gates was every unpleasantness, and the prince feared to enter, saying to himself, "When I go in, they will eat me!"

However, the gates opened and he entered. He stepped into the first room, the second, several more rooms, and then came to the last room of all. There sat his sister. "Greetings, sister!"

"Greetings, Prince Ivan."

He related how the wind had torn away his dog. But his sister remarked, "Sit under the chair. A snake with thirty heads will fly up."

He sat under the chair. And now the wind rose and tore the roof from the house, and a snake with thirty heads flew up. "Phoo, Phoo," it said. "I smell a Russian, and truly he is our brother."

This snake tapped against the ground and became more magnificent than Ivan. They took the prince, fed him, gave him plenty to drink, and put him to sleep. He rose early, but his brother-in-law was sewing on him three peacock's feathers.

Ivan said, "Brother, why are you making me a present of these peacock's feathers?"

The brother-in-law replied, "They will be useful in time."

When Ivan's sister gave him a tablecloth and a small golden egg, he said, "Why do you give me these things?"

She replied, "When you wish to eat and drink, the tablecloth will unfold. Take the egg beyond the gates and let it go. Follow it wherever it rolls."

He went out past the gates and let the egg roll freely. Wherever it went, Prince Ivan followed.

Climbing a steep hill, he grew tired. There he found a crystal house with everything objectionable on its gates. He approached and the gates opened. He entered the first room, and the second room, then passed through several rooms, and in the last one of them, found his sister.

"Greetings, sister!"

"Greetings, brother!"

He related how the wind had torn away his dog, and his sister said, "Get under the couch. A snake with forty heads will fly here."

He took his place beneath the couch. Suddenly the wind rose and tore the roof off the house. A forty-headed snake flew up and said, "Phoo, Phoo, there is a Russian odor. Truly our brother is here."

This snake tapped against the ground and became in appearance finer than Ivan. Then the prince received drink and was fed and put to sleep. Ivan got up early and found his brother-in-law sewing three peacock's feathers on him.

Ivan said, "Why are you giving me these three feathers?"

His sister also gave him a self-flying carpet and a small egg and said, "When you wish to eat and drink, this carpet will unfold. Go beyond the gates and set the egg free. Follow wherever it rolls."

He went through the gates, and freeing the egg, took care to follow it. Some horses were running in a meadow, and Ivan caught one of them. But Princess Maria saw, and cried, "My dear servants, drag him to prison!"

Ivan was led to a prison where peasants were sitting, who said, "They will bring us some straw."

Ivan whispered to himself, "I'm not losing courage."

When the party wished to eat, he said, "Napkin, unfold, unroll. I'm hungry and thirsty."

The napkin unfolded, and the peasants drank and ate heartily and became noisy.

Maria said to the servant, "The prisoners are trying to escape. Go and see what they are doing."

The servants went and said, "Who is there?"

Ivan replied, "Prince Ivan."

The servant told Maria the prisoner's name.

"Go," she directed, "and ask what he is doing."

The man arrived and said, "Is anyone here doing anything?"

One of the peasants remarked, "There is such a wonderful napkin here!"

The servant said, "Ivan, sell it to Maria!"

And Ivan said, "I will sell it, but it must be gazed at three hours."

Maria thought awhile and said to the servant, "Send him here."

The prince came. Maria took out a watch and wore it. Ivan looked at Maria, and Maria looked at the watch. When three hours had passed, Maria said, "Good servants, drag him back to the prison."

The order was obeyed. The peasants said, "Ivan, we are lost!"

Ivan replied, "Don't fear; we are not lost."

They wished to eat, and Ivan said, "Tablecloth, unfold, unroll. I'm hungry and thirsty."

The tablecloth unrolled, and corks flew up to the ceiling. They all ate their fill and drank and became noisy.

Then Maria said, "My prisoners are trying to escape. Go, my servant, and see what they are doing."

The man went and said, "Who is here?"

Ivan replied, "Prince Ivan."

The servant enquired, "What are you doing?"

"We have such a wonderful tablecloth!"

The servant reported thus to Maria, "Prince Ivan is there and he has a tablecloth."

Maria sent the servant to say, "Would Prince Ivan not sell his tablecloth?"

Ivan replied, "I will sell the tablecloth, if I may visit Maria for three hours."

Maria thought awhile and said, "Go and bring Ivan here."

Ivan came. Maria took out a watch and wore it. Ivan looked at Maria, and Maria looked at the watch. When three hours had passed, Maria said, "Good servants, take him back to the prison."

The servants led Ivan to the prison. But some peasants were sitting there and said, "Now we are lost, Ivan!"

He replied, "Have no fear; we are not lost. Let's enjoy ourselves! Self-flying carpet, unfold, unroll! I'm thirsty and hungry."

The carpet unfolded, and corks struck the ceiling. The peasants rode away on horses and Ivan's dog appeared.

Maria said, "Good servants, my prisoners wish to break out."

The servants went and said, "Who is here?"

And Ivan replied, "Prince Ivan is here."

"What are you doing?"

"There is a flying carpet here."

The servant returned and said to Maria, "He has a flying carpet."

She said, "Go and buy it."

The servant went and said, "Ivan, Maria wishes to purchase your flying carpet. How much do you ask for it?"

Ivan replied, "Let her marry me!"

The servant reported to Maria what Ivan said.

Maria pondered and said, "Bring him here."

Ivan came, and they were married. Maria gave Ivan the keys and said, "Go into all the storerooms except one of them; into that you must not enter."

Ivan opened all the rooms except one. He approached this room and wondered what it contained, and said at last, "I'll open it."

He opened it. There sat a Deathless Skeleton-Man on horseback. The horse was chained to a cauldron.

The Deathless Skeleton said, "Ah, Ivan, I have long waited for you to come. Unchain my horse, and I will deliver you from three deaths."

Ivan unchained the horse, which the Skeleton-Man mounted and rode off, taking Maria with him.

Ivan arrived, and saying, "Where is Princess Maria?" heard from the servants that the Deathless Skeleton-Man had carried her off.

Ivan went after Maria. She sat in the Skeleton Man's house very ill. Scarcely recognizing her, Ivan said, "Come with me!"

"No, the Skeleton-Man will overtake us!"

"Let's go!" he said.

They went. But the Deathless Skeleton-Man arrived and asked his horse this question. "Where is Princess Maria?" and the horse replied, "Ivan has taken her away."

The Skeleton Man asked his horse if it would be possible to overtake the fugitives.

"It will be possible if you give me a round loaf of bread and two buckets of beer."

The Skeleton-Man supplied his horse with these refreshments and then mounted and rode off. He took Maria from Ivan and departed.

The prince again returned for Maria and said, "Come with me." But she objected that they would be overtaken. "Don't worry. He won't overtake us!"

They set out, but the Skeleton-Man arrived and said, "Dear horse, where is Princess Maria?"

The horse replied, "Prince Ivan took Princess Maria away."

"Is it possible to overtake them?"

"It's possible. Give me two round loaves of bread and four buckets of beer, and I will overtake them." The Skeleton-Man provided these refreshments and, when they had been consumed, he mounted and rode away. Again, he took Maria from Ivan and departed.

But Ivan pursued and said, "Maria, will you come with me?"

She replied, "We shall be overtaken."

"Have no fear," said the prince, "he won't overtake us." They started.

The Skeleton-Man arrived and asked his horse, "Where is Princess Maria?"

"Prince Ivan took her away."

"Is it possible to overtake them?"

"It is, if you give me six round loaves and three buckets of beer."

The Skeleton-Man gave the provisions and, when the horse had finished drinking, the pursuit was begun again.

Once more Maria was seized by the Skeleton-Man, and once more recovered by Ivan. The horse now demanded four round loaves and eight buckets of beer for his services. The Skeleton-Man came up with the fugitives, cut Ivan down, took Maria with him, and departed.

Ivan's brothers-in-law came and said, looking at his body, "This is our brother!"

Some cranes now flew near, and the brothers caught one of them and were about to eat it. But the other cranes said, "Don't eat our crane, and we will return your kindness."

The cranes flew away, but returned with some Water-of-Life and Water-of-Death. The brothers sprinkled Ivan with the Water of Death, and he became whole. Next, they sprinkled him with the Water-of-Life, and he got up and said, "Ah, brothers, how long have I slept?"

Their reply was, "If it had not been for us, you would have slept longer."

They sent him to Baba-Yaga to watch her mares and said, "Take, not a mare, but a scabby foal!"

Ivan went to Baba-Yaga, who wished to know why he had come.

"To take care of the mares," he replied.

Baba-Yaga fed him, and he went to guard the mares; but they ran like the wind and dispersed; he could not collect them. Then some cranes flew near, and Ivan caught one of them and made ready to eat it.

Then they said, "If you don't eat this crane, we'll pursue the mares."

They pecked the mares all over and collected them into a crowd and said, "Now, Ivan, take a stick and drive them!"

Ivan drove the mares and Baba-Yaga fed him. When evening came, the mares separated. But some bees approached, and Ivan caught one and was about to eat it.

The bees said, "Don't eat our little bee, and we'll drive the mares to you." The bees bit the horses all over, and said to Ivan, "Now take a stick and drive them."

Ivan drove the mares, and then Baba-Yaga gave him plenty of food and drink and put him to sleep. In the morning he got up early and again went off to guard the mares, which separated and ran like the wind.

A frog came up with its young, and Ivan having caught the young, wished to kill it.

But the parent-frog said, "Be merciful, and I will drive the mares." Having taken them into a marsh and then out of it, the frog said, "Now drive them with a stick."

Ivan took a stick and drove the mares. Baba-Yaga fed him and put him to sleep. He woke early.

Baba-Yaga washed the mares and said, "Now take whichever you wish."

He replied, "No, I won't take one of the mares. Give me a scabby foal!"

Baba gave him a foal. Ivan rode and took Maria and carried her off on the foal. The Skeleton-Man on his horse could not overtake them, and was thrown to the ground. Then Prince Ivan and Princess Maria began to live and to amass riches.

Source: Coxwell, *Siberian and Other Folk-tales*, 775-781.

Ivan Tsarevitch and the Gray Wolf

Far away and many years ago, a mighty tsar named Demyan Danilovitch wisely ruled in his tsardom. He had three courageous sons, and the eldest was named Klym Tsarevitch, and the second was Pyotr Tsarevitch, and the youngest was Ivan Tsarevitch. And he loved his sons more than everything, and after them he loved the beautiful apple tree that grew in his palace garden and bore him golden fruit.

But in an evil hour a thief came and plundered his tree, and the Tsar became sorrowful. He couldn't eat and he couldn't sleep. He brought his sons into his presence and said to them, "Friends of my heart and my beloved sons, the time has come when you can serve me well. A thief has made his way into my garden at night and stolen fruit from my golden tree. I'm sick at heart. I'd gladly rather suffer death than lose my dearest treasure. Therefore, pay attention. Whoever captures the thief, on him I'll bestow half of my tsardom while I live and half when I die."

His three sons consulted with one another, and they decided to take turns each night to watch for the bold thief. On the first night, Klym Tsarevitch went into the garden, and lay down in the soft grass beneath the apple tree. For a while, he scanned the ground and sky, but no thief appeared. Soon he fell asleep and didn't wake until the noonday sun blazed in the sky.

Loudly yawning, he went before the Tsar and said, "Sire, I watched last night beside your tree, but no thief appeared to pluck the golden apples."

Pyotr Tsarevitch, on the second night, went into the garden and lay down in the soft grass beneath the apple tree. For a while, he scanned the ground and sky, but no thief appeared. Soon he fell asleep and didn't wake until the noonday sun blazed in the sky.

Loudly yawning, he went before the Tsar and said, "Sire, I watched last night beside your tree, but no thief appeared to pluck the golden apples."

On the third night, Ivan Tsarevitch took his turn in the garden to wait for the thief. He stood motionless beneath the tree, and waited to see what would happen. At midnight, the garden was lit suddenly as if by a flame. From the east, swift as a falling star, a bird of fire flew toward the apple tree. Her feathers were brighter than the sun and turned night into day.

Ivan Tsarevitch pressed close against the tree, not daring to breathe, and the bird of fire landed and plucked a golden apple from the branch. And she plucked a second and a third, and when she had plucked twelve, Ivan Tsarevitch came out of his hiding place and seized her by the tail.

She dropped the golden apples and beat her wings, trying in vain with all her might to free herself. Before she could loosen his hold, Ivan Tsarevitch plucked from her shining tail a single feather that lit the entire garden with its splendor.

Ivan Tsarevitch went before his father and said, "Sire, I watched last night beside your tree, and the thief that steals the golden apples is no man but a bird of fire. I bow before you and show you this shining feather plucked from her tail."

Rejoicing, Tsar Demyan embraced his son. From that point onward, the golden apples grew undisturbed, and the Tsar regained health, and ate well and slept from dusk to dawn.

But now he longed for the bird of fire. He summoned his elder sons before him and said, "My children, you now have the strength of adulthood, and it's time you should get to know my people and be known by them. Go out then into the white world, and with my blessing and the help of God, win glory for your names, and look for the wondrous bird of fire whose feathers light the earth. Whoever accomplishes this task will have half of all my tsardom while I live, half when I die."

They bowed before the Tsar, didn't wait long, but set forth into the white world.

Soon Ivan Tsarevitch came before his father, saying, "Great Tsar and Sire, Demyan Danilovitch, I beg you to let me follow my brothers, because it's time I should know your people and be known by them. Give me your blessing and, with the help of God, I will win glory for my name, and seek for you the wondrous bird of fire."

The Tsar replied, "You are too young, my son, and your strength is the strength of a green sapling that bows before the storm. Wait a little while, for your time will come. Don't forsake me now. I'm getting old, and if some evil should rob me of your brothers, who would rule my tsardom and my people?"

But Ivan Tsarevitch wouldn't be denied, and in the end, the Tsar gave Ivan his blessing, and so he set forth into the white world.

And traveling, he came to a crossroad that led in three directions. He saw a pillar with these words: "He that goes straight will suffer cold and hunger. He that turns right will perish, but his horse will live. He that turns left will lose his horse, but he will live." And Ivan Tsarevitch turned to the left and traveled farther.

Before he had gone the length of a field of grain, a gray wolf sprang from the thicket, pounced on his horse and killed him, and then went away. Ivan Tsarevitch bowed his head in sorrow and traveled farther.

In a moment the gray wolf appeared again before him and spoke in a human voice. "I grieve for you, Ivan Tsarevitch, and for your unlucky horse. But you did read the words of destiny and have to live with the result of your choice. But now take care, because I will be your horse and be of faithful service to you. Get on my back, and tell me where you are going and why."

Ivan Tsarevitch climbed onto the gray wolf's back and said, "I'm looking for the bird of fire."

The gray wolf replied, "With the Lord's help, I'll bring you where she is." And he took off, and his flight was swifter than the flight of eagles.

At midnight they paused before a wall of stone, and the gray wolf said, "Beyond the wall the bird of fire sits in her golden cage. Go softly, and bring her here. But beware. Don't touch the golden cage, because disaster will follow."

Ivan Tsarevitch scaled the wall, and he saw the bird of fire in her golden cage. The entire garden was lit by her feathers as if by the noonday sun. He took hold of her and would have fled again, but suddenly thought, "How will I bring her to my father's tsardom?" He forgot the gray wolf's wise counsel and he grabbed the golden cage.

Touching it, he heard a sound like the humming of golden harp strings. Two sturdy guardsmen seized him by either hand and led him before Tsar Afron.

Afron said, "Where do you come from and who are you?"

He answered, "Ivan Tsarevitch, son of the noble Tsar Demyan Danilovitch, who rules wisely over his far-reaching lands. Your bird of fire had come at night into my father's garden and plucked the golden apples from his tree. Therefore, I have come here to capture her."

Afron answered, "Whether you are indeed Ivan Tsarevitch, son of the Tsar Demyan Danilovitch, I don't know. But this I know—you are not acting princely. If you had come openly and said, 'Give me the bird of fire, Tsar Afron,' I would have freely given her to you, out of the love I bear the Tsar your father. But now you're just a thief and villain, and all the world will know of your dishonor. But wait! If you'll travel beyond the thrice ten tsardoms to the land of Tsar Kasim and bring me his daughter, whom men call Helen the Fair, I'll have mercy on you and give you in return the bird of fire."

Ivan Tsarevitch bowed his head in shame, and went to where the gray wolf waited for him.

The gray wolf said, "I love you well, Ivan Tsarevitch. If I didn't, you would have only found my smell waiting for you here. Yet to rebuke you won't undo your foolishness. Get on my back, and with God's help I'll bring you to the land of Tsar Kasim. Once there, remain outside, and I'll go in and do what needs to be done."

He took off, and his flight was swifter than the flight of seagulls. At midday they reached the land of Tsar Kasim, and the gray wolf said, "The garden of the Tsar is nearby. Wait for me under this green oak until I return."

He leapt over the garden wall and hid beneath the hedge, waiting there until Helen and her maids would walk around.

In the cool of day they came, Helen the Fair, daughter of Tsar Kasim, all her rosy maidens, and all her train of nurses and attendants. They strolled along the garden paths and tossed their colored balls. Their laughter pealed like the peal of silver bells, and their happy cries filled the air.

The gray wolf kept watch and saw that Helen, tiring of her play, sat by herself. He sprang up from beneath the hedge, seized her, and flung her onto his back. God gave to his limbs the swiftness of the wind.

In the garden a wild cry burst from the rosy maidens and from the nurses and attendants, and out of the palace rushed the ministers and courtiers and boyars, and at their head was the great Tsar Kasim. When he heard that a gray wolf had seized his daughter, he ordered his huntsmen to call their hounds and hurry in pursuit.

But though they hunted for nine days and nights, they couldn't find a trace of the gray wolf. Tsar Kasim mourned for the loss of Helen the Beautiful. Meanwhile, the gray wolf sped onward while the maiden, fainting from terror, lay motionless against the prince's breast. Soon her white lids fluttered, and her cheeks were stained with the faint bloom that steals upon the eastern sky at dawn. In the end, she opened her eyes wide and looked at Ivan Tsarevitch. Her face glowed like a flower. So great was the love each felt for the other, that it cannot be told in a tale nor written down with a pen.

Ivan Tsarevitch suffered from torment and thought, "How can I give her up to Tsar Afron?"

The gray wolf read his sorrow and replied, "You're crying for nothing, Ivan Tsarevitch, since I'll prevent that which you fear. This task will be easier than eating a rabbit. After this, there will be a more serious task."

Having reached the tsardom of Afron, he said, "I'll transform myself into a woman and you'll bring me to the Tsar Afron. When you've received the bird of fire in return, leave and wait for me with your bride in the secret place I'll show you. I'll hurry, so you two won't have to wait long."

The gray wolf showed them the secret place, then struck the earth and transformed into a beautiful woman. Ivan Tsarevitch brought her to the palace and gave her to Tsar Afron, and in return he took the bird of fire and went to the secret place where Helen the Beautiful waited for him.

Tsar Afron commanded that the church be decorated and the wedding feast prepared, for he would marry his beautiful bride right away. When he went to kiss her white forehead, sharp bristles pierced his mouth, and his nose was seized in the grip of strong jaws. Terrified, he saw before him no beautiful woman but a great gray wolf.

The nobles shouted, "After him! Seize him! Don't let him escape!"

But the gray wolf knocked down the Tsar with a blow from his tail, and plunged down the long hall and through the palace gates. No one could grab onto him. And so he reached the place where Helen the Beautiful and Ivan Tsarevitch waited for his return.

They got on his back, and swift as an arrow from the bow he sped, until they came to where the bones of the dead horse lay as they had been left.

The gray wolf said, "Alas, Ivan Tsarevitch, we must part. I have been faithful to you, and you have been great company. Even if my years outnumber the shining stars, I won't forget you, and that which I destroyed I will make whole." And with these words he breathed upon the bones, and the gallant horse rose and pawed the earth.

The gray wolf said, "Now mount your horse and go with Helen the Beautiful and the bird of fire back to your father's tsardom. I will pray that no hardship befalls you on the way. Trust no one you meet, not even your brothers. Go with God." And the gray wolf vanished into the forest.

Ivan Tsarevitch wept to see him go, then turned his horse and galloped homeward. Helen the Beautiful rode in front of him and the bird of fire behind.

From a distance he saw the domes of his father's city, but in a nearby meadow a tent was pitched. His brothers came out of the tent and welcomed him. Joyfully he clasped them in his arms, but envy like a creeping snake writhed in their hearts when they saw the treasures he had won.

They asked Ivan Tsarevitch to enter the tent, so he could rest. Being tired, he entered and lay down and slumbered. With their sharp-edged swords, his brothers killed him and seized the bird of fire and the woman, and fled. They flung Ivan Tsarevitch into the swamp, and his faithful horse lifted his head and cried aloud for comfort.

The hours passed and the night fell, and a black raven with his fledgling hovered above the prince's lifeless form. But when they would have landed on his breast, from nowhere the gray wolf appeared and seized the elder raven by the tail.

The raven begged for mercy, crying, "Release me, good gray wolf, and I'll leave Ivan Tsarevitch undisturbed in the swamp."

The gray wolf answered, "I won't release you unless you send your fledgling to bring me the waters of life and death."

The raven called his fledgling and drew two flasks from beneath his wing and said, "Take these flasks and fly with them beyond the edge of the white world to the springs of life and death, and fill them and bring them here again." And the fledgling spread his wings and flew away.

But his sire remained behind, and talked about the wonders he had seen, and all the treasures of his hidden tales he spread before the wolf. The gray wolf marveled at his wisdom, but didn't loosen his hold on the tail, and crushed it even more between his paws, as who should say, "You are wise, black raven, yet for all your wisdom, the gray wolf holds you still."

The sun sank, the night waxed and waned, and with the dawn the fledgling returned, bearing beneath his wing the waters of life and death. The gray wolf took the flagons and set the raven free. With his fledgling, he soared high into the sky and vanished.

The gray wolf sprinkled Ivan Tsarevitch with the water of death, and all his wounds were healed. Then he sprinkled him with the water of life, and Ivan Tsarevitch sprang to his feet and cried, "I have slept long, my brothers."

"And longer would you have slept, Ivan Tsarevitch, except for my coming. For your false brothers took your life and left you in the swamp, but the gray wolf has made you whole again. He has served you with all his cunning and with all his strength, but from now on you must serve yourself. Kostchei the Deathless has killed your brothers and cast a spell of everlasting sleep upon your father's realm. Helen the Beautiful and the bird of fire are captives within his palace walls. He can't harm your bride, because she is protected by a powerful spell. But only his death can free her, and where his death lies hidden is known to Baba Yaga and to none beside. Then mount your horse and travel to the east, and seek her in the ancient forest where no beast prowls nor any bird takes flight. Her dwelling is a hut on chickens' legs, her horse a mortar, and with a broom she sweeps from behind her the traces of her flight. May God protect you and, if it be His will, I will dance at your bridal feast." And the gray wolf vanished into the forest, and Ivan Tsarevitch mounted his horse and traveled to the east.

He rode for a day and a second and a third, and came at dusk to the ancient forest and entered in. The oaks and cedars towered to the sky, but no bird stirred in their branches, no beast prowled in their shade, nor any insect crept among their roots. The leaves hung motionless on the still air, and only the hoofbeats of the flying horse disturbed the silence.

Ivan Tsarevitch stopped before the hut that turned on chickens' legs and cried aloud, "Stand with your back to the forest, hut, your face to me!" And the hut obeyed, and stood with its back to the forest and its face to Ivan Tsarevitch, and he dismounted and bowed in greeting at the threshold and entered in.

The Baba Yaga lay on the floor of her hut, and her feet were thrust into the chimney-place. She heard the sound of his footsteps and said, "I smell a Russian smell, and this is strange, for until now no soul has found his way into my forest, no beast stirred in the thicket, nor bird among the trees. What brings you here, Russian? Do you come gladly or does sorrow drive you?"

And Ivan Tsarevitch was angered and he cried, "Shame on you, foolish witch, is this your welcome? Give me something to eat and drink, lead me to a soft couch so I can rest my weary bones, and ask me questions afterwards."

The Baba Yaga bathed and anointed him, spread rich food in front of him, and let him rest on a silken couch. And she said, "Sleep, brave hero, in peace under my roof. The morning is wiser than the night, and tomorrow I'll give you advice."

Ivan Tsarevitch prayed to the Lord and slept, not waking until the sun shone in the sky.

Baba Yaga stood at his side and said, "What can I do for you?"

"I seek the death of the vile wizard, Kostchei the Deathless."

"Ech, young Tsarevitch, you have undertaken a perilous task. Yet, by my wisdom and the grace of God, you will find what you're looking for. To help you, I'll give you three treasures—a cap that makes both man and beast invisible, a club that beats its master's enemies, and a cloth that will provide you with food and drink. And now listen. On an island that is called Buyan, which lies in the midst of the sea, an old oak grows, beneath whose roots a chest, bound with iron bands, is buried deep. In the chest sleeps a velvety rabbit, and in the rabbit lies a young gray duck, and in the duck an egg is hidden, and in the egg lies the death of great Kostchei the Deathless. When you have found the egg, go to the palace gates where a dragon with twelve heads keeps an endless watch. Don't draw your sword against him, because no sword can kill him, but put on the cap and send the club to beat him, and you'll see strange things. Then scale the mountain, and in the presence of Kostchei the Deathless, hurl to the ground the egg that holds his death, and he'll perish. One task remains. The dulcimer, which hangs on the willow and sings by itself, alone is powerful enough to break the curse cast by Kostchei on your father's realm. Take it and flee with Helen the Beautiful and the bird of fire, Don't stop until you've reached the foot of the mountain. And now farewell, and when you have reached the end of all your troubles, think kindly about her who helped you with her cunning and her strength."

Ivan Tsarevitch thanked Baba Yaga and, mounting his horse, continued on his journey. And soon the ancient forest lay far behind him and the blue sea before him. He saw a net, where a silver pike struggled to free herself. When the pike saw Ivan Tsarevitch, she cried in a human voice, "Kind youth, free me from the net, and when you need me, I'll befriend you." And so he freed her from the fisher's net. Flapping her tail in thanks, she swam away.

Ivan Tsarevitch guided his horse close to the water's edge, and the noble charger plunged into the waves, battling against their fury without tiring until he had brought his master to the island that is called Buyan and lies in the midst of the sea.

Ivan Tsarevitch let him eat in the green pasture, and he went alone to where the old oak grew and shook it once. But the great tree stood firm. He shook it again, and its branches groaned as though they wrestled with a mighty storm. Once more he shook it, and the oak fell crashing to the earth, while its uptorn roots, like crawling serpents, spread over all the land.

Where the tree had stood, a chasm yawned, and in the chasm a chest bound with iron bands lay buried deep. Ivan Tsarevitch brought the chest up and shattered the bolt and seized the velvety rabbit by the ears and tore him in half. The gray duck flew swiftly out to sea but, more swiftly still, Ivan Tsarevitch drew his bow and shot an arrow into the gray duck's heart. Cackling, she let fall the egg that sank like a boulder underneath the waves. Ivan Tsarevitch cried aloud in sorrow, because he didn't know how to get it from the depths of the blue sea.

But through the troubled waters, the silver pike flashed like a ray of light and vanished and reappeared. In her mouth she bore the egg in which lay buried the death of great Kostchei the Deathless. She gave the egg into the Prince's hand and said, "In your hour of need, Ivan Tsarevitch, I have befriended you," and flapping her tail, she swam far out to sea.

He placed the egg close to his chest and mounted his horse, who plunged again into the ocean, and having brought his master safe to shore, sped toward the land of Tsar Kostchei.

Whether the journey was little or long, they came at length to a high mountain, a palace on its summit, and at its foot great gates of iron that were guarded by a dragon with twelve heads. Six heads slept and six heads watched in turn, and the tongues spat black venom and flames burst from the throats, so that no one, even if he was the bravest in the realm, dared to venture close. No man could overpower the dragon, for it was written that he would kill himself.

Ivan Tsarevitch put on the magic cap that rendered invisible both man and beast and crept up to the dragon, whose sleeping heads lay stretched on the ground, while those that waked curled on their twisting necks and looked every way at once.

Ivan Tsarevitch whispered to his club, "Now to your task, stout friend!"

The club beat up the dragon, and struck the heads that slept and those that were awake. The dragon leapt into the air and hissed and snorted, but to no avail, because still the club kept at its task and did nothing else. The dragon ran up and down and lashed his tail and roared in agony, spitting black venom and hot fumes of rage and tearing at the earth. And still the club hit him, neither hurrying nor slowing its steady pace. In the end, the dragon, consumed with anger, drove his bitter fangs deep into his own breast and tore his flesh. Bellowing so that the mountain trembled, he fell to the earth and died.

Ivan Tsarevitch commanded the club to stop and, spreading his magic cloth on the ground, he said, "Good cloth, comfort my tired horse with food and water until I return." He shouldered his club and went forth to scale the mountain. The way was long and troublesome but, although his limbs grew heavy, he didn't tire or stop until he heard at last the sweet strains of the dulcimer that hung from a willow branch and played by itself.

Drawing near, he entered a garden where fountains splashed and peacocks spread their tails. Underneath the willow, Helen the Beautiful moaned her fate. Ivan Tsarevitch took off his magic cap and stood before her. Her eyes grew big with joy, but when she would have fled into his embrace, he placed his hand in warning to his lips and whispered, "I bring the death of great Kostchei the Deathless. When I have found him and doled out his doom, I will return to you." And he replaced the cap upon his head and went his way.

But now the wizard came to greet his captive and said, "Fret no longer, maiden, for you have seen your bridegroom killed at his brothers' hands, and your tears won't restore him. Become the bride of great Kostchei, and you'll live at ease and share the glory of his deathless name."

Ivan Tsarevitch, returning to the garden, heard his words and whispered to his club, "Beat him!" And the club did his bidding, and struck Kostchei upon his back and shoulders, and struck his head and hands, until he rolled in anguish at Helen's feet and howled for mercy.

But Ivan Tsarevitch cried, "No, beat him, brother, beat him without mercy! You thief and dog Kostchei, you toad-faced monster, will you steal maidens now and set a dragon with twelve heads to guard them? Or cast a curse of everlasting sleep on my father's realm? Beat him, good club, for he has done great evil! And even if you beat him for thrice nine years, you couldn't purge him of half of all his crimes."

Kostchei cried, "Where are you and who are you? Let me see your face!"

Ivan Tsarevitch took off his cap and looked at Kostchei, then drew the egg from his breast and dashed it to the ground. The egg shattered into many fragments, and Kostchei the Deathless turned on his back and died.

Ivan Tsarevitch embraced his bride and from the tree branch he took the dulcimer that played by itself. He left the garden, the club on his back, Helen the Beautiful on his right side, and underneath his arm the bird of fire.

They descended into the valley, and scarcely had they reached the foot of the mountain when a mighty roaring sounded in their ears, as though the earth would tear itself in two. Turning, they saw the palace of Kostchei tottering on its height, and with a crash that echoed to the farthest edge of the white world, the mountain fell. In its place, a lake of bubbling pitch spread its foul odors over all the land.

Ivan Tsarevitch mounted his horse, and Helen sat before him, and they set out on their way home. When they were hungry, the magic cloth served them with meat and drink, and the dulcimer played for them when they were weary. The bird of fire made the darkness bright, and at the portals of their tent the club kept faithful watch.

In this way they traveled until they reached the tsardom of the great Tsar Demyan Danilovitch. When they crossed his border, they saw that everything slumbered. Here, a peasant slept in his half-ploughed field behind his sleeping oxen, while in midair the whirling whip was checked before it could fall. And there a knight dreamed on his dreaming horse, and the dust was a quiet cloud about his feet. They rode through cities and through villages, and all were chained in the power of Kostchei's spell—men in their doorways, and black flies on the wall, and plumes of smoke that neither rose nor fell, but stood in rings above the chimney pots.

And so they came to the Tsar's city, at whose gates Ivan Tsarevitch saw the bodies of his false brethren, slain by the wizard's hand. They dismounted in the palace court and passed the sleeping guard and entered.

The great Tsar Demyan Danilovitch slept on his throne. His nobles, whose unseeing gaze was fixed upon their lord, surrounded him, while a minister stood open-mouthed before him, his honeyed phrases stilled upon his tongue.

Ivan Tsarevitch approached the throne and cried, "Play, dulcimer!"

The dulcimer obeyed, and as its first notes sounded sweet and clear, the court awakened, and the nobles fixed their gaze upon the Tsar, and the minister bowed down before him, uttering sage counsel.

But when the Tsar saw Ivan Tsarevitch, he was as one lacking sober wit. And, weeping, he embraced him, and listened to the tale of his adventures and wept again. But in the end, he put aside his tears and, joyfully he danced with his son's fair bride.

Guns were fired from the city walls, and bells pealed from the steeples, and heralds hurried up and down the land and cried, "Be it known to all his people that the great Tsar Demyan Danilovitch gives to his well-loved son, Ivan Tsarevitch, the half of all his kingdom while he lives, half when he dies. Moreover, you are invited tomorrow—soldiers and merchants, beggars and gentlefolk—you rich and poor, you lowborn and highborn alike—to eat and celebrate at the wedding feast of Helen the Beautiful with Ivan Tsarevitch."

The next day Ivan Tsarevitch married his bride. All the nobles saluted them, and the people thronged at the palace gates, and whirled and swirled like a stormy sea. Their clamor was as the clamor of mighty waters. And they cried, "Long life to Tsar Demyan Danilovitch! Long life to Ivan Tsarevitch and to his bride, Helen the Beautiful!"

The magic cloth spread fruits and mead and many savory foods. The guests ate and partied in the streets. And the guards and sentinels were welcomed to the feast, while the club took over for them, beating so fiercely the thieves who would have plundered the joyful city that they stole no more but walked in righteousness. And the dulcimer played melodies so sweet that no one had heard their like, for they were as the song of birds at dawn and the music of running streams and the sound of winds that blow through a lonely forest.

And Tsar Demyan Danilovitch arose and raised his golden goblet, and silence fell upon the multitude. Before he could shape the words he would have spoken, a blare of trumpets rang out in the court, and a coach appeared, bright with gold trappings, attended by pages and outriders, and drawn by prancing horses, that arched their necks and came to rest before the palace gate.

Ivan Tsarevitch went forward to greet his guest, and the gray wolf came out of the coach and clasped Ivan Tsarevitch in his arms. He was dressed in splendor, with scarlet pants and a velvet coat, a tasseled cap tied with ribbons underneath his chin, and a tie of fine silk. On his paws were gauntlets, and his tail was bound in a hood of silver, embellished with rare pearls. In this outfit did the gray wolf appear, to pay his duty to the great Tsar Demyan Danilovitch, and dance at the wedding feast of Helen the Beautiful with Ivan Tsarevitch.

Ivan Tsarevitch led him before his father, who kissed him on either cheek. Then, arm in arm, they passed down the long hall, and the gray wolf saluted the wedding guests and gave them compliments. And so mild was his stance and gracious his demeanor that everyone was charmed who looked upon his face and heard his speech.

And so they feasted, and the gray wolf sat at the right hand of Ivan Tsarevitch. When darkness fell, the wondrous feathers of the bird of fire lit the city streets.

The next morning the gray wolf came to say goodbye to the Prince, but Ivan Tsarevitch begged him to share his fortune and take up his residence within the palace, vowing that he would be exalted in rank above the highest, and wear on his breast the ribbons of all the noble orders of the land. In the end Ivan Tsarevitch convinced the gray wolf to do his will, and the gray wolf, as a symbol of his agreement, laid his hairy paw in the Prince's hand.

And so for many years they lived in joy, until the Tsar Demyan Danilovitch, having ruled long and gloriously, died, and Ivan Tsarevitch was in power over his broad domain. Helen the Beautiful ruled at his side, and the Lord blessed them with devoted sons and beautiful daughters, whom the gray wolf nursed. He told them tales of knights and bogatyrs, and taught them to ride swiftly and speak the truth, and many things besides, things proper for young hearts to know.

The gray wolf lived to a ripe old age, and when he died, he was mourned by young and old. In his papers was found a chronicle of the adventures that had happened to him in the depths of the great forest. And from his chronicle this tale is told.

Source: Zeitlin, *Skazki; Tales and Legends of Old Russia*, 91-122.

The Blind Man and the Cripple

*I*n a certain kingdom there lived a king and queen. They had a son, Prince Ivan, and to look after that son was appointed a tutor named Katoma Dyadka of the oaken cap. The king and queen lived to a ripe old age, but then they fell ill, and despaired of ever recovering. So they sent for Prince Ivan and strictly commanded him, "When we are dead, always respect and obey Katoma. If you obey him, you'll prosper; but if you choose to be disobedient, you'll perish like a fly."

The next day the king and queen died. Prince Ivan buried his parents and lived according to their instructions. Whatever he had to do, he always consulted his tutor about it.

Some time passed by. The Prince gained adulthood and began to think about getting married. One day he went to his tutor and said, "Katoma, I'm tired of living alone. I want to marry."

"Well, Prince! What's to prevent you? You've reached an age where it's time to think about a bride. Go into the great hall. There's a collection there of the portraits of all the princesses in the world. Look at them and choose for yourself. Whichever one pleases you, to her send a proposal of marriage."

Prince Ivan went into the great hall and began examining the portraits. The one that pleased him best was that of the Princess Anna the Fair—such a beauty! The like of her wasn't to be found in the whole world! Underneath her portrait were written these words: "If anyone asks her a riddle, and she doesn't guess it, him shall she marry; but he whose riddle she guesses shall have his head chopped off."

Prince Ivan read this inscription, became greatly afflicted, and went off to his tutor. "I've been in the great hall," he said, "and I picked out for my bride Anna the Fair. Only I don't know whether it's possible to win her."

"Yes, Prince, she's hard to get. If you go alone, you won't win her anyhow. But if you take me with you, and if you do what I tell you, perhaps the affair can be managed."

Prince Ivan begged Katoma to go with him and gave his word of honor to obey him whether in joy or grief.

They got ready for the journey and set off to make a plea for the hand of the Princess Anna the Fair. They traveled for one year, two years, three years, and traversed many countries. Prince Ivan said, "We've been travelling all this time, uncle, and now we're approaching the country of Princess Anna the Fair, and yet we don't know what riddle to propose."

"We'll manage to think of one in good time," replied Katoma.

They went a little farther. Katoma was looking down at the road, and on it lay a purse full of money. He lifted it up right away, poured all the money out of it into his own purse, and said, "Here's a riddle for you, Prince Ivan! When you come into the presence of the Princess, propose a riddle to her in these words: 'As we were coming along, we saw Good lying on the road, and we took up the Good with Good, and placed it in our own Good!' That riddle she won't guess in a lifetime; but any other one she would find out directly. She would only have to look into her magic book, and as soon as she had guessed it, she'd order your head to be cut off."

At last Prince Ivan and his tutor arrived at the lofty palace in which lived the fair Princess. She happened to be out on the balcony, and when she saw the newcomers, she sent out to know where they came from and what they wanted.

Prince Ivan replied, "I have come from such-and-such a kingdom, and I wish to pursue the hand of the Princess Anna the Fair."

When she was informed of this, the Princess gave orders that the Prince should enter the palace, and there in the presence of all the princes and boyars of her council should propose his riddle.

"I've made this compact," she said "Anyone whose riddle I cannot guess, him I must marry. But anyone whose riddle I can guess, him I may put to death."

"Listen to my riddle, fair Princess!" said Prince Ivan. "As we came along, we saw Good lying on the road, and we took up the Good with Good, and placed it in our own Good."

Princess Anna the Fair took her magic book and began turning over its leaves and examining the answers of riddles. She went right through the book, but she didn't get at the meaning she wanted. Therefore, the princes and boyars of her council decided that the Princess must marry Prince Ivan. She wasn't at all pleased, but there was nothing she could do, and so she began to get ready for the wedding. Meanwhile, she thought about how she could spin out the time and do away with the bridegroom, and she thought the best way would be to overwhelm him with tremendous tasks.

She called Prince Ivan and said to him, "My dear Prince Ivan, my destined husband! It is right that we should prepare for the wedding. Please do this small request for me. On such and such a spot of my kingdom there stands a high iron pillar. Carry it into the palace kitchen and chop it into small chunks for fuel for the cook."

"Excuse me, Princess," replied the Prince. "Was it to chop fuel that I came here? Is that the proper sort of employment for me? I have a servant for that kind of thing, Katoma Dyadka of the oaken cap."

The Prince immediately called for his tutor and ordered him to drag the iron pillar into the kitchen, and to chop it into small chunks for fuel for the cook. Katoma went to the spot indicated by the Princess, seized the pillar in his arms, brought it into the palace kitchen, and broke it into little pieces, but four of the iron chips he put into his pocket, saying, "They'll prove useful sooner or later!"

The next day the Princess said to Prince Ivan, "My dear Prince, my destined husband, tomorrow we have to go to the wedding. I'll drive in a carriage, but you should ride on a heroic horse, and you should break him in beforehand."

"Break a horse in myself! I keep a servant for that."

Prince Ivan called Katoma and said, "Go into the stable and tell the grooms to bring out the heroic horse. Sit on him and break him in. Tomorrow, I have to ride him to the wedding."

Katoma fathomed the subtle device of the Princess, but, without stopping long to talk, he went into the stable and told the grooms to bring out the heroic horse. Twelve grooms were gathered, and they unlocked twelve locks, opened twelve doors, and brought out a magic horse bound in twelve iron chains.

Katoma went up to him. No sooner had he managed to seat himself than the magic horse leapt up from the ground and soared higher than the forest—higher than the standing forest, lower than the flitting cloud. Katoma sat firm, with one hand grasping the mane; with the other he took from his pocket an iron chunk and began taming the horse with it between the ears. When he had used up one chunk, he took out another. When two were used up, he took out a third. When three were used up, the fourth came into play.

So grievously did he punish the heroic horse that it could not hold out any longer, but cried aloud with a human voice, "Batyushka Katoma! Don't completely deprive me of life in the white world! Whatever you wish, order me. I'll do everything you say."

"Listen, O meat for dogs!" answered Katoma. "Tomorrow Prince Ivan will ride you to the wedding. Now when the grooms bring you out into the wide courtyard, and the Prince goes up to you and lays his hand on you, stand quietly, not moving so much as an ear. When he is seated on your back, sink into the earth right up to your fetlocks, and then move under him with a heavy step, just as if an immeasurable weight had been laid upon your back."

The heroic horse listened to the command and sank to earth scarcely alive. Katoma seized him by the tail and flung him close to the stable, crying, "Hey there, coachmen and grooms, carry off this dog's meat to its stall!"

The next day arrived; the time drew near for going to the wedding. The carriage was brought around for the Princess, and the heroic horse for Prince Ivan. The people were gathered together from all sides— a countless number. The bride and bridegroom came out from the white stone halls. The Princess got into the carriage and waited to see what would become of Prince Ivan, whether the magic horse would fling him to the wind and scatter his bones across the open plain.

Prince Ivan approached the horse, laid his hand upon its back, placed his foot in the stirrup—the horse stood just as if petrified, without so much as twitching an ear! The Prince got on its back, and the magic horse sank into the earth up to its fetlocks. The twelve chains were taken off the horse, and it began to move with a steady, heavy pace, while the sweat poured off it just like hail.

"What a hero! What immeasurable strength!" cried the people as they gazed upon the Prince.

So the bride and bridegroom were married, and then they began to move out of the church, holding each other by the hand. The Princess decided to make one more trial of Prince Ivan, so she squeezed his hand so hard that he couldn't bear the pain. His face turned red, and his eyes disappeared beneath his brows.

"A fine sort of hero you are!" thought the Princess. "Your tutor has tricked me splendidly, but you won't get off for nothing!"

Princess Anna the Fair lived for some time with Prince Ivan as a wife ought to live with a God-given husband, flattered him in every way in words, but in reality never thought of anything except how she might get rid of Katoma. With the Prince, without the tutor, there'd be no difficulty in settling matters! she said to herself.

But whatever slanders she might invent, Prince Ivan never allowed himself to be influenced by what she said, but always felt sorry for his tutor. At the end of a year, he said to his wife one day, "Beautiful Princess, my beloved spouse, I would like to bring you to my own kingdom."

"By all means," she replied, "let's go. I myself have long been wishing to see your kingdom."

They got ready and went off. Katoma was given the position of coachman. They drove and drove, and as they drove along Prince Ivan went to sleep. Suddenly, the Princess Anna the Fair awoke him, loudly complaining, "Listen, Prince, you're always sleeping; you hear nothing! But your tutor doesn't obey me a bit, drives the horses on purpose over hill and dale, just as if he wanted to put an end to us both. I tried speaking to him, but he jeered at me. I won't go on living any longer if you don't punish him!"

Prince Ivan, between sleeping and waking, got angry with his tutor and handed him over to the Princess, saying, "Deal with him as you please!"

The Princess ordered his feet to be cut off. Katoma submitted patiently to the outrage.

"Very good," he thought. "I shall suffer, it's true; but the Prince also will know what it's like to lead a wretched life!"

When both of Katoma's feet had been cut off, the Princess glanced around, and saw that a tall tree stump stood on one side. She called her servants and ordered them to set him on that stump. As for Prince Ivan, she tied him to the carriage by a cord, turned the horses around, and drove back to her own kingdom. Katoma was left sitting on the stump, weeping bitter tears.

"Farewell, Prince Ivan!" he cried. "You won't forget me!"

Meanwhile Prince Ivan was running and leaping behind the carriage. He knew well enough by this time what a mistake he had made, but there was no turning back for him. When the Princess Anna the Fair arrived in her kingdom, she set Prince Ivan to take care of the cows. Every day he went into the field with the herd in the early morning, and in the evening he drove them back to the royal yard. At that hour the Princess was always sitting on the balcony, and looking out to see that the number of the cows was all right.

Katoma remained sitting on the stump one day, two days, three days, without anything to eat or drink. To get down was utterly impossible. It seemed as if he must die of starvation.

But not far away from that place there was a dense forest. In that forest was living a mighty hero who was quite blind. The only way he could get himself food was this: whenever he perceived by the sense of smell that any animal was running past him, whether a hare, or a fox, or a bear, he immediately started to chase it, caught it—and dinner was ready for him. The hero was exceedingly swift-footed, and there was not a single wild beast that could run away from him.

One day it fell out thus. A fox slunk past. The hero heard it, and went after it immediately. It ran up to the tall stump and turned sharp off on one side, but the blind hero hurried on, took a spring, and thumped his forehead against the stump so hard that he knocked the stump out by the roots.

Katoma fell to the ground and asked, "Who are you?"

"I'm a blind hero. I've been living in the forest for thirty years. The only way I can get my food is this: to catch some game or other and cook it over a wood fire. If it hadn't been for that, I would have starved to death long ago!"

"You haven't been blind all your life?"

"No, not all my life. Princess Anna the Fair put my eyes out!"

"There now, brother," said Katoma, "it's thanks to her, too, that I'm left here without any feet. She cut them both off, the accursed one!"

The two heroes had a talk and agreed to live together and work together to get their food. The blind man said to the lame one, "Sit on my back and show me the way. I'll serve you with my feet, and you me with your eyes."

So he took the cripple and carried him home, and Katoma sat on his back, kept a look out all around, and cried out from time to time, "Right! Left! Straight on!" and so forth.

They lived for a while in the forest in that way and caught hares, foxes, and bears for their dinner. One day the cripple said, "Surely, we can never go on living all our lives without a soul to speak to. I've heard that in such and such a town lives a rich merchant who has a daughter; and that merchant's daughter is exceedingly kind to the poor and crippled. She gives alms to everyone. Suppose we carry her off, brother, and let her live here and keep house for us."

The blind man took a cart, seated the cripple in it, and rattled it into the town, straight into the rich merchant's courtyard. The merchant's daughter saw them out of the window and immediately ran out and came to give them alms.

Approaching the cripple, she said, "Take this, in Christ's name, poor fellow!"

He seemed to be going to take the gift, but he seized her by the hand, pulled her into the cart, and called to the blind man, who ran off with it at such a pace that no one could catch him, even on horseback. The merchant sent people in pursuit—but no, they couldn't catch up with him.

The heroes brought the merchant's daughter into their forest hut, and said to her, "Be in the place of a sister to us, live here and keep house for us. Otherwise, we poor sufferers will have no one to cook our meals or wash our shirts. God won't desert you if you do that!"

The merchant's daughter remained with them. The heroes respected her, loved her, acknowledged her as a sister. They went out hunting all day, but their adopted sister was always at home. She looked after all the housekeeping, prepared the meals, washed the linen.

But after a while, a Baba Yaga took to haunting their hut and sucking the breasts of the merchant's daughter. No sooner had the heroes gone off to hunt, than the Baba Yaga was there in a moment. Before long the fair maiden's face began to fall away, and she grew weak and thin. The blind man could see nothing, but Katoma remarked that things weren't going well. He spoke about it to the blind man, and they went together to their adopted sister and began questioning her. But the Baba Yaga had strictly forbidden her from telling the truth. For a long time, she was afraid to tell them about her trouble. For a long time, she held out, but at last her brothers convinced her, and she told them everything without hesitation.

"Every time you go away to hunt," she said, "there immediately appears in the cottage a very old woman with a most evil face and long gray hair. And she makes me brush her hair, and meanwhile she sucks my breasts."

"Ah!" said the blind man, "that's a Baba Yaga. Wait a bit. We'll take care of her. Tomorrow we won't go hunting, but we'll try to trap her and grab her!"

So the next morning, the heroes didn't go out hunting.

"Now then, Uncle Footless," said the blind man, "you get under the bench and lie ever so still, and I'll go into the yard and stand under the window. As for you, sister, when the Baba Yaga comes, sit down just here, close by the window, and as you brush her hair, quietly separate the locks, and throw them outside through the window. Just let me grab hold of her by those gray hairs of hers!"

What was said was done. The blind man grabbed hold of the Baba Yaga by her gray hair and cried, "Hey there, Uncle Katoma, come out from under the bench and grab hold of this viper of a woman, while I come into the hut!"

The Baba Yaga heard the bad news and tried to jump up to get her head free. (Where are you off to? That's no go, sure enough!) She tugged and tugged, but it did no good!

Just then from under the bench crawled Uncle Katoma. He fell upon her like a mountain of stone, started strangling her until the heaven seemed to her to disappear. Then into the cottage bounded the blind man, crying to the cripple, "Now we must heap up a great pile of wood and burn this accursed one with fire and fling her ashes to the wind!"

The Baba Yaga began begging them, "My fathers! my darlings! forgive me. I'll be good."

"Very good, old witch! Then show us the fountain of healing and life-giving water!" said the heroes.

"Only don't kill me, and I'll show it to you right away!"

Katoma sat on the blind man's back. The blind man took the Baba Yaga by her back hair, and she led them into the depths of the forest, brought them to a well, and said, "That is the water that cures and gives life."

"Be careful, Uncle Katoma!" cried the blind man. "Don't make a mistake. If she tricks us now, we won't be right for the rest of our lives!"

Katoma cut a green branch off a tree and flung it into the well. The bough hadn't so much as reached the water before it all burst into flames!

"Ha! So you're still up to your tricks," said the heroes and began to strangle the Baba Yaga, with the intention of flinging her, the accursed one, into the fiery well. More than ever did the Baba Yaga beg for mercy, swearing a great oath that she wouldn't deceive them this time.

"On my honor, I'll bring you to good water," she said.

The heroes consented to give her one more try, and she took them to another well.

Uncle Katoma cut a dry branch from a tree and flung it into the well. The branch had not yet reached the water when it already turned green, budded, and put forth blossoms.

"Come now, that's good water!" said Katoma.

The blind man wetted his eyes with it and immediately saw. He lowered the cripple into the water, and the lame man's feet grew again. Then they both rejoiced greatly and said to one another, "Now the time has come for us to make everything right! We'll get everything back again that we used to have! Only first we must put an end to the Baba Yaga. If we pardon her now, we would always be unlucky; she'd be scheming mischief all her life."

Right away they went back to the fiery well and flung the Baba Yaga into it. Didn't it soon make an end of her!

After this, Katoma married the merchant's daughter, and the three companions went to the kingdom of Anna the Fair in order to rescue Prince Ivan. When they drew near to the capital, what did they see but Prince Ivan driving a herd of cows!

"Stop, herdsman!" said Katoma. "Where are you driving these cows?"

"I'm driving them to the Princess's courtyard," replied the Prince. "The Princess always sees for herself whether all the cows are there."

"Here, herdsman, take my clothes and put them on, and I'll put on yours and drive the cows."

"No, brother, I can't do that. If the Princess found out, I'd suffer harm!"

"Don't worry. Nothing will happen! Katoma will guarantee you that."

Prince Ivan sighed and said, "Ah, good man! If Katoma had been alive, I wouldn't have been feeding these cows in the field!"

Then Katoma disclosed to him who he was. Prince Ivan warmly embraced him and burst into tears. "I never expected to see you again," he said.

So they exchanged clothes. The tutor drove the cows to the Princess's courtyard. Anna the Fair went onto the balcony, looked to see if all the cows were there, and ordered them to be driven into the sheds. All the cows went into the sheds except the last one, which remained at the gate. Katoma sprang at it, exclaiming, "What are you waiting for, dog's-meat?"

Then he seized it by the tail, and pulled it so hard that he pulled the cow's hide right off! The Princess saw this and cried with a loud voice, "What is that brute of a cowherd doing? Seize him and bring him to me!"

Then the servants seized Katoma and dragged him into the palace. He went with them, making no excuses, relying on himself. They brought him to the Princess. She looked at him and asked, "Who are you? Where do you come from?"

"I am he whose feet you cut off and whom you set on a stump. My name is Katoma Dyadka of the oaken cap."

"Well," thought the Princess, "now that he's got his feet back again, I mustn't deceive him in the future."

And she began to beg him and the Prince to forgive her. She confessed all her sins and swore to always love Prince Ivan and obey him in all matters. Prince Ivan forgave her and began to live with her in peace and harmony. The hero who had been blind remained with them, but Katoma and his wife went to the house of her father the rich merchant and took up their abode under his roof.

Source: Ralston, *Russian Folk-tales*, 240-252.

The Realms of Copper, Silver and Gold

nce upon a time there was an old man and his old wife, and they had three sons. One was called Egorushko Zalyot (a bold flyer); the second was called Misha Kosolapy (bowlegged); and the third was called Ivashko Zapechnik (sitting behind the stove). The parents wanted to secure wives for them, and sent the eldest son out to seek a bride. He went for a long time, and saw many maidens, but he took none to wife, for he liked none well enough. On the way he met a three-headed dragon and was very frightened.

The dragon asked him, "Where are you going, brave youth?"

"I'm going courting, but I cannot find a bride."

"Come with me. I'll take you where you can find one."

So they journeyed together until they came to a great heavy stone.

The dragon said to him, "Lift that stone off, then you'll find what you're seeking."

Egorushko tried to lift the stone away, but he failed.

Then the dragon said, "I have no bride for you here."

So Egorushko went back home, and he told his father and mother all he had gone through. The parents thought about it for a long time. They at last sent Misha Kosolapy on the same journey. He met the dragon after many days, and asked him to show him how he should get a bride. The dragon told him to go with him, and they came to the stone. Mísha tried to lift it away, but in vain, so he returned to his parents and told them all he had gone through.

This time the parents were at an utter loss what they should do. Ivashko Zapechnik wouldn't have any better luck. But still Ivashko asked his parents for permission to go to the dragon. After some reluctance, he obtained it.

Ivashko met the three-headed dragon, who asked him, "Where are you going, brave youth?"

"My brothers set out to marry, but they could find no brides. It's now my turn."

"Come with me. Perhaps you may win a bride."

So the dragon and Ivashko went up to the stone, and the dragon commanded him to lift the stone up.

Ivashko thrust the stone, and it flew up from its bed like a feather, as though it were not there. It revealed an opening in the earth, with a rope ladder.

"Ivashko," said the dragon, "go down that ladder. I'll let you down into the three kingdoms, and in each of them you'll see a fair maiden."

So Ivashko went down, deeper and deeper, right down to the realm of copper, where he met a maiden who was very fair.

"Greetings, strange guest! Sit down wherever you can find room, and tell me where you come from."

"Oh, fair maiden, you have given me nothing to eat and drink, and you ask me for my news!"

So the maiden gave him all manner of meat and drink and set them on the table. Ivashko had a drink, and then said, "I'm seeking a bride. Will you marry me?"

"No, fair youth! Go farther on into the silver kingdom. There lives a maiden who is much fairer than I." Right away, she gave him a silver ring.

The youth thanked her for her kindness, said farewell, and he went farther until he reached the silver kingdom. There he saw a maiden who was fairer than the former, and he prayed and bowed down low. "Good day, fair maiden!"

"Good day, strange youth! Sit down and tell me where you come from and what you're looking for."

"But, fair maiden, you have given me nothing to eat or drink, and you ask my news!"

So the maiden put rich drink and food on the table, and Ivashko ate as much as he could. Then he told her that he was seeking a bride, and he asked her if she would be the bride.

"Go farther into the golden realm; there lives a maiden who is much fairer than I!" the girl said, and she gave him a golden ring.

Ivashko said farewell, and went farther, went deeper still, into the golden realm. There he found a maiden who was much, very much fairer than the others, and there he said the right prayer, and he greeted the maiden.

"Where are you going, fair youth; and what are you looking for?"

"Fair maiden, give me something to eat and drink, and I'll tell you my news."

So she gave him so fine a meal that no better meal on earth could be desired, and she was so fair that no pen could write and no tale could tell. Ivashko then told his tale.

"I'm seeking a bride. If you will marry me, come with me!"

The maiden consented, and she gave him a golden ball. Then they went on and on together, until they reached the silver realm, where they took the maiden who was there. Then they went on and on and on from there to the copper realm, and took this maiden with them as well. Finally, they came to the hole through which they had to climb out. The rope ladder stood ready, and there stood the elder brothers, who were looking for him. Ivashko tied the maiden from the copper realm to the ladder, and the brothers lifted her out, and they let the ladder down again. Then Ivashko took hold of the maiden from the silver realm, and she was drawn up, and the ladder let down again. This time the maiden from the golden realm came and was also drawn up.

The steps were let down again, and Ivashko sat on them, and the brothers drew it up. When they saw that this time it was Ivashko Zapechnik who sat on it, they began to think, "If we let him out, perhaps he won't give us any of the maidens." So they cut the steps, and Ivashko fell down. He wept bitterly, but it was no good. He went down farther, and he then came across a tiny old man, who sat on a tree-branch and had a long white beard. Ivashko told him what had happened.

The old man advised him to continue on once more. "You'll come to a little hut. Enter it and you'll see a long man lying in it from one corner to the other. Ask him how you can reach Russian land once more."

So Ivashko went up to the hut, stepped in, and said: "Strong giant, spare me, and tell me how I can get home again."

"Fi, fo, fum, you Russian bones!" said Idolishche. "I didn't summon you, and still you have come. Go to the thrice-tenth sea. In that place stands a hut on cocks' legs in which the Baba Yaga lives. She has an eagle that can carry you."

The young man went on and on, a far way, to the hut, and he stepped in.

The Baba Yaga cried out at once, "Fi, fo, fum, Russian bones, why have you come here?"

"Oh, mother, the giant Idolishche sent me to ask you to lend me your mighty eagle to carry me to Russia."

"Go," said Baba Yaga, "into the garden. At the gate there stands a watchman; take his keys and pass through seven doors, and when you open the last one, the eagle will flap his wings. Sit on his back if you aren't afraid, and fly away. But take meat with you and give it to him to eat whenever he turns around."

Ivashko did as he was told, sat on the eagle, and flew away. The eagle flew on, flew on, then he soon turned his head around, and Ivashko gave him a bite of flesh. Then the eagle flew on afar, and turned around again, and Ivashko fed him. He fed him until he had nothing more left, and Russia was still far off. Then the eagle turned around, and as he had no flesh, he tore a fragment out of Ivashko's back and ate it up. But they had already reached the opening. When Ivashko parted from the eagle, he spat a bit of flesh out and told Ivashko to put it on himself. Ivashko did so, and his body healed. Ivashko went home, took the maiden from the golden realm from his brothers, and they then lived happily, and may still be living if they are not dead.

I was there and I drank beer. I drank the beer, and it flowed up to my moustache, but none of it reached my mouth.

Source: Afanas'ev, *Russian folk-tales*, 225-229.

By Command of the Prince Daniel

nce upon a time there was an aged queen who had a son and a daughter. They were fine, strong children. But an evil witch couldn't endure them, and she began to devise plans on how she might bring about their downfall.

She went to the old Queen and said, "Dear Gossip, I'm giving you a ring. Put it on your son's hand, and he will then be rich and generous: only he must marry the woman this ring fits."

The mother believed her and was extremely glad. On her deathbed, she ordered her son to marry only the woman whom the ring fit.

Time went by, and the boy became a man and looked at all the maidens. He liked many of them, but as soon as he put the ring on their finger, it was either too broad or too narrow. So he traveled from village to village and from town to town. He searched out all the fair damsels, but he couldn't find his chosen one, so he returned home in a reflective mood.

"What's the matter, brother?" his sister asked him.

So he told her of his trouble, explained his sorrow.

"What a wonderful ring you have!" said the sister. "Let me try it on."

She tried it on her finger, and the ring was firmly fixed as if it had been soldered on, as though it had been made for her.

"Oh, sister, you are my chosen bride, and you must become my wife."

"What a horrible idea, brother! That would be a sin."

But the brother wouldn't listen to a word she said. He danced for joy and told her to get ready for the wedding. She wept bitter tears, went in front of the house, and sat on the threshold and let her tears flow.

Two old beggars came up, and she gave them something to eat and drink. They asked what her trouble was, and that she needed to tell the two. "Now, don't cry, but do what we say. Make up four dolls and put them into the four corners of the room. After your brother calls you in for the betrothal, go. If he calls you into the bridal chamber, ask for time, trust in God, and follow our advice." And the beggars departed.

The brother and sister were betrothed, and he went into the room and cried out, "Sister of mine, come in!"

"I'll come in in a moment, brother. I'm taking off my earrings."

And the dolls in the four corners began to sing:

"Coo-Coo—Prince Danilo
Coo-Coo—Govorilo
Coo-Coo—'Tis a brother
Coo-Coo—Weds his sister:
Coo-Coo—Earth must split asunder
Cooo—And the sister lie hid under."

Then the earth rose up and slowly swallowed the sister.

And the brother cried out again, "Sister of mine, come in to the feather-bed!"

"In a minute, brother. I'm undoing my girdle."

Then the dolls began to sing:

"Coo-Coo—Prince Danilo
Coo-Coo—Govorilo
Coo-Coo—'Tis a brother
Coo-Coo—Weds his sister:
Coo-Coo—Earth must split asunder
Cooo—And the sister lie hid under."

Now she had vanished, all but her head.

And the brother cried out again: "Come into the feather-bed."

"In a minute, brother. I'm taking off my shoes."

And the dolls went on cooing, and she vanished under the earth.

And the brother kept crying, and crying, and crying. When she never returned, he became angry and ran out to fetch her. He could see nothing but the dolls, which kept singing. He knocked off their heads and threw them into the stove.

The sister went farther under the earth, and she saw a little hut standing on cocks' feet and turning around. "Hut," she cried out, "stand as you should with your back to the wood."

So the hut stopped and the doors opened, and a fair maiden looked out. She was knitting a cloth with gold and silver thread. She greeted the guest friendlily and kindly, but sighed and said, "Oh, my darling,

126

my sister! I'm so glad to see you. I'll be happy to look after you and to care for you as long as my mother isn't here. As soon as she flies in, woe to you and me, for she is a witch."

When she heard this, the maiden was frightened, but couldn't flee anywhere. She sat down and began helping the other maiden at her work. They chattered along, and soon, at the right time before the mother came, the fair maiden turned her guest into a needle, stuck her into the besom, and put it on one side. Scarcely had she done this, when Baba Yaga came in.

"My fair daughter, my little child, tell me at once, why does the room smell of Russian bones?"

"Mother, there have been strange men traveling past who wanted a drink of water."

"Why didn't you keep them here?"

"They were too old, mother, much too tough a snack for your teeth."

"From now on, entice them all into the house and never let them go. I must leave again and look for other booty."

As soon as ever she had gone, the maidens set to work knitting, talking, and laughing.

Then the witch came into the room once more. She sniffed about the house, and said, "Daughter, my sweet daughter, my darling, tell me at once, why does it smell of Russian bones?"

"Old men who were just passing by wanted to warm their hands. I did my best to keep them, but they wouldn't stay."

The witch was angry, scolded her daughter, and flew away. In the meantime, her unknown guest was sitting in the besom.

The maidens once more set to work, sewed, laughed, and thought how they might escape the evil witch. This time they forgot how the hours were flying by, and suddenly the witch stood in front of them.

"Darling, tell me, where have the Russian bones crept away?"

"Here, my mother; a fair maiden is waiting for you."

"Daughter of mine, darling, heat the oven quickly. Make it very hot."

The maiden looked up and was frightened to death. For Baba Yaga with the wooden legs stood in front of her, and her nose rose to the ceiling. The mother and daughter carried firewood in, logs of oak and maple, and made the oven ready until the flames shot up merrily.

Then the witch took her broad shovel and said in a friendly voice, "Go and sit on my shovel, fair child."

The maiden obeyed, and the Baba Yaga was going to shove her into the oven. But the girl stuck her feet against the wall of the hearth.

"Will you sit still, girl?"

But it was no good. Baba Yaga couldn't put the maiden into the oven. She became angry, thrust her back, and said, "You are simply wasting time! Just look at me and see how it's done."

Down she sat on the shovel with her legs nicely stuck together. The maidens instantly put her into the oven, shut the door, and slammed her in. They took their knitting with them, and their comb and brush, and ran away.

They ran away fast, but when they turned around, there was Baba Yaga running after them. She had set herself free. "Hoo, Hoo, Hoo, there run the two!"

The maidens, out of necessity, threw the brush behind them, and a thick, dense grove arose which Baba Yaga couldn't break through. She stretched out her claws, scratched herself a way through, and again ran after them.

Where should the two poor girls flee? They flung their comb behind them, and a dark, murky oak forest grew up, so thick, no fly could ever have flown its way through. Then the witch whetted her teeth and set to work. And she went on tearing up one tree after another by the roots, and she made herself a way, and again set out after them, and almost caught up with them.

Now the girls had no strength left to run, so they threw the cloth behind them, and a broad sea stretched out, deep, wide, and fiery. The old woman rose up, wanting to fly over it, but fell into the fire and was burned to death.

The poor maidens, poor homeless doves, they didn't know where to go. They sat down to rest, and a man came and asked them who they were. He then told his master that two little birds had fluttered onto his estate, two fairest women similar in form and shape, eye for eye and line for line. One was his sister, but which was it? He couldn't guess. So the master went to both of them. One was the sister—which?

The servant had not lied. He didn't know them. But his sister was angry with him and didn't speak.

"What shall I do?" asked the master.

"Master, I'll pour blood into an ewe-skin and put that under your armpit. You go talk to the women. In the meantime, I'll pass by and stab you in the side with my knife. Blood will flow. Then your sister will betray herself who she is."

"Very well!"

As soon as it was said, it was done. The servant stabbed his master in the side, and the blood poured forth, and he fell down.

Then his sister flung herself over him and cried out, "Oh, my brother! My darling!"

Then the brother jumped up again healthy and well. He embraced his sister, gave her a proper husband, and he married her friend, for the ring fit her just as well. So they all lived splendidly and happily.

Source: Afanas'ev, *Russian folk-tales*, 64-69.

The Story of Yvashka with the Bear's Ear

In a certain kingdom, in a certain government, there lived a peasant whose wife bore him a son who had the ear of a bear, on which account he was called Yvashka, or Jack with the Bear's Ear. Now when Jack with the Bear's Ear was beginning to attain his full growth, he used to walk in the street and attempt to play with the children. If he seized a child by the hand, he was sure to tear it off, and if he seized one by the head, he would tear it off.

The other peasants, not being able to put up with such horrors, told Jack's father that he must either make his son behave or not allow him to go out into the street to play with the children. The father for a long time struggled to reform Jack, but seeing that his son didn't improve, he decided to send him away, and said to him, "Leave and go wherever you please. You can't stay in my house any longer, because I'm terrified something terrible will happen to me because of you."

So Jack with the Bear's Ear, left his father and mother and went on his way. He traveled for a long time until he reached a forest, where he saw a man cutting oak boards. He went up to him and said, "Good man, what's your name?"

"Quercillo," the other replied.

They became sworn brothers and proceeded farther. Arriving at a rocky mountain, they saw a man hewing the rock, to whom they said, "God help you, honest lad. What's your name?"

"My name is Montano," he replied.

They called him their brother and suggested that he should stop digging the mountain and agree to go with them right away. He agreed to their request. All three immediately continued on their way and journeyed for some time. Arriving at the bank of a river, they saw a man sitting. He had a pair of enormous moustaches with which he fished for his living.

All three of them said to him, "God help you brother in your fish-catching."

"Thank you, brothers," he replied.

"What's your name?" they asked.

"Moustacho," he answered.

They also called him their brother and invited him to join their company, which he did not refuse. And so these four continued their journey, and whether they traveled long or short, far or near, my tale will be soon told, though the undertaking was a long time in doing. At last, they arrived at a forest, where they saw a cabin standing on crow's feet, which kept turning here and there.

They went up to it, and said, "Cabin, cabin, stand with your rear to the wood and your front to us."

The cabin instantly obeyed them. Then, having entered it, they began to decide how they should live there. After that they all went into the forest, killed some game, and prepared food for themselves. On the second day they left Quercillo at home to cook the dinner, while the rest of them went into the forest to hunt. After Quercillo got the dinner ready, he sat by the window and waited for his brethren to return.

At that moment, Baba Yaga came riding on an iron mortar, which she urged on with the pestle. With her tongue lolling out of her mouth, she drew a mark on the earth as she went. Upon entering the cabin, she said,

" 'Till now ne'er a Russian wight

I've heard with ear, or seen with sight,

Now full clear I see and hear."

Then turning to Quercillo, she asked, "Why did you come here, Quercillo?"

Immediately, she began to beat him, and continued beating him until he was half dead. After that, she devoured all the food he had prepared, and then rode off.

When Quercillo's companions returned from the hunt, they asked him for their dinner. Not informing them that Baba Yaga had been there, he said that he had fainted and had got nothing ready.

In the same manner did Baba Yaga treat Montano and Moustacho. At last, it was Jack with the Bear's Ear's turn to sit at home. He remained while his companions went out to hunt game. Jack cooked and roasted everything. Having found in Baba Yaga's cabin a pot of honey, he placed a post by the bench. Having split the post at the top, he thrust in a wedge and emptied the honey over the post. He then sat on the bench, hiding behind the post while he prepared three iron rods.

After a little time, Baba Yaga arrived and screamed forth,

" 'Till now ne'er a Russian true

I've heard with ear, or seen with view,

Now I do both hear and view."

"Why have you come here, Jack with the Bear's Ear. And why do you waste my provisions?"

At which point, she began to lick the post. No sooner did her tongue touch the crack than Jack snatched the wedge from out of the post, and trapped her tongue. He leapt up from the bench and beat her with the iron rods until she begged him to let her go, promising she would leave him alone and never come back.

Jack agreed to her request. He freed her tongue and placed Baba Yaga in a corner while he sat by the window waiting for his companions. They soon returned and imagined that Baba Yaga had done to him the same as she did with them. But seeing that he had the food prepared, they were quite astonished. After dinner he told them how he had dealt with Baba Yaga, and laughed at them because they were unable to handle her.

At last, wishing to show them the defeated and beaten Baba Yaga, he led them to the corner, but she was no longer there. So, they resolved to go after her. Having arrived at a stone, they lifted it up and saw a deep abyss, down which they'd have to descend. But as none of his companions had courage enough to do this, Jack with the Bear's Ear said he'd go. They began to construct a rope, and having made a canoe for him to sit in, they let him down into the hole.

Meanwhile Jack commanded them to wait for him a whole week. If, during that time, they didn't hear back from him, to stop waiting. "If I'm alive and pull the rope, draw up the canoe if it's light, but if it's heavy, cut the rope so you won't draw up Baba Yaga instead of me." Then having said goodbye, he descended into the deep subterranean abyss.

He remained there for a long time. After a time, he arrived at a cabin. When he entered, he saw three beautiful women embroidering with gold. These were Baba Yaga's daughters.

As soon as they noticed Jack with the Bear's Ear, they said, "Good youth, what's brought you here? Baba Yaga, our mother, lives here. As soon as she arrives, you're a dead man, for she'll certainly kill you. But if you'll free us from this place, we'll tell you how to save your life."

He promised to get them out of that abyss, and they said to him, "As soon as our mother arrives, she'll throw herself at you and begin to fight. After that, she'll stop and run into the cellar, where she has two pitchers filled with water. In the blue pitcher is the water of strength and in the white that of weakness."

Barely had Baba Yaga's daughters finished speaking when they heard their mother coming on the iron mortar, driving it with the pestle. With her tongue lolling out of her mouth, she drew a mark as she went.

Baba Yaga, having arrived, screamed out,

" 'Till now ne'er a Russ have I

Heard with ear or seen with eye.

Now do I both hear and spy."

"Why are you here, Jack with the Bear's Ear? Did you decide to bother me here also?"

Then hurling herself suddenly at him, she began to fight. Both battled for a considerable time, and at length they fell to the ground. Baba Yaga jumped up and ran into the cellar, while Jack rushed after her. Without looking, she seized the white pitcher and Jack the blue one, which had been switched, and both drank. After that, they left the cellar and continued their battle.

Jack, having overpowered her, seized her by the hair and beat Baba Yaga with her own pestle. She began to beg Jack to have pity on her, promised to live at peace with him, and at that very moment to leave the place. Jack with the Bear's Ear agreed and stopped beating Baba Yaga.

As soon as she left, he went to her daughters, thanked them for their information, and told them to prepare to leave. While they were packing their things, he went to the rope, and having pulled at it, his companions instantly let down the canoe. He placed the eldest sister in it first, and by her sent word to them to draw them all up. Jack's comrades having drawn up the woman were much astonished at her. After learning from her the whole matter, they hoisted up her other sisters.

At last, they let down the canoe for Jack. By this time, he had packed into the canoe many clothes and a great deal of money. He then seated himself inside. His companions, feeling the weight, imagined that it was Baba Yaga who sat there. They cut the rope and left poor Jack in the abyss. They themselves agreed to marry the damsels, and lost no time in doing so.

In the meantime, Jack with the Bear's Ear walked for a long time around the abyss, looking for a way out. At last, with luck, he found in the gloomy place an iron door, which he broke open. He proceeded for a long time in the darkness until he finally saw a light at a distance. Heading straight toward it, he emerged from the cavern.

After this, he determined to seek his companions, whom he soon found. The three were already married. Upon seeing them, Jack asked them why they had left him in the hole. His terrified companions told Jack that Moustacho had cut the rope, and Jack immediately slew him and took his wife to be his own. Then they all lived together, and acquired great riches.

Source: Borrow, *The Works of George Borrow*, 11-23.

Baba Yaga and Zamoryshek

nce upon a time there lived an old man and his old wife, and they had no children, and what on earth did they not do to get them! How they begged God! But for all that the wife bore no children. One day the old man went into the forest to look for mushrooms, and another old man met him.

"I know your thoughts. You're thinking about children," he said. "Go to the village and collect one little egg from every house and put a brood hen over them, and, what will happen, you'll see for yourself."

Now there were forty-one houses in the village. The old man went and collected the eggs and put a brood hen over them. Two weeks later he and his wife went to see, and they found that there were children born of the eggs, and they looked again and they found that forty of the children were fine, strong, and healthy, and there was one who was a weakling.

The old man gave them names. But he had no name left for the last, so he called him Zamoryshek (Runt). And these children grew up not by days, but by hours, and they shot up fast and began to work and to help the mother and father. The forty of them used to go into the fields while Zamoryshek stayed at home. When the harvesting season arrived, the forty began making the haystacks, and in a single week all the stacks were put up. They came back home to the village, lay down, slept, and ate of the food God provided.

The old man looked at them and said, "Young and green, goes far, sleeps sound, and leaves the work undone!"

"Go and look, Father," said Zamoryshek.

So, the old man went into the fields and saw forty stacks standing. "Ah, these are fine boys of mine! Look at all they have harvested in one week!" The next day he went out again to gloat on his possessions and found one stack was missing. He came home and said, "One stack has vanished."

"Never mind, Father," said Zamoryshek, "we'll catch the thief. Give me a hundred rubles, and I'll do it."

Then Zamoryshek went to the blacksmith and asked for a chain big enough to cover a man from head to foot.

And the blacksmith said, "Certainly."

"Very well, then, if the chain holds, I'll give you one hundred rubles; if it breaks, your labor's lost."

The blacksmith forged the chain. Zamoryshek put it around himself, stretched it, and it broke. So the smith made a second iron chain. Zamoryshek put it around his body, and it broke again. Then the smith made a third chain, three times as strong, and Zamoryshek could not break it.

Zamoryshek then went and sat under the haystack and waited. At midnight a sudden storm rose and the sea raged, and a strange mare rose out of the sea, ran up to the stack and began to eat it. Zamoryshek bound her neck around with chains and mounted her. The mare began to gallop over the valleys and over the hills, and she reared, but she could not dislodge the rider.

At last, she stopped and said in a human voice, "Now, good youth, since you maintained your seat on me, you may become master of my foals."

Then she ran under the sea and neighed, and the sea opened and up ran forty-one foals. They were such fine foals, every single horse was better than every other horse. You might go around the entire earth and never see any horses as good.

The next morning, the old man heard neighing outside his door, and wondered what the noise was, and there was his son Zamoryshek with the entire herd.

"Good!" he said. "Now, my sons, you had better go and search for brides."

So off they went. The mother and father blessed them, and the brothers took to the road and set off on their distant journey. They rode far in the white world in order to seek their brides, for they would not marry separately. But what mother could they find who should boast of having forty-one daughters?

They went across thirteen countries, and they then saw a steep mountain which they ascended. There stood a white stone palace with high walls around and iron columns and gates where they counted forty-one columns. They tied their knightly horses to each of the stakes, and they entered.

Then the Baba Yaga met them and said, "O you unlooked-for, uninvited guests, how dare you tie your horses to my stakes without permission?"

"Come on, old lady, what are you complaining about? First of all, give us food and drink, start a bath for us, and then ask us for our news, before you question us."

The Baba Yaga served them food and drink, conducted them to the bath, and then afterwards she asked them, "Have you come to do deeds, young men, or to flee from deeds?"

"We have come to do deeds, grandmother," they said.

"What are you looking for?"

"We are seeking brides."

Then she replied, "I have daughters." And she burst into the upper rooms and brought out her forty-one daughters.

They were then betrothed, and began to feast together and celebrate the marriage.

When evening came, Zamoryshek went to look at his horse. The good horse saw him and spoke with a human voice, "Be careful, my master. When you lie down with your young wives, dress them in your clothes, and put on your wives' clothes; otherwise, you'll all be killed."

They all went and lay down, and went to sleep, only Zamoryshek took care to keep his eyes open.

And at midnight Baba Yaga cried out in a loud voice, "Hey, my faithful servants, will you cut off the heads of my insolent and uninvited guests?" And so the servants ran and cut off the daughters' heads.

Zamoryshek woke his brothers and told them what had happened. They took the heads with them, put them on the forty-one stakes, armed themselves, and galloped off.

In the morning the Baba Yaga got up, looked through her little window, and saw the heads on the stakes. She was very angry and she called for her fiery shield. She chased after the men and waved her fiery shield in all directions to the four winds.

Where could the youths hide themselves? In front of them was the blue sea and behind them the Baba Yaga. And she burned everything in front of her with her fiery shield. They might have had to die, but Zamoryshek was an inventive youth. He hadn't forgotten to take Baba Yaga's handkerchief. He shook the handkerchief in front of him and built a bridge across all the blue sea, so the fine lads crossed the sea safely. Then Zamoryshek shook the handkerchief on the left-hand side, and the bridge vanished. The Baba Yaga had to turn back, but the brothers went home safely.

Source: Afanas'ev, *Russian folk-tales*, 48-51.

Ivan Tsarevich and Bailoi Polyanyin

In a certain kingdom, in a certain land, there lived a Tsar who had three daughters and one son, Ivan Tsarevich. The Tsar grew old and died, and Ivan Tsarevich took the crown. When neighboring kings heard of this, they collected a countless army and went to war against him.

Ivan Tsarevich didn't know what to do. He went to his sisters and asked, "My dear sisters, what can I do? All of the neighboring kings have risen against me."

"Oh, you brave warrior!" said the oldest sister. "Why are you afraid? Look at Bailoi Polyanyin. He's been fighting with Baba Yaga, Golden Leg, thirty years. He never gets off his horse, and he lives without rest, but you're frightened about nothing."

Ivan Tsarevich saddled his good horse, put on his war armor, took his sword, Kladyenets, his lance of long measure, and his silken whip, prayed to God, and rode out to meet his enemies. He killed not so many with the sword as he trampled with his horse. He destroyed the hostile army, went home, lay down to rest, and slept three days and nights without waking. On the fourth day, he woke up and went out to look at the open field. The kings had collected more men than before. Their army was under the walls of the city.

Ivan Tsarevich didn't know what to do. He went to his sisters and asked, "Oh, my sisters, what am I to do? I destroyed one army, but now another stands under the city walls and threatens me worse than the first one did."

"What sort of a warrior are you, to fight one day and sleep three days and nights without waking? Look at Bailoi Polyanyin. He's been fighting with Baba Yaga, Golden Leg, for thirty years. He never gets off his horse, and he lives without rest, but you're frightened about nothing."

Ivan Tsarevich went to the white-walled stable, saddled his good horse, his heroic horse, put on his battle armor, and strapped on his magic sword. In one hand he took his lance of long measure, in the other, a silken whip. He prayed to God and went to meet his enemy.

It was not a bright falcon flying toward a flock of geese, swans, and gray ducks, but rather Ivan Tsarevich bearing down on the enemy's army. He killed not so many himself as his horse trampled. He slew a great warrior force; then he went home and lay down and slept six days and six nights without waking. On the seventh day, he rose and went out to look on the open field. The kings had collected a greater force than before and had surrounded the city. It was a fearsome sight.

Ivan Tsarevich went to his sisters and asked, "Dear sisters, what am I to do? I have destroyed two mighty forces, now the third one stands under the walls and threatens me worse than the first and the second did."

"Oh, what a brave warrior! You fought one day and slept six days and nights without waking. Look at Bailoi Polyanyin. He's been fighting with Baba Yaga, Golden Leg, for thirty years. He never gets off his horse. He lives without rest."

This was bitter for the Tsarevich to hear. He hurried to the white-walled stables, saddled his good horse, put on his battle armor, strapped on his magic sword, took in one hand his lance of long measure, in the other, his silken whip, prayed to God, and rode out to meet his enemy.

It was not a bright falcon flying toward a flock of geese, swans, and gray ducks, but Ivan Tsarevich coming down on the hosts of the enemy. Not so many did he slay himself as his good horse trampled. He killed a mighty warrior force, then returned to his castle, lay down to sleep, and slept nine days and nine nights without waking.

On the tenth day he rose up, called his ministers and officers, and said, "My ministers and officers, I have decided to visit strange lands. I'm going to look for Bailoi Polyanyin. I ask you to give judgment, govern, and settle all questions honestly."

Then he left his sisters, mounted his horse, and rode away on his way. Whether it was long or short, he came to a dark forest. In that forest was a cabin, and in the cabin lived an old man.

Ivan Tsarevich went to him and said, "Hello, grandfather!"

"Hello, Russian Tsarevich! Where is God taking you?"

"I'm looking for Bailoi Polyanyin. Do you know where he is?"

"I don't know myself, but I'll summon my faithful servants and ask."

The old man went to the door of the cabin and began to play on a silver flute. Right away, birds flew to him from every direction. There flew together seen and unseen. They covered the sky with a dark cloud.

The old man cried with a loud voice and whistled a hero's whistle, "My faithful servants, passing birds, have you seen, have you heard of Bailoi Polyanyin?"

"We haven't seen him; we haven't heard about him," they answered.

"Well, Ivan," said the old man, "go to my brother. Maybe he'll tell you something. Take this ball. Let it go before you. Wherever it rolls, turn your horse that way."

Ivan Tsarevich mounted his good horse and dropped the ball to the ground. It rolled on, and he rode after it. Whether it was long or short, he came to a cabin. In the cabin sat an old man as gray as a kite.

"Hello, grandfather!" said Ivan.

"Hello, Russian Tsarevich. Where are you going?"

"I'm looking for Bailoi Polyanyin. Do you know where he is?"

"I don't know, but I'll call my trusty servants and ask them."

The old man went to the door and blew his silver horn. Right away, beasts gathered to him from all sides.

He whistled a hero's whistle, then cried with a loud voice, "My faithful servants, racing beasts, have you heard of Bailoi Polyanyin?"

"We haven't seen him. We haven't heard about him," answered the beasts.

"Count up, maybe you're not all here."

The beasts counted themselves. The lame she-wolf wasn't there. The old man sent a messenger for her and soon she came.

"Tell me, lame she-wolf, do you know where Bailoi Polyanyin lives?"

"Of course I know since I live near him. He slays armies and I feed on the dead."

"Where is he now?"

"He is on a great mound in the open field, sleeping in his tent. He has been fighting with Baba Yaga, Golden Leg, and after the fight he has lain down to sleep for twelve days and twelve nights."

"Guide Ivan Tsarevich to him."

The she-wolf ran on, and Ivan galloped after her. He came to the great mound and entered the tent. Bailoi Polyanyin was resting in a deep sleep.

Ivan said, "My sisters told me that this hero fought without rest, but he has lain down to sleep for twelve days and nights. Shouldn't I sleep also?"

He thought and thought, and at last he lay down at the side of Bailoi Polyanyin.

A small bird flew into the tent, fluttered around the pillow, and said these words, "Rise! wake up, Bailoi Polyanyin, and give my brother, Ivan Tsarevich, to a cruel death. If not, he will kill you!"

Ivan Tsarevich sprang up, caught the bird, tore off her right leg, threw her out of the tent, and again lay down at the side of Bailoi Polyanyin.

He had not fallen asleep when another small bird flew in, fluttered around, and said, "Rise! wake up, Bailoi Polyanyin, and give my brother, Ivan Tsarevich, to a cruel death. If not, he will kill you!"

Ivan Tsarevich sprang up, caught the bird, tore off her right wing, threw her out of the tent, and lay down again.

A third small bird came flying and fluttering around, and said, "Rise! wake up, Bailoi Polyanyin, and give my brother, Ivan Tsarevich, to a cruel death. If not, he will kill you!"

Ivan sprang up, caught the bird, tore off her bill, threw her out, and then lay down, and slept soundly as before.

The time came, and Bailoi Polyanyin woke up. He saw that at his side was lying an unknown hero. He seized his sharp sword and was going to give him to a cruel death, but he halted.

"No," he thought, "this hero came while I was sleeping, and he didn't put blood upon his sword. It would not be honorable or praiseworthy for me to destroy him now. A sleeping man is the same as a dead one. I will wake him."

He woke Ivan Tsarevich and asked, "Are you a good or a bad man? Speak! What's your name, and why have you come?"

"They call me Ivan Tsarevich, and I have come to look at you and try your strength."

"You are bold, Ivan Tsarevich. Unbidden, you've entered my tent; without asking, you've slept by my side. I might have killed you for that."

"Ah, Bailoi Polyanyin, don't boast before you've cleared the ditch. You may stumble. You have two hands, and my mother didn't bear me with one. We will fight."

They mounted their heroic horses, rushed at each other, and struck with such force that their lances broke into splinters and their good horses fell to their knees. Ivan Tsarevich knocked Bailoi Polyanyin out of his saddle and raised his sharp sword above him.

Bailoi Polyanyin begged, "Don't kill me; let me live. I'll call myself your younger brother. I'll honor you in place of a father."

Ivan Tsarevich took him by the hand, raised him from the earth, kissed him, and called him younger brother. "I have heard, my brother," he said, "that you have been fighting thirty years with Baba Yaga, Golden Leg. Why this war?"

"She has a daughter, a beauty. I want to marry her."

"If we are friends, then one should give aid to the other. Let's go fight against Baba Yaga."

They mounted their horses and rode to the field. Baba Yaga, Golden Leg, had put out an uncountable fighting force. Those two were not bright falcons flying at a flock of doves, but they were strong mighty heroes rushing down on an army of enemies. Not as many did they slay with swords as they trampled with their horses. Baba Yaga rushed off in flight, but Ivan Tsarevich pursued her. He had almost caught her, when suddenly she ran into a deep ravine, raised an iron slab, and disappeared under the earth.

Ivan Tsarevich and Bailoi Polyanyin bought a great herd of oxen, killed them, took off their hides and made straps of them. They fastened the straps together and made a strap so long that one end of it was in this world and the other in the underground world.

Ivan said to Bailoi Polyanyin, "Let me down quickly and don't pull up the rope until I jerk it."

Ivan reached the underground world, looked around, and went in search of Baba Yaga. He journeyed and traveled, walked and walked on, looked, and behind a grating tailors were sitting.

"What are you doing there?" asked Ivan.

"We're sitting and sewing an army for Baba Yaga, Golden Leg."

"How do you sew an army, brothers?"

"This is how. What we prick with a needle is a Cossack with a pipe. He mounts his horse, stands in line, and goes to make war on Bailoi Polyanyin."

"Oh, brothers, you do it quickly, but not firmly. Stand in a row, and I'll show you how to sew firmly."

They stood in a row. Ivan Tsarevich drew his sword, and the heads flew. He killed the tailors and walked on and on. Whether it was long or short, he came to a grating and behind it shoemakers were sitting.

"What are you doing?" asked Ivan Tsarevich.

"We are sitting and making an army for Baba Yaga, Golden Leg."

"How do you make an army, brothers?"

"This is how. What we prick with an awl is a warrior with a sword. He mounts a horse, stands in line, and goes to war against Bailoi Polyanyin."

"Oh, brothers, you do it quickly, but not well. Stand in a row, and I'll show you how to do it better."

They stood in a row. Ivan Tsarevich drew his sword, and the heads flew. He killed the shoemakers and went on. Whether it was long or short, he came to a great city. In the city was a Tsar's castle, and in the castle sat a maiden of indescribable beauty. When she saw Ivan, his dark curls, his falcon eyes, and his heroic bearing pleased her. She asked where he came from and why.

"I'm seeking Baba Yaga, Golden Leg," said Ivan.

"Ivan Tsarevich, I'm her daughter. She has lain down to rest for twelve days and nights."

Ivan Tsarevich went to Baba Yaga, Golden Leg. He found her asleep, struck her with his sword, and cut off her head.

The head rolled, and said, "Strike again, Ivan Tsarevich."

"A single blow from a hero is enough," answered the Tsarevich and went back to the castle to see the beautiful maiden.

He sat with her at the oaken table at the spread cloth. They ate and drank, then he asked her, "Is there in the world any one stronger than I am, or fairer than you are?"

"Oh, Ivan Tsarevich, what sort of a beauty am I? Beyond the thrice ninth land in the thirtieth kingdom lives, with the Tsar of the Serpents, a maiden of unspeakable beauty. She washed her feet and I bathed in that water."

Ivan Tsarevich took the white hand of the maiden and led her to the palace where the rope was hanging. He gave the sign, and Bailoi Polyanyin pulled and pulled, and drew out the Tsarevich and the maiden.

"Hello, Bailoi Polyanyin!" said Ivan Tsarevich, "here is your bride. Live and be happy. I'm going to the Serpent Kingdom."

He mounted his heroic horse, said goodbye to Bailoi Polyanyin and his bride, and galloped away beyond the thrice ninth land to the thirtieth kingdom. Whether it was long or short, high or low, a tale is soon told, but a deed is not soon done. Ivan Tsarevich came to the Serpent Kingdom, slew the Tsar of the Serpents, liberated the beautiful Tsarevna, and married her. After that he came home, lived with his young wife and earned great wealth.

Source: Curtin, *Fairy Tales of Eastern Europe*, 49-60.

Snow-child

An old man and an old woman, who were married, had no children. Deciding to visit a fortune-teller, the old woman walked a long way and found a small house, which she entered.

Although Baba-Yaga lay in the house, her head was in the cattle stall, one of her feet was on the stove, and the other on the plank bed in the attic; one of her hands was in front of the house and the other before the stove.

The old woman entered and said, "Greetings, Baba-Yaga!"

"If you had not greeted me," replied the witch, "I would have torn you in two and swallowed you without effort."

"I have no children, Baba-Yaga," said the old woman.

"Go and roll a ball of snow and place it in a cradle. It will become a child when you rock the cradle!"

The old woman returned home. She rolled a snow ball and placed it into a cradle, which she rocked. She heard a child's cry. Looking into the cradle, she found in it a baby girl. Husband and wife rejoiced and discussed what they should call the child. They called her Snow-child. Snow-child grew and became plump and sensible and pretty.

Once some of Snow-child's girl friends came to her mother and said, "Let Snow-child come into the forest with us to pick berries."

The mother would on no account let Snow-child go. But Snow-child and her friends came together to her mother and finally got permission.

The girls entered the forest and gathered a number of berries. It had already begun to get dark when the children came together and left the forest. They saw a small house covered with nettles and standing on the edge of the forest. Entering, they said, "Let's sleep here and go home tomorrow."

Almost immediately, Bear Great-mouth entered. The little house belonged to him.

"Sleep, sleep!" said Bear Great-mouth, "and tomorrow I'll prepare your breakfast."

The next day Bear Great-mouth rose early and heated the house. All the children slept except Snow-child, who, peeping from under her hands, with which she covered her face, saw how Bear Great-mouth was engaged. Bear Great-mouth was cooking some soup. He poured water into an iron vessel, scraped scabs from himself (he was covered with mange), put the scabs into the iron vessel, and set the vessel to boil.

The bear woke the children, and they all ate the soup, except Snow-child, who knew how it had been made.

When the children had eaten, the bear said, "I'll let all who have eaten go home, but anyone who hasn't eaten must stay with me." The bear allowed them all to go except Snow-child.

Bear Great-mouth brought in a sleigh, hung it up like a cradle, lay down in it and said, "Snow-child, rock me!"

Snow-child rocked the bear until he fell asleep, but she remained standing and weeping.

An eagle flew to the window and said, "Snow-child, what are you doing?"

"I'm standing here and weeping."

"Take a seat on me, and I'll carry you home!" said the eagle.

The eagle flapped its wings and flew away and Bear Great-mouth woke up. He guessed where Snow-child was and started in pursuit. After flying some time, the eagle grew tired and descended to rest. At this point, Bear Great-mouth arrived, tore the eagle's feathers, and took Snow-child back.

Snow-child's little friends, when they returned home, told Snow-child's mother what had happened and how Bear Great-mouth had kept the child with him.

The mother sat down on the stump of a tree in the yard and gave way to her grief.

A scurfy, scabby bullock, having on his back two spikes, came to Snow-child's mother and said, "Don't weep. I'll steal Snow-child from Bear Great-mouth."

The next time Bear Great-mouth went to sleep in the sleigh, Snow-child once more sat at the window and wept.

The scurfy, scabby bullock approached and said to her, "Snow-child, why do you weep?"

"Bear Great-mouth won't let me go home."

"Climb on me. I'll get you home," answered the scabby, scurfy bullock.

"Where can you take me? Even the eagle couldn't carry me off," answered the child, but she took her seat on the bullock, and he started out immediately.

Bear Great-mouth woke and began a pursuit.

But the bullock said to Snow-child, "Draw a spike from my back."

Snow-child took out a spike from the back part of the bullock, and he tore the bear's eyes and face with it. The bear stopped and wiped his face, and the bullock galloped away. After the bear had wiped his eyes and face, he renewed the pursuit of the bullock and Snow-child.

The bear again overtook them, and the bullock said, "Draw from my back a second spike."

Snow-child took out the second spike, and the bullock tore the bear from head to foot with it. The bear stopped to wipe the torn parts, and meanwhile the bullock and Snow-child reached home.

Source: Coxwell, *Siberian and Other Folk-tales*, 579-581.

The Snake-Tsarevna

A Cossack rode one night through the dark forest and lost his way. He wandered for a day and a night, and a second day and a night, and on the evening of the third day, he reached a clearing where a haystack rose among the trees. He wanted to rest his weary limbs, so, leaping from his horse, he sat beside the haystack and lit his black pipe.

For an hour he smoked and rested, not noticing that a spark from his black pipe kindled the hay. Having regained his energy, he mounted his horse and traveled farther.

But before he had gone ten steps, a great light burst on the blackness of the forest. He turned and saw the haystack on fire, and on its summit a lovely maiden stood, a ring of fire encircling her.

The maiden stretched out her white arms and cried, "Good Cossack, save me from a bitter death!"

The Cossack answered, "How can I save you? The fire's too hot and will consume me before I can reach your side."

"Simply thrust your spear into the flames, and I'll save myself."

The Cossack thrust his spear into the flames but turned his head aside, for his flesh couldn't endure the fire's heat. In that moment, the maiden transformed into a snake and, slipping through the flames, she glided along the spear until she reached the Cossack. She then coiled her body twice around his throat and grasped her tail between her sharp, white teeth.

The Cossack paled with fear and would have plucked her from his throat but his strength failed him. The serpent spoke in a human voice and said, "You have no need to fear me, handsome youth. I won't harm you. Even so, for seven years and seven days you must endure to have me lie around your throat. Also, you must roam through the four corners of the world to search for the copper palace. Ask the way from all the winds that blow, the storms of winter and the autumn blasts, the breeze of summer and the breath of spring. When you find the palace, you'll know joy from then on."

So the Cossack searched for the copper palace. Many days passed by and many waters flowed into the sea, while he roamed through the four corners of the world. He asked the way from all the winds that blew.

At the end of seven years, he arrived at a high mountain, and a palace of red copper gleamed on its summit. A white wall surrounded the palace on every side.

The Cossack spurred his horse up the high mountain, and the white wall opened to receive him and closed again. He found himself within the palace court. Then the snake fell from the Cossack's throat and struck the earth, and was transformed into the lovely maid he had saved from the flames.

She led his weary horse into the stable, but the Cossack she led into a high chamber, whose walls were mirrors and whose marble floor was strewn with tapestries and rich brocades.

The maiden said, "I'm the daughter of a mighty Tsar and a wicked dragon has enchanted me. For seven long years you have served me well, good Cossack, and now only seven days of your service remain, which you must spend within these mirrored walls. You'll have food and drink but, if you love me, I beg you not to venture beyond the threshold, nor seek to read the riddle of anything that you'll see. Listen to my request, and when the spell is ended in seven days, I'll return to you." Striking the ground, she was transformed into a snake and slipped away.

The Cossack looked about him and sighed. "Eh, what a place this is! Mirrors and tapestries and rich brocades, but no sign of honest food and drink! It's clear that I'll die of hunger here, before half of seven days are over."

As he spoke a copper barrel appeared and rolled to the right, and a feast lay spread before him such as his eyes had never seen nor his thoughts pictured. He ate heartily and drank his fill, but still the platters were heaped high with food, and the tankards brimmed with ale.

The Cossack eventually cried, "I can eat no more."

The barrel rolled to the left, and the table and its burden disappeared.

The Cossack said, "Eh, what a place is this! It's certain that I might live here for three times seven years, and come to the end of my feasting."

For six days he lived within the chamber and feasted. On the seventh day, he thought, "Today I leave the palace with my bride, and through the white world we'll ride together. What harm then if I take this copper barrel, so that we can live in plenty, and not worry about tomorrow?"

When the barrel appeared and he had feasted, he grabbed hold of it. But the barrel rolled from underneath his hand to the chamber door, with the Cossack in pursuit. After crossing the threshold, he seized it in his arms. At that moment, a mighty roaring sounded in his ears. The mountain rocked, and the palace crashed to the earth, leaving the Cossack standing beneath the open sky, his whimpering horse beside him and in his arms the magic copper barrel. Far above his head, a dragon soared, carrying between his fiery wings the snake-Tsarevna.

Now he thought about the maiden's words and, weeping for his crime, he vowed to search for her through all the tsardoms of the earth and free her from the dragon's evil power. Mounting his horse, he set forth on his way. He traveled near and far, and he traveled little and long. At length, he met an aged man whose beard was as white as milk.

The old man said, "Long life to you, Cossack! Will you give me food and drink?"

The Cossack rolled his barrel to the right, and a table appeared that held three whole roast oxen and three huge vats of beer. The old man ate the oxen and drank the beer and wiped the foam from his lips.

He said, "Another ox would have been welcome, but the Lord's will be done. Thank you, good Cossack, for bread and salt. Where are you traveling?"

"I go wherever my eyes look in search of the snake-Tsarevna. Do you know, grandsire, where she's hidden?"

"Why shouldn't I know, Cossack? I know it well."

"And will you tell me?"

"Why should I tell you? For even if you knew where she's hidden, or know not where, what does it matter, since you will never find her?"

"Tell me anyway, and I'll give you my magic barrel, and say a prayer for you night and morning."

"It's a good barrel, and I'll use it well. As for the maid, look for the Baba Yaga with bony legs. She is sister to the dragon that stole your bride. Every evening, when the moon is high, she travels in her mortar through the forest to visit her brother's cave. If you can follow her, you will reach your goal, and this is all my advice. Take, in return for your gift, my sword of might, since your need is far greater than mine. Nothing can resist its strength, as you'll see."

He cried, "Cut down the forest, sword!"

The sword leapt from its sheath. With a single stroke, it cut down great trees, and split vast rocks apart. In a moment, it had laid waste to the forest as far as the eye could see.

The old man cried, "Return to the scabbard, sword!" And the sword obeyed.

The Cossack took the sword, and gave its master his magic barrel. He went to look for the Baba Yaga with bony legs. As he rode, a brown bear crossed his path, and she was as high as a mountain. He would have thrust his spear into her heart, but she cried in a human voice, "Spare me, good Cossack, and I'll serve you afterward."

The Cossack said, "Why not?" and went his way.

As he rode, a falcon flew before him. Her outspread wings were as wide as the broad blue sea. He would have thrust his spear into her heart, but she cried in a human voice, "Spare me, good Cossack, and I'll serve you afterward."

The Cossack said, "Why not?" and went his way.

As he rode, he came to the bank of a stream, and a fish flashed through the waters. She was as long as a tale that is never done. He would have thrust his spear into her heart, but she cried in a human voice, "Spare me, good Cossack, and I'll serve you afterward."

The Cossack said, "Why not?" and went his way.

And now the moon rode high in the deep heavens, and the ground at the Cossack's feet trembled and broke, and the earth heaped itself on either side. Out of the pit a mortar rose and sailed through the air, bearing the Baba Yaga with bony legs to the dragon's cave.

The Cossack whispered in his good horse's ear, "Follow, my heart! Her mortar outstrips the wind, but a Cossack's horse can fly more swiftly still."

And the horse followed so hard upon her track that, though she swept it from behind her with her broom, she could not sweep as swiftly as he ran.

In the end, they reached the blue sea-ocean and paused on the sandy shore. The Baba Yaga mocked the Cossack's plight as her mortar sailed above the tranquil waves, and she cried, "Let your horse plunge into the waters, Cossack! Maybe it will cool his heated limbs."

From the sea, a fish rose to the surface. She was as long as a tale that is never done. She said, "How can I serve you?"

The Cossack answered, "I need to cross the sea, and not lose the track of that foul witch with bony legs that travels in her mortar."

The fish struck the sea with her mighty tail, and a bridge spanned the water whose like the Tsar himself had never seen. For its girders were of silver, its gates of gold, and its floor of shining crystal, so that one trod upon it as on a mirror. The hoofs of the Cossack's horse rang on the crystal, and so they crossed the sea to the farther shore. And the bridge of wonder vanished.

The Cossack said, "I thank you, fish."

The fish replied, "My duty to you, Cossack," and swam away.

Again, they followed the track of the Baba Yaga, until they came to a barren mountain. The Baba Yaga mocked the Cossack's plight as her mortar sailed over the peak, and she cried, "Let your horse scale the barren mountain, Cossack! Maybe he will graze at its crest."

A falcon swooped from the sky. Her outspread wings were as broad as the broad blue sea. She said, "How can I serve you?"

The Cossack answered, "I need to cross the mountain, without losing track of that vile witch with leather skin that travels in her mortar."

The falcon bore the Cossack and his horse across the barren mountain and set them down on the farther side.

The Cossack said, "I thank you, falcon."

The falcon answered, "My duty to you, Cossack," and flew away.

Again, they followed the track of the Baba Yaga, until they came to a forest so dense that a bee might not crawl through its branches. The Baba Yaga mocked the Cossack's plight as her mortar sailed above the tree-tops, and she cried, "Let your horse wander through the forest, Cossack! Maybe he will rest beneath its shade."

The Cossack cried, "Cut down the forest, sword!"

The sword of might leapt from its sheath, and with a single stroke hewed down the forest. But still the Cossack couldn't travel through it, because the fallen trees lay strewn so thick about him that they reached the sky.

Out of the forest a brown bear came forth. The bear was as high as a mountain. She said, "How can I serve you?"

The Cossack answered, "I need to cross the forest, and not lose track of that accursed witch, with eyes like coals, that travels in her mortar."

The brown bear bent to her task, and flung the trees aside, to make a path for the Cossack and his horse. It was a task that might have wearied the strongest, but the brown bear toiled without rest. When she was tired, she drank at the stream that flowed through the wood and returned again to her labor. In the end, she made a path for the Cossack and his horse.

The Cossack crossed the forest and said, "I thank you, bear."

The bear replied, "My duty to you, Cossack, and a word of advice. Your foot stands now, on the edge of the dragon's realm, but over everyone who enters, he casts the spell of everlasting sleep. If you can outwit him and keep your eyes from sleep, you'll arrive at the end of your journey and find the snake-Tsarevna." And the bear ran away.

When the Cossack entered the dragon's realm, his limbs were stricken with heaviness, and the head of his horse hung lifeless on his breast. But before the spell had overpowered him, the Cossack drew from his pouch a box of snuff, and filled each nostril. He sneezed so violently that his eyes flew open, and his horse ran more swiftly than before, and sleep left him as though a hand had taken it away.

The Cossack laughed aloud and cried, "Good friend, this is the time to fight and not to sleep. And for your spell, it might frighten children, but never a Russian Cossack!"

And so he came at length to the dragon's cave, guarded by boulders and the trunks of trees. He knocked on the door with his spear, but no answer came. Then he cried, "Cut down the barrier, sword!" And the sword cut down the tree-trunks and the boulders, and the Cossack entered.

The snake-Tsarevna, in a crown of gold and a jeweled sarafan, sat on a stone while the dragon's evil head lay in her lap, and she told him tales of wonder.

But now the dragon raised his head and cried, "What rash fool enters here to face my fury and meet his death between my hungry jaws?"

"No rash fool, dragon, but a Russian Cossack, whom you have deeply wronged."

"Hey, Russian Cossack, I'll lay one paw on you and crush you with the other, until nothing remains of you except a fleck of blood."

"Tsars and the sons of tsars tremble before you—princes and generals bow to your might—but the Cossack fears you as little as the hare that runs across his path in the deep forest."

The dragon raised his head from the maiden's lap and leapt upon his enemy. But the Cossack cried, "Cut down the monster, sword!" And the sword leapt from its sheath and slew the dragon with a single blow.

The Cossack would have taken his bride into his arms, but she had vanished. In her place, a snake lay coiled on the rock.

The Cossack cried, "I have crossed the blue sea and the barren mountain and the wilderness, and I have slain the dragon that held you captive. What task remains undone, before the crime I committed against you is atoned for?"

The snake replied, "Until I am bathed in the spring of the water of life, the spell won't be undone."

"And where can I seek the spring of the water of life?"

"Ask the Baba Yaga with bony legs!"

The Cossack saw the Baba Yaga where she crouched behind a boulder. He plucked her up and cried, "If you want to live, lead me right away to the spring of the water of life."

She answered, "Master, I will," and led the way.

The snake coiled herself about the Cossack's throat and grasped her tail between her sharp, white teeth. He mounted his horse and followed the Baba Yaga.

Whether the way was long or short, swiftly told is the tale, but the deed is slowly done. In time, they arrived at a spring in a sunny clearing.

The Baba Yaga cried, "There lies the spring of life."

She would have fled, but the Cossack seized the mortar and held it fast. He flung a dry branch into the spring, and the dry branch burned to ashes.

He said to the Baba Yaga, "Now, you'll die!"

She answered, "No, master, if I die, how will you find the spring?"

Again, she led the way to a sunny clearing and cried, "There lies the spring of life."

She would have fled, but the Cossack held her fast. He flung a dry branch into the spring, and the dry branch withered to dust.

He said to the Baba Yaga, "Now, surely, you'll die a horrid death."

She answered, "Release me, master, and honestly, I'll lead you to the spring of the water of life."

He released her, and she led the way to a dark forest where a spring welled between two rocks. She cried, "There lies the spring of the water of life!"

The Cossack flung a dry branch into it, and the branch blossomed and bore golden fruit. Then the Baba Yaga with bony legs vanished in smoke.

The Cossack bathed the snake in the water of life, and the scales fell from her body, and she was changed into a beautiful maiden.

She laid her hand in his and said, "Your crime has been paid, Cossack, and you can marry me."

And so, they traveled to her father's tsardom, where they were greeted with shouts and rejoicing. The Tsar gave the Cossack a royal palace and many servants, and he lived in ease and plenty all his days.

And so, I tell you the tale as I have heard it—neither too long nor too short, but as long as from you to me.

Source: Zeitlin, *Skazki; Tales and Legends of Old Russia*, 309-326.

The Bewitched Princess

A soldier in a certain kingdom had served in the mounted guards honestly and faithfully twenty-five years. The king rewarded him for his good conduct, by giving him at the time of his discharge the horse on which he had ridden in his regiment, together with the saddle and bridle.

Having said farewell to his comrades, the soldier went off to his own district. He traveled all of one day, a second day, and a third day; even during a whole week, a second week, and a third week. Finally, he had no money to support either himself or his horse, and his home was still far away. The matter was serious, because the soldier was hungry. Looking around, he saw, in a certain direction, a great castle.

"Well now," he thought, "why shouldn't I call there? Perhaps I may be taken into service for a while and earn something."

He turned to the castle and, having entered the courtyard, fed his horse in a stable, and entered the palace. There he found a table laden with wine and eatables, everything a person could desire!

When he had eaten and drunk to his heart's content, the soldier thought, "I can now take a nap."

But suddenly a she-bear appeared and said, "Don't fear me, my brave fellow! You're in luck. I'm not a cruel bear, but a beautiful maiden, a bewitched princess. If you remain and stay three nights here, the spell will be broken, and I'll become a princess again. Then I'll marry you."

The soldier having agreed, the she-bear left, and he was alone. However, he became so tired that he didn't care to look at the world. His tiredness grew as time went on. If it hadn't been for the wine, he probably wouldn't have endured it a single night.

On the third day the tiredness had so increased that the soldier decided to forget everything and leave the castle, but, however much he tried and searched, he couldn't find the way out. He was forced to remain against his will. He stayed the third night, and in the morning the princess, with indescribable beauty, appeared before him. She thanked him for his service and commanded him to get dressed for the wedding. After which ceremony, which was immediately performed, the pair began to live together in complete happiness.

After a while, the soldier thought about his own country, but the princess opposed his wish to return there.

"Stay here, my dear," she said. "Don't go away! What more could you want than what you now have?"

But no, she couldn't talk him out of it, and so she said farewell to her husband and, giving him a little bag filled with seeds, said, "On whatever road you travel, throw some of these seeds on both sides. Wherever the seeds fall, trees will spring there in a minute. The trees will bear rare fruits, various birds will sing, and cats from beyond the seas will tell fairy tales."

The good and brave fellow soon mounted his faithful horse and set out. Wherever he went, he threw seeds on both sides of the road, and immediately forests arose in his tracks. They sprang continually from the moist ground.

Having traveled one day, a second day, and a third day, he saw a caravan which had stopped in an open area. Some merchants were sitting on the green grass and amusing themselves with cards. A kettle stood beside them and, although beneath it there was no fire, the soup was boiling vigorously.

"What a marvel!" thought the soldier. "The soup in this kettle never stops boiling. I must see what's going on."

Leaving his horse, he approached the merchants and said, "Greetings, worthy gentlemen!"

He had no idea that instead of being merchants, they were unclean spirits. "That's a good trick of yours, a kettle that boils without any fire under it! But I have something better."

He took out of his bag a small grain and threw it down. In an instant a full-grown tree sprang from the ground and displayed rare fruits, while various birds sang and cats from beyond the seas related fairy tales.

Through his boasting, the unclean spirits recognized him. "Ah," they said among themselves, "this is the man who freed the princess! Brothers, for that let's drug him with an herb, so that he'll sleep for half a year."

After entertaining the soldier, they drugged him with a magic herb. He fell on the grass and slept soundly, as if he would never wake, while the merchants, the caravan, and the kettle instantly vanished.

About this time the princess went into her garden for a stroll. She saw that the tops of all the trees had begun to wither.

"This means something bad," she thought. "Clearly some evil has happened to my husband."

Three months passed. The time had come for the soldier's return, but as he remained absent, the princess got ready and went to look for him. She took the same road that her husband had passed along. On both sides of her, forests had sprung up, birds were singing, and cats from over the seas recounted fairy tales. She reached a place where no more trees were growing, and the road wound along in an open area.

"Where can he have gone?" she asked herself. "He cannot have sunk into the ground!"

Behold, a wonderful tree stood near her, and beneath it lay her dear husband. She ran forward and began to push him, for she felt that she must wake him. But he didn't move! She began to pinch him and to stick pins into his sides. But however much he was pinched or pricked, he felt no pain; he lay motionless as if dead.

The princess became angry, and in her wrath pronounced this curse: "May you in your worthless sleep be caught up by a violent wind and borne off to an unknown country."

She had scarcely spoken these words, when suddenly winds whistled and roared, and in a second, the soldier was snatched up by a terrible whirlwind and carried out of the princess' sight.

Afterwards, regretting that she had uttered such an evil wish, she wept bitter tears, and returning home, began to lead an utterly lonely existence.

But the soldier was taken far by the whirlwind, beyond the thrice ninth land, into the thrice tenth empire, and thrown onto a neck of land between two seas. The sleepy man fell on such a narrow place that if he had turned to the left or to the right, he would immediately have fallen into the sea and so met with his end.

The good and brave young fellow had slept for half a year and not moved a finger; but at last, he woke and sprang suddenly to his feet. When he looked, waves were rising on both sides of him, and the sea appeared limitless.

He stood, bewildered, and asked himself, "By what miracle have I fallen here? Who brought me?"

He passed along the strip of land and reached an island, on which was a mountain so high and steep that its summit reached the clouds. On the mountain lay a great stone. Approaching the mountain more nearly, he saw three devils fighting. Blood was pouring from them, and tufts of hair were flying about.

"Stop, accursed ones," he said. "Why are you fighting?"

"Well, the day before yesterday our father died, and left behind him three wonderful things: a flying carpet, swift-bearing boots, and a cap of invisibility. Unfortunately, we can't divide them."

"Oh, you cursed ones, to think that you've decided to fight about such small matters! If you wish, I'll divide your shares. You'll be satisfied, and I won't offend anybody."

"Very well, countryman, please divide them!"

"I will!" was the reply. "Run quickly to the pine woods and bring here, each of you, two tons of pitch."

The devils rushed through the pine forest and collected six tons of pitch and brought them to the soldier.

"Now drag up from hell its largest cauldron."

The fiends dragged up an enormous cauldron, which would contain about forty barrels! They put all the pitch in it. The soldier lit a fire, and as soon as the pitch had melted, he ordered the fiends to drag the cauldron up the hill and pour it down from there. They did this in a second.

"Now," said the soldier, "push this stone. Roll it downhill and let the three of you run after it with all your might. Whoever first overtakes it will be the first to choose for himself one of the three marvels. The second in the race will then choose one of the two remaining marvels, and the third marvel will belong to the last of you."

The devils pushed the stone, and it rolled down hill at a great rate. They all three rushed after it, and one of them, having outstripped the others, stuck fast to it. The stone immediately turned around, and drawing the devil under itself, drove into the pitch. The second fiend also overtook the stone, and then the third was successful, but both suffered the fate of the first. They stuck firmly to the pitch.

The soldier took under his arm the swift-bearing boots and the cap of invisibility, and having sat on the flying carpet, fled away to find his own country. After a while, he reached a cottage and entered it. Baba Yaga-bony-legs was sitting there, old and toothless.

"Greetings, grandmother! Tell me how I can find my beautiful princess."

"I don't know, my dear. I have neither seen nor heard of her. But go over many seas and lands to where my middle sister lives. She has more knowledge than I have, and perhaps she'll tell you."

The soldier sat on the flying carpet and flew away. He had to travel far. If he wished to eat or drink, he put on his cap of invisibility and then let himself down into a town and entered various shops. When he had taken whatever his soul desired, he traveled farther on the carpet.

Reaching a second cottage, he went in. There sat Baba Yaga-bony-legs, the old and toothless.

"Greetings, grandmother! Do you know where I can find my beautiful wife?"

"No, my dear, I don't know, but go across many seas and many lands to where my elder sister is living. Perhaps she knows."

"You old hag! In spite of the years you have lived in the world, and you have lived so long that all your teeth have fallen out, you know nothing!"

He got on his flying carpet and flew to the elder sister. He traveled long and far. Many were the lands and seas he saw. At last, he came to the edge of the world. There stood a cottage beyond which it was impossible to go, since beyond it was only extreme darkness; nothing was visible.

"Well," he thought, "if I don't get satisfaction here, I can't get it by flying farther."

The soldier entered the cottage. There sat Baba Yaga-bony-legs, the gray-haired and toothless.

"Greetings, grandmother! Tell me where I can find my princess."

"Wait a little! I'll summon all my Winds and ask them. You see, they blow over the whole world, and therefore ought to know where she is living."

The old woman crossed the threshold and screamed in a loud voice, then she whistled with great force. Suddenly from all sides, boisterous Winds arose and blew so that the cottage shook.

"Quietly, quietly," cried Baba-Yaga, who, as soon as the Winds had gathered, began to question them. "My boisterous Winds, you blow over the whole world. Have you seen the beautiful princess?"

"We have not seen her anywhere," answered the Winds with one voice.

"Are you all present?"

"We are all here except the South Wind."

A little later the South Wind flew up.

The old woman said to him, "Where have you been spending your time? I have waited for you."

"I'm sorry, grandmother! I called at the new kingdom, where the beautiful princess is living. Her husband is lost. There is no news of him, so now various tsars and princes and kings and the sons of kings seek her in marriage."

"And how far is it to the new kingdom?"

"It will take a walker thirty years. Anyone who uses wings will lessen the time to ten years. But if I blow, I can take you there in three hours."

With tears in his eyes, the soldier prayed that the South Wind would carry him to the new kingdom.

"Very well," said the South Wind, "I'll carry you, if you give me the freedom to blow as I like in your kingdom for three days and three nights."

"For three weeks, if you wish!"

"Agreed! I'll rest two or three days and gather my strength, and then start."

The South Wind rested for two or three days and then collecting his power, said to the soldier, "Now, brother, get ready. Let's start at once. Don't worry. You won't be hurt."

Immediately, a strong whirlwind, roaring and whistling, raised the soldier into the air and carried him across mountains and seas, under the very clouds. In exactly three hours, he arrived in the new kingdom where the beautiful princess was living.

The South Wind said to him, "Farewell, my good and brave fellow. As I pity you, I won't blow in your kingdom."

"Why?"

"Because, if I indulged myself freely, not a single house in the town and not a single tree in the gardens would remain standing. All would be thrown upside down."

"Farewell, and thank you," said the soldier.

He put on his cap-of-invisibility and went into the white stone palace. Before he came into the kingdom, all the trees in the gardens had stood with dry tops, but when he arrived, they freshened and began to flower. He entered a great room in which were sitting at a table various tsars and kings and princes, who had come to court the beautiful princess. As they sat, they were entertained with sweet wines. But if any would-be bridegroom filled his glass and raised it to his lips, the soldier immediately struck the glass with his fist and knocked it away. The guests were astounded at this, but the beautiful princess guessed the truth at once.

"It is clear," she said to herself, "that my husband has returned."

She looked through the window into the garden. The tops of all the trees had revived!

Then she set her guests this riddle, "I had a self-made casket and a golden key; I lost the key and, now contrary to my expectation, have found it. I will marry whoever shall guess this riddle."

Tsars and kings and princes for a long while racked their brains, but couldn't figure it out. The princess said, "Appear, my dear husband!"

The soldier removed his cap-of-invisibility, took her white hands, and kissed her sweet lips.

"Behold the solution!" said the beautiful princess. "I am the self-made casket, and my true husband is the golden key."

Becoming uncomfortable, the suitors left to their own castles, and the princess and her husband began to enjoy life and to grow wealthy.

Source: Coxwell, *Siberian and Other Folk-tales*, 674-679.

The Sea Tsar and Vasilisa the Wise

nce a Tsar lived with his Tsaritsa beyond thrice-nine lands in the thrice-tenth kingdom. He liked to go hunting and shooting the wild beasts. One day the Tsar went out hunting and saw a young eagle sitting on an oak.

He was just going to shoot him down, when the eagle begged him, "Don't shoot me, Tsar my master; rather take me with you. At some time or other I can be of service to you."

The Tsar thought and thought, and he said, "How can you be of any service to me?" Again, he wanted to shoot him.

The eagle said to him a second time, "Don't shoot, Tsar my master, rather take me with you. Someday, I can be of service to you."

The Tsar thought and thought, and again he couldn't imagine whatever service the eagle would be to him, and he still wanted to shoot him.

For the third time, the eagle spoke to him, "Don't shoot me, Tsar my master. Rather take me with you and feed me for three years. At some point, I can be of service to you."

The Tsar was convinced. He took the eagle with him, and he fed him one year and another year. The eagle ate up so much, ate up all the cattle, and left the Tsar with neither a sheep nor a cow.

Then the eagle said to him, "Let me go free." The eagle tried his wings, but no, he couldn't fly, and he asked him, "Now, Tsar my master, you have fed me for two years, as I asked. Now feed me one more year. Only go on and feed me, and you won't lose."

The Tsar did this.

"Go and hire cattle and feed me. You won't lose."

The Tsar did this. From all the neighboring countries he went and hired cattle, and every one helped him to feed the eagle. Afterwards, he let him go free of his own will.

Then the eagle rose higher and higher, and he flew and flew, and then he came down to earth and said, "Now, Tsar my master, come and sit on me; we'll fly together."

The Tsar sat on the eagle, and they flew on and on. Maybe much time went by, maybe little, but they at last flew to the border of the blue sea. Then the eagle shook the Tsar off himself, and he fell into the sea, and he was wet up to his knees.

The eagle didn't let him drown, but supported him on his wing and asked, "Why, Tsar my lord, why are you frightened?"

"I was frightened," said the Tsar, "in case I drowned."

Once more they flew on, until they came to another sea. And the eagle shook the Tsar off into the middle of the sea, and the Tsar was wet up to his waist.

The eagle supported him by his wing and asked him, "Why, Tsar my master, why are you frightened?"

"I was frightened," said the Tsar, "and I was thinking, you might never drag me out."

And again they flew on, and they arrived at the third sea, and the eagle threw the Tsar into the great depths, and he was immersed in the water up to his very neck.

Again, the third time, the eagle held him by the wing and asked him, "Why, Tsar my master, why are you frightened?"

"I was," said the Tsar, "I was thinking if only you would rescue me!"

"Now, Tsar my master, you have learned the fear of death. All this shall be for you in the past, and shall be an old tale. You may recall how I was sitting on the oak and you wished to kill me. Three times you took up your gun to shoot me, but I asked you to spare me. I was thinking in my mind, maybe you wouldn't destroy me but have pity and take me with you!"

He then flew across thrice-nine lands, for a very long flight. And the eagle said, "Come and see, Tsar my master, what is over us and what is under us."

And the Tsar looked. "Over us," he said, "is the sky, and under us the earth."

"Look once more. What is there on the left and right-hand sides?"

"On the right-hand side there is an open field and on the left-hand side there is a house."

"We'll fly there," said the eagle. "My youngest sister lives there."

So they flew straight to the courtyard, and the sister came to meet them and received her brother, seated him on an oaken table. But she wouldn't look at the Tsar—she left him outside in the courtyard and she let the fleet dogs out to eat him.

But the eagle was very angry, and he leapt up from the table, grabbed hold of the Tsar and flew, yet farther. They flew and flew, and the eagle said to the Tsar, "Look, what is there behind us?"

The Tsar turned around and looked, and said, "Behind us there is a beautiful house."

Then the eagle said to him, "It is the house of my youngest sister that glitters. She wouldn't receive you, but let you be food for the fleet hounds."

So they flew and flew on, and the eagle asked him again, "Look, Tsar my master, what is there over us, and what under us?"

"Over us the sky and under us the earth."

"Look, what is there on the right-hand, and what is there on the left?"

"On the right-hand side there is the open field, and on the left-hand side there stands a house."

"There my younger sister lives. We'll fly there and be her guests."

So they came down to the open courtyard, and the younger sister came and received her brother, and she seated him on an oaken stool. But she left the Tsar in the courtyard, and she released the fleet hounds on him.

And the eagle was angry, leapt up from the table, grabbed hold of the Tsar, and flew with him yet farther. They flew on and on, and the eagle said to the Tsar, "Look, what is there behind us?"

"Behind us there is a beautiful house."

"It is the house of my younger sister that glitters," said the eagle. "Now we'll fly where my mother and eldest sister live."

So they flew there, and the mother and eldest sister were ever so glad to see them, and they received the Tsar with honor and affection.

"Now, Tsar my master," said the eagle, "come and rest with us. Afterwards, I'll give you a ship, and I'll repay you all I ate up while I was with you. And you can go home with God's aid."

He gave the Tsar a ship and two chests; one was red and the other green. And he said, "Be careful, don't open the chests until you reach home. Open the red chest in the back courtyard and the green chest in the front courtyard."

The Tsar took the two chests, said farewell to the eagle, and went on the blue sea. He went on and he arrived at an island, where the ship stopped. He got out on the shore, and he remembered the two chests and began to wonder what was in them, and why the eagle had told him not to open them. He thought and thought, and his patience gave out. He so badly wanted to know, and so he took the red chest, put it on the ground, and opened it. Out of it all sorts of cattle came out, so many that the eye couldn't count them all. They almost filled the entire island.

When the Tsar saw this, he was sorry and began to weep and say, "What can I do now? How can I collect all of this herd into such a tiny chest?"

Then he saw that out of the water came a man, who went up to him and asked him, "Why are you weeping so bitterly, Tsar my master?"

"Why shouldn't I weep?" answered the Tsar. "How can I put all this great herd into this tiny chest?"

"If you want, I can help you. I'll collect all this herd, only on the condition that you give me what you don't know of at home."

The Tsar began to think. "What do I not know of at home? It seems to me that I know of everything." He thought, and he considered it, and he said, "Go and gather them together, and I'll give you what I don't know of at home."

Then the man gathered all of the cattle into the box, and the Tsar went on board and sailed on his own journey.

When he reached home, he saw that a son had been born to him, the Tsarevich, and he began to kiss him and to fondle him. But then he began to weep bitter tears.

"Tsar my master," said the Tsaritsa, "why do you weep such bitter tears?"

"Out of joy," he said, for he feared to tell her the truth that he must give up the Tsarevich.

Then he went into the courtyard and opened the red chest, and out of it came oxen and cows, sheep and rams. There was a multitude of all sorts of cattle. All the barns and the folds were full. He then came to the forecourt and he opened the green chest, and in front of him a wonderful garden spread out with every kind of tree in it. The Tsar was so joyous he forgot to give his son up.

Many years went by. One day the Tsar wanted to take a walk, and he went to the river. Just then, that same man peered up out of the water and said, "You are a very forgetful person, Tsar my master. You should pay your debts."

Then the Tsar went home with grief in his groaning heart, and he told the Tsaritsa and the Tsarevich the truth, and they were troubled. They all wept together and decided that something had to be done, and that they must give up the Tsarevich. So, they took him to the seashore and left him by himself.

The Tsarevich looked around and he saw a path. He went down it, trusting God wouldn't lead him astray. He went on and on, and he lost his way in the slumberous forest, and he saw a little hut in the forest. In the hut there lived the Baba Yaga.

"I'll go in," thought the Tsarevich, and he went into the hut.

"Good-day, Tsarevich," said Baba Yaga: "Is it work on your way, or for sloth do you stray?"

"Hey, granny, give me food and drink, and ask me afterwards."

She then gave him food and drink, and the Tsarevich told her all his problems without hiding anything—where he was going and why.

Then Baba Yaga said to him, "Go, my child, to the sea. There you'll find twelve spoonbills flying in the air. They'll turn into fair maidens, who will bathe. Go and hide, and seize the shirt of the eldest maiden. When you've made friends with her, go to the Sea Tsar."

The Tsarevich said goodbye to Baba Yaga, went to the spot she named on the seashore, and he hid himself behind the bushes. Then twelve spoonbills flew along, struck the gray earth, and turned into fair maidens, who began bathing. The Tsarevich stole the maiden's shirt, sat behind the bush, and never stirred. The maidens came out of the sea and went on shore. Eleven of them struck the earth, turned into birds, and flew home. One was left alone, the eldest—Vasilísa the Wise.

When she saw that her sisters flew away, she said, "Don't look for me, my dear sisters, but fly home. I'm to blame. It's all my own fault. I didn't look, and I must pay the cost."

So the sisters, the fair maidens, struck the gray earth and turned into spoonbills, spread their wings, and flew far away. Vasilisa the Wise was left by herself, and she looked around and said, "Whoever he is who now has my shirt, let him come here. If he's an old man, he'll be as my own father. If he's a middle-aged man, he'll be as my beloved brother. If he's of my age, he'll be my lover."

As soon as he heard this, Ivan Tsarevich came out of his hiding place. She gave him a golden ring and said, "Ivan Tsarevich, how long it's taken you to come. The Sea Tsar is angry with you. That is the road that leads to the kingdom under the sea. Go along it bravely. There you'll find me as well, for I am Vasilisa the Wise, the daughter of the Sea Tsar."

Then Vasilisa the Wise, the eldest, struck the earth, turned into a spoonbill, and flew away from the Tsarevich.

Then Ivan went under the sea, and he saw light there as it is above, fields and meadows and green arbors. And the sun was hot.

Then he came to the Sea Tsar, and the Sea Tsar shrieked out at him, "Why have you been so long? You have been guilty, and you must do me this task. I have a piece of waste ground 20 miles long and broad. There is nothing on it except ditches, ravines, and sharp stones. By tomorrow morning, all this must be as smooth as the palm of my hand. Rye must be sown and grow so high that a jackdaw can hide in it. But if you fail, your head will roll off your shoulders."

Ivan Tsarevich left the Sea Tsar and wept a sea of tears. Out of the window of her room, from a lofty turret, Vasilisa the Wise saw him and asked, "Hello, Ivan Tsarevich. Why are you weeping?"

"Why shouldn't I weep?" answered Ivan. "The Sea Tsar has commanded me in a single night to level the ravines and clear the stones from a piece of land 20 miles long and broad, and grow rye on it so high that a jackdaw can hide in it."

"That's easy enough. This is no trouble—trouble is still ahead. Come and lie down in peace. The morning is wiser than the evening. All will be ready."

So Ivan Tsarevich went and lay down, and Vasilisa the Wise went to a little window and cried in a loud voice, "Hello, my faithful servants, go and level the deep ravines, take away the sharp stones, sow the ground with full-eared rye, so that in the morning it grows so high that a jackdaw can hide in it."

In the morning, Ivan Tsarevich awoke, and when he looked out, it was all done. There were no ravines and no crevasses, and the field was as flat as the palm of his hand, and the rye on it was red and so high that a jackdaw could hide in it. He went to report his completion of the task to the Sea Tsar.

"Thank you," said the Sea Tsar. "You have been able to complete for me this task. Here is your second one. I have thirty haystacks, and each haystack contains as much as thirty piles of white-eared barley. Thresh for me all the barley until it's clean, quite clean to the last grain, only don't destroy the haystacks nor beat down the sheaves. If you don't do this, your shoulders and your head will part company."

"I'll obey your Majesty," said Ivan Tsarevich, and again he went to the courtyard and was lost in tears.

"Why are you weeping so bitterly, Ivan Tsarevich?" Vasilisa the Wise asked him.

"Why shouldn't I weep? The Sea Tsar has commanded me to thresh clean thirty haystacks of barley without destroying a haystack or a single sheaf, and all in a single night."

"That's an easy task. Harder tasks are to come. Sleep peacefully, for the morning is wiser than the evening."

So Ivan Tsarevich went and lay down.

Vasilisa went to her window and cried out in a threatening voice, "Hello, you creeping ants, as many as there are of you in the white world, all creep here and pick out all the corn of my father's haystacks quite cleanly."

In the morning, the Sea Tsar asked Ivan Tsarevich if he had done this service.

"I have, your Majesty."

"Let's go and see."

So they went to the barn floor, and there all the haystacks stood untouched. They went to the granary, and all the lofts were filled to the top with corn.

"Thank you, brother," said the Sea Tsar. "Now you must make me a church out of white wax, to be ready tonight, and this shall be your last task."

Once again, Ivan Tsarevich went to the courtyard and began to weep.

"Why are you weeping, Ivan Tsarevich?"

"Why shouldn't I weep? The Sea Tsar has commanded me in a single night to build a church of white wax."

"That's an easy task. Harder tasks are close at hand. Lie down peacefully, for the morning is wiser than the evening."

So Ivan Tsarevich went to sleep.

Then she went to her window and called to her all the bees in the white world, "Hello, you bees my servants. Go and build me a church with your white wax, and let it be finished before the morning."

In the morning. Ivan got up, looked, and saw that the church stood there made of clean wax, and he went to the Sea Tsar and reported the task.

"Thank you, Ivan Tsarevich. Of all the servants I have had, none of them have been able to do as well as you. Now be my heir and the preserver of my kingdom. Select for yourself a bride out of my twelve daughters. They are all alike, face for face, hair with hair, clothing with clothing. If you guess three times the same one, she shall be your bride. If you don't, you'll suffer."

Vasilisa the Wise learned of this, chose her opportunity, and said to the Tsarevich, "The first time I'll wave my dress, the second time I'll smooth my dress, and the third time there will be a fly buzzing around my head."

Therefore, he was able to guess Vasilisa all three times. They were betrothed, and there was a merry feast for three days.

Time went by, maybe little, maybe much. Ivan Tsarevich grew anxious to see his father and mother, and he wished to go back to Holy Russia.

"Why are you so mournful, Ivan Tsarevich?"

"Oh, Vasilisa the Wise, I'm suffering for my father and my mother, and desire to behold Holy Russia."

"If we go away, there will be a great chase after us. The Sea Tsar will be angry and will kill us. We must be clever."

So Vasilisa spat in three corners, and the doors of her room opened, and she, with Ivan Tsarevich, ran into Sacred Russia. On the second day, very early, an embassy came from the Sea Tsar to gather the young couple and summon them into the palace.

They knocked on the door. "Wake up. Get up from your sleep. Your father is calling you."

"It's too early. We haven't slept yet. Come back later," one pool answered.

The ambassadors retired, and they waited one hour and another hour, and they knocked again. "This isn't the time and season to sleep. This is the time and season to get up."

"Be patient. We'll get up. We're dressing," the second pool answered.

The third time the envoys came, saying that the Sea Tsar was angry. "Why is it taking you so long to get ready?"

"We'll be down soon," answered the third pool.

The messengers waited and waited and then knocked again. There was no answer and no reply, so they broke down the door, and all was empty. They left and sent word to the Sea Tsar that the young folk had run away. He was very angry, and he set a great hunt after them.

But Vasilisa the Wise, with Ivan Tsarevich, was already very far ahead. They were leaping on swift horses without stopping, without taking a breath. "Now, Ivan Tsarevich, bend your head down to the gray earth and listen. Is there any noise of a hunt from the Sea Tsar?"

Ivan Tsarevich leapt down from his horse, put his ear to the ground, and said, "I hear the talk of people, and the tramp of horses."

"This is the hunt after us," said Vasilisa the Wise. She at once turned the horses into a green meadow, Ivan Tsarevich into an old shepherd, and herself into a brooding lamb.

The hunt passed by.

"Hey, old man, have you seen a strapping youth with a fair maiden galloping by?"

"No, good folk, I haven't seen them," said Ivan Tsarevich. "It has been forty years that I've been pasturing on these fields. Not one bird has ever flown by, not one wild beast has ever rambled by."

So, they returned home.

"Your Imperial Majesty, we saw no one on the road. We only saw a shepherd feeding a little sheep."

"Why didn't you take it? That was them!" said the Sea Tsar. And he sent out a second hunt.

But Ivan Tsarevich and Vasilisa the Wise were leaping far off on their swift horses. "Now, Ivan Tsarevich, put your head to the gray earth and listen to hear if there is a hunt from the Sea Tsar."

Ivan Tsarevich leapt off his horse, put his ear to the gray earth, and said, "I hear the talk of people and the hoppety-hop of horses."

"This is the chase; that is the horses," said Vasilisa the Wise. She turned herself into a church, and Ivan Tsarevich into an elderly pope, and the horses into trees.

So the hunt went by.

"Ho, batyushka, have you seen a shepherd with a little lamb passing by?"

"No, good people, I have not. I have been working for forty years in this church. Not one bird has flown by; not one beast has rambled by."

So, the hunt went back and reached home.

"Your Imperial Majesty, we couldn't find the shepherd with the little lamb. The only thing we saw on the road was a church and an old man as pope."

"Why didn't you break down the church and capture the pope? That was them!" the Sea Tsar exclaimed. He himself leapt out to hunt after Ivan Tsarevich and Vasilisa the Wise.

They went far, and again Vasilisa the Wise said, "Ivan Tsarevich, put your ear to the ground. Can you hear any hunt?"

Then the Tsarevich leapt down, put his ear to the gray earth, and said, "I hear the talk of people and the thunder of horses' hooves faster than before."

"This is the Sea Tsar himself who is galloping."

Vasilisa the Wise turned the horses into a lake, Ivan Tsarevich into a drake, and herself into a duck. The Sea Tsar came up to the lake and he instantly guessed who were the duck and the drake, so he struck the gray earth and turned into an eagle. The eagle wanted to strike them to death. It might well have been, but, as soon as he struck at the drake, it dove into the water. Whenever he struck at the duck, the duck dove into the water. Whatever he tried to do was all in vain.

The Sea Tsar galloped back to his own kingdom under the seas, and Vasilisa the Wise with Ivan Tsarevich waited a while and then returned to Sacred Russia. It may be long, it may be short, at last they came into the thrice-ninth realm. When they arrived home, his father and mother were overjoyed to see Ivan Tsarevich, for they had given him up as lost. And they made a great feast and celebrated the marriage.

Source: Afanas'ev, *Russian folk-tales*, 243-255.

The Frog Princess

This is a story from Poland, and Baba Yaga here is called Jandza.

There was once a king, who was very old, but he had three grown-up sons. He called them to him, and said, "My dear sons, I'm very old, and the cares of government press heavily upon me. I must therefore give them over to one of you. But as it is the law among us, that no unmarried prince may be King, I wish you all to get married, and whoever chooses the best wife shall be my successor."

They determined each to go a different way, and settled it thus. They went to the top of a very high tower, and each one at a given signal shot an arrow in a different direction to the others. Wherever their arrows fell, they were to go in search of their future wives.

The eldest prince's arrow fell on a palace in the city, where lived a senator, who had a beautiful daughter, so he went there and married her.

The second prince's arrow struck upon a country-house, where a very pretty young lady, the daughter of a rich gentleman, was sitting, so he went there, and proposed to her, and they were married.

But the youngest prince's arrow shot through a green wood, and fell into a lake. He saw his arrow floating among the reeds, and a frog sitting there, staring at him.

The marshy ground was so unsafe that he couldn't venture upon it, so he sat down in despair.

"What's the matter, prince?" asked the frog.

"What's the matter? Why, I cannot reach that arrow on which you are sitting."

"Take me for your wife, and I'll give it to you."

"But how can you be my wife, little frog?"

"That is just what has got to be. You know that you shot your arrow from the tower, thinking that where it fell, you would find a loving wife. So, you'll have her in me."

"You are very wise, I see, little frog. But tell me, how can I marry you, or introduce you to my father? And what will the world say?"

"Take me home with you, and let nobody see me. Tell them that you have married an Eastern lady, who must not be seen by any man, except her husband, nor even by another woman."

The prince considered a little. The arrow had now floated to the margin of the lake. He took the arrow from the little frog, put her in his pocket, carried her home, and then went to bed, sighing very deeply.

The next morning the king was told that all his sons had got married. He called them all together, and said, "Well children, are you all pleased with your wives?"

"Very pleased indeed, father and king."

"Well, we shall see who has chosen best. Let each of my daughters-in-law weave me a carpet by tomorrow, and the one whose carpet is the most beautiful shall be queen."

The elder princes hastened at once to their ladies, but the youngest, when he reached home, was in despair.

"What's the matter, prince?" asked the frog.

"What's the matter? My father has ordered that each of his daughters-in-law shall weave him a carpet, and the one whose carpet proves the most beautiful shall be first in rank. My brothers' wives are most likely working at their looms already. But you, little frog, although you can give back an arrow and talk like a human being, won't be able to weave a carpet, as far as I can see."

"Don't be afraid," she said. "Go to sleep, and before you wake the carpet will be ready."

So he lay down and went to sleep.

But the little frog stood on her hind-legs in the window and sang:

"Ye breezes that blow, ye winds that sigh,
Come hither on airy wing;
And all of you straight to my dwelling hie,
And various treasures bring.
Two fleeces I crave of the finest wool,
And of the loveliest flowers a basketful;
From the depths of the ocean bring sands of gold,
And pearl-drops of luster manifold;
That so I may fashion a carpet bright,
Adorned with fair flow'rets and gems of light,
And weave it in one short day and night,
When my true love's hands must the treasure hold."

There was a gentle murmur of the breezes, and from the sunbeams descended seven lovely maidens, who floated into the room, carrying baskets of various colored wools, pearls, and flowers. They curtsied deeply to the little frog, and in a few minutes, they wove a wonderfully beautiful carpet. Then they curtsied again and flew away.

Meanwhile, the wives of the other princes bought the most beautifully colored wools, and the best designs they could find, and worked hard at their looms all the next day.

Then all the princes came before the king and spread out their carpets before him.

The king looked at the first and the second, but when he came to the third, he exclaimed, "That's the carpet for me! I give the first place to my youngest son's wife, but there must be another trial yet."

And he ordered that each of his daughters-in-law should make him a cake the next day, and the husband of the one whose cake proved the best should be his successor.

The youngest prince came back to his frog wife. He looked very thoughtful and sighed deeply.

"What's the matter, prince?" she asked.

"My father demands another proof of skill, and I'm not so sure that we'll succeed so well as before, because how can you bake a cake?"

"Don't be afraid," she said. "Lie down and sleep. When you wake, you'll be in a happier frame of mind."

The prince went to sleep. The frog sprang up to the window and sang:

"Ye breezes that blow, ye winds that sigh,
Come hither on airy wing;
And all of you straight to my dwelling hie,
These various gifts to bring.
From the sunbeams bright
Bring me heat and light;
And soft waters distil
From the pure flowing rill.
From the flowers of the field
The sweet odors they yield.
From the wheatfields obtain

Five full measures of grain,
That so I may bake
In the night-time a cake,
For my true love's sake."

The winds began to rise, and the seven beautiful maidens floated down into the room, carrying baskets, with flour, water, sweetmeats, and all sorts of dainties. They curtsied to the little frog, and got the cake ready in a few minutes; they curtsied again and flew away.

The next day the three princes brought their cakes to the king. They were all very good, but when he tasted the one made by his youngest son's wife, he exclaimed, "That's the cake for me! Light, floury, white, and delicious! I see, my son, you have made the best choice, but we must wait a little longer."

The two elder sons went away much depressed, but the youngest greatly elated. When he reached home, he took up his little frog, stroked and kissed her, and said, "Tell me, my love, how was it that you, being only a little frog, could weave such a beautiful carpet or make such a delicious cake?"

"Because, my prince, I'm not what I seem. I am a princess, and my mother is the renowned Queen of Light, and a great enchantress. But she has many enemies, who, as they could not injure her, were always seeking to destroy me. To conceal me from them, she was obliged to turn me into a frog. For seven years, I have been forced to stay in the marsh where you found me. But under this frog-skin, I'm really more beautiful than you can imagine. But until my mother has conquered all her enemies, I must wear this disguise. After that takes place, you'll see me as I really am."

While they were talking, two courtiers entered, with the king's orders that the young prince come to a banquet at the king's palace and bring his wife with him, as his brothers were doing with theirs.

He didn't know what to do, but the little frog said, "Don't be afraid, my prince. Go to your father alone. When he asks for me, it will begin to rain. You must then say that your wife will follow you, but she is now bathing in May-dew. When it lightens, say that I'm dressing, and when it thunders, that I'm coming."

The prince, trusting her word, set out for the palace. The frog jumped up to the window and, standing on her hind-legs, began to sing:

"Ye breezes that blow, ye winds that sigh,
Come hither on airy wing;
And all of you straight to my dwelling hie,
These several gifts to bring.
My beauty of yore;
And my bright youth once more;
All my dresses so fair;
And my jewels so rare;
And let me delight
My dear love by the sight."

Then the seven beautiful damsels, who were the handmaidens of the princess—when she lived with her mother—floated on the sunbeams into the room. They curtsied, walked three times around her, and pronounced some magical words. Then the frog-skin fell off her, and she stood among them a miracle of beauty, and the lovely princess she was.

Meanwhile, the prince, her husband, had arrived at the royal banquet-hall, which was already full of guests. The old king welcomed him warmly and asked him, "Where is your wife, my son?"

Then a light rain began to fall, and the prince said, "She won't be long. She's now bathing herself in May-dew."

Then came a flash of lightning, which illuminated all the palace, and he said, "She's now adorning herself."

But when it thundered, he ran to the door exclaiming, "Here she is!"

And the lovely princess came in, seeming to bring the sunshine with her. They all stood amazed at her beauty.

The king couldn't contain his delight. She seemed to him all the more beautiful, because he thought her the very image of his long-deceased queen. The prince himself was no less astonished and overjoyed to find such loveliness in her, whom he had only as yet seen in the shape of a little frog.

"Tell me, my son," said the king, "why you didn't let me know what a fortunate choice you had made?"

The prince told him everything in a whisper, and the king said, "Go home, then, my son, at once. Pick up that frog-skin of hers. Throw it into the fire and come back here as fast as you can. Then she'll have to remain just as she is now."

The prince did as his father told him. He went home and threw the frog-skin into the fire, where it was at once consumed.

But things didn't turn out as they expected, because the lovely princess, on coming home, looked for her frog-skin. Not finding it, she began to cry bitterly. When the prince confessed the truth, she shrieked aloud, and taking out a green poppy-head, threw it at him. He went to sleep at once, but she sprang up to the window, sang her songs to the winds, upon which she was changed into a duck and flew away.

The prince woke up in the morning and grieved sadly, when he found his beautiful princess gone. Then he got on horseback and set out to find her, asking everywhere for the kingdom of the Queen of Light—his princess's mother—to whom he supposed she must have fled.

He rode on for a very, very long time, until one day he came into a wide plain, all covered with poppies in full flower, the odor of which so overpowered him, that he could barely sit up in his saddle. Then he saw a queer little house, supported on four crooked legs. There was no door to the house, but knowing what he ought to do, he said:

"Little house, move
On your crooked legs free;
Turn your back to the wood,
And your front door to me."

The hut with the crooked legs made a creaking noise, and turned around, with its door toward the prince. He went straight in and found an old fury, whose name was Jandza. She was spinning from a distaff and singing.

"How are you, prince?" she said. "What brings you here?"

The prince told her, and she said, "You have done wisely to tell me the truth. I know your bride, the beautiful daughter of the Queen of Light. She flies to my house daily, in the shape of a duck, and this is where she sits. Hide under the table and watch your opportunity to grab hold of her. Hold her tight, whatever shapes she assumes. When she's tired, she'll turn into a spindle. You must then break the spindle in half, and you'll find what you're looking for."

Presently the duck flew in, sat beside the old fury, and began to preen her feathers with her beak. The prince seized her by the wing. The duck quacked, fluttered, and struggled to get loose. But seeing this was useless, she changed herself into a pigeon, then into a hawk, and then into a serpent, which so frightened the prince, that he let her go. She became a duck again, quacked aloud, and flew out of the window.

The prince saw his mistake, and the old woman cried aloud, "What have you done, you careless fellow? You've frightened her away from me forever. But as she is your bride, I must find some other way to help you. Take this ball of thread, throw it in front of you, and wherever it goes, follow after it. You'll then come to my sister's house, and she'll tell you what to do next."

So the prince went on day and night, following the ball of thread, until he came to another queer little house, like the first, to which he said the same rhyme, and going in, found the second old fury, and told her his story.

"Hide under the bench," she exclaimed. "Your bride is just coming in."

The duck flew in, as before, and the prince caught her by the wing. She quacked and tried to get away. Then she changed herself into a turkey, then into a dog, then into a cat, then into an eel, so that she slipped through his hands and glided out of the window.

The prince was in despair, but the old woman gave him another ball of thread, and he again followed it, determining not to let the princess escape again so easily. So going on after the thread, as it kept unwinding, he came to a funny little house, like the first two, and said:

"Little house, move
your crooked legs free;
Turn your back to the wood,
And your front door to me."

The little house turned around, so that he could go in, and he found a third old fury, much older than her sisters and having white hair. He told her his story and begged for help.

"Why did you go against the wishes of your clever and sensible wife?" said the old woman. "You see she knew better than you what her frog-skin was good for, but you must have been in such a hurry to display her beauty, to gain the world's applause, that you have lost her; and she was forced to fly away from you."

The prince hid himself under the bench, and the duck flew in and sat at the old woman's feet. He again caught her by the wings. She struggled hard, but she felt his strength was too great for her to resist, so she turned herself into a spindle at once. He broke it across his knee. And lo and behold, instead of the two halves of the spindle, he held the hands of his beautiful princess, who looked at him lovingly with her beautiful eyes and smiled sweetly.

And she promised him that she would always remain as she was then, because since her mother's enemies were now all dead, she had nothing to fear.

They embraced each other, and went out of the old fury's hut. Then the princess spoke some magical spells. In the twinkling of an eye, there appeared a wonderful bridge, reaching from where they stood hundreds of miles, up to the very gallery of the palace, belonging to the prince's father. It was all made of crystal, with golden hand-rails and diamond bosses upon them.

The princess spoke some more magical words, and a golden coach appeared, drawn by eight horses, and a coachman, and two tall footmen, all in golden liveries. And there were four outriders on splendid horses, riding by the side of the coach, and an equerry, riding in front, and blowing a brazen trumpet. A long procession of followers, in splendid dresses, came after them.

Then the prince and princess got into the golden coach and drove away, thus accompanied, along the crystal bridge, until they reached home. When the old king came out to meet them, he embraced them both tenderly. He appointed the prince his successor. Such magnificent festivities were held on the occasion, as never were seen or heard of before.

Source: Gliński, *Polish Fairy Tales*, 1-14.

The Frog Princess (in Verse)

Once, a tsar and his tsaritsa
Ruled a kingdom in an empire.
They had sons just three in number,
Each courageous and unmarried,
Hitherto described by no one,
Neither writer, nor yet speaker;
And the prince named John was youngest.

Having called his sons together,
Thus the tsar one day addressed them;
"Each of you select an arrow;
Lifting up your bows well tightened,
Shoot in various directions!
In the place where falls your arrow,
Or in home, or court, or mansion,
Seek a bride, become a suitor!"

Now the eldest's missile landed
Near a noble maiden's dwelling;
And the middle brother's arrow
Came to earth within a courtyard
Where a wealthy merchant's daughter,
Oh, a maid of soul and beauty!
Stood erect beside the entrance.

Then the youngest used his weapon,
And his arrow fell in marshes
Where, forthwith, a frog secured it.
Straightway, John addressed his father:
"Can I mate with such a croaker
That in nothing is my equal?"
"Take her," said the father promptly,
"You are fated to obtain her."

One by one, the princes married:
This, the daughter of the noble;
That, the wealthy merchant's daughter;
And the youngest, froggy-croaker.

Next, the tsar the brothers summons,
Says their wives must bake, get ready
Bread the whitest for the morrow.

John, the prince, came home despondent,
Hung his head in manner helpless.
Then the frog said, "Kva, Kva, husband,
Wherefore so o'ercome by sorrow?
Has your father spoken harshly?"

"How should I escape from grieving?
When the tsar has stern commanded:
That you bake, before to-morrow
Bread the whitest?" "Prince, have courage,
Go to rest and peaceful slumber;
Morning is than evening wiser."

When she saw her husband sleeping,
She without delay, completely,
Shed her frog's skin: stood with others,
As a maid of soul and beauty,
Vasilissa, the sagacious.

In the mansion now the princess
Loudly cried, "Come hither, women,
Get to work, and quickly show me
Whitest bread, the kind exactly
That was eaten at my father's."

When the prince awoke from slumber,
He perceived the bread beside him;
And the clever really cannot
Faintly fancy its consistence;
In but fairy tales 'tis eaten.
It was furbished with devices,
Such as royal towns and gateways,
And the tsar was very grateful,
Thanked the prince for bread so wondrous.
But he gave a further order
To his sons, who all were married:
In a single night their wives must
Skillfully produce a carpet.

John the prince returned unhappy,
With his head indeed low hanging.
"Kva-Kva, Kva-Kva," said his consort,

"Why, my prince, a prey to sorrow?
Has your father spoken roughly?"

"How can I to-day be merry,
When my father-tsar has ordered
You to weave, before to-morrow,
Now, a carpet, soft and silky."

"Do not worry! prince and husband!
But retire to rest and slumber,
Morning is than evening wiser."
While he slept, she cast her frog's skin,
And became the beauteous maiden,
Vasilissa, the sagacious.
Forth she went and loudly uttered
On the balcony this order:
"Women! quickly here assemble,
Get to work and weave a carpet,
Silky, like the one I sat on
In my childhood, at my father's."

As she ordered, 'twas accomplished.
When the prince awoke, the carpet
Long ago had been completed,
And its marvels were so mighty,
You could scarcely them imagine,
Though in fairy tales you'll meet them.
It was worked with gold and silver,
Patterns intricate presented,
Blazed with colors, all combining.

For the gift the tsar was grateful,
Thanked the prince for such an effort;
But he next his sons commanded
To appear at court before him,
And each son must bring his consort.

Once again the prince was gloomy,
Hung his head, when home returning.
"Kva-Kva, why, my prince, this sadness?
Has your father spoken rudely?"

"How can I to-day be happy
When my lord, the tsar, has ordered
Your attendance for inspection?
Can I show you to the people?"

"Do not be uneasy, husband,
Go alone to see your father,
I will follow; but remember!
If you hear a noise like thunder,
Say, 'Behold, my little froggy
To us comes within her casket.' "

Lo! arrived the elder brothers
With their wives bedecked and splendid,
And they stood and laughed, surveying
John the prince. "Good gracious, brother,
You have come without your lady,
Have not put her in a kerchief!
Where did you unearth the beauty?
Probably in lonely marshes!"

Swiftly rose a crash and pealing,
So that all the palace trembled.
Every guest was seized with terror;
All the seats at once grew vacant,
Everybody acted wildly.
John the prince, still speaking calmly,
Sought to dissipate the terror.
"It is nothing but my dearest
Coming in her little casket."

Dashing to the palace entrance,
Quickly stopped a gilded carriage.
Drawn along by six fine horses.
Forth emerged sage Vasilissa,
Of a beauty past conception,
Only found in fairy stories.

Then the prince his wife led proudly,
Led her to a table covered
Richly with a cloth embroidered.
Now, the guests began their supper,
Ate and drank, mid merry laughter;
But, although sage Vasilissa
Lifted up her wine and sipped it,
She contrived the greater portion
In her sleeve should fall unnoticed;
And, although she ate some swan's flesh,
She the little bones let tumble
In the second sleeve on purpose.
Lo! the elder prince's consorts
Closely watched, and did as she did.

Later, Vasilissa dancing,
Raised her arm, and freely waved it;
Then, a lake arose before her!
Next she waved her arm the other;
Swans appeared upon the water!
Tsar and guests began to marvel.

Soon the elder wives were dancing,
Waved their arms without cessation,
But they failed in their endeavor,
To compete with Vasilissa:
They the guests with wine besprinkled,
Overwhelmed the tsar with swan bones;
So he drove them forth dishonored.

John the prince, ere long had managed
Home to speed and find the frog's skin
And consign it to a furnace.
But, at once, sage Vasilissa
Coming back, the loss discovered,
Grew depressed and sad and wretched.
"John the prince! I now am ruined,
Dearest, had you waited longer,
I had lived with you forever;
As it is, farewell! Yet, seek me
In the thrice-ninth land, my husband!
Seek me in the thrice-tenth kingdom;
With the skeleton that's deathless."
Forth she flew, a swan in semblance.

John the prince, in bitter sorrow,
Moving first in all directions,
Prayed and, next, went straight before him.
Going, maybe, to a distance,
(Or not far; 'tis unimportant)
He to meet an old man happened
Who, with words of kindly greeting,
Asked him whither he was speeding,
Listened to his sad adventure.

"Prince! you dared to burn the frog's skin,
You that were without the puissance
To inflict it, or remove it!
Vasilissa the sagacious
Had more wisdom than her father;
So he, stirred by envy, ordered
Her to be three years a croaker!

You should find her through my counsel;
Have a care this ball to follow;
If it runs, pursue it boldly!"

John the prince was duly grateful,
And was led to open country,
Where a bear appeared before him.
"I will kill," said John, "this creature."
But the bear remarked with meaning,
"Strike me not, and I will serve you!"

Further on the prince, up gazing,
Saw a drake in flight approaching.
John upraised his bow, would use it,
Till the bird, in accents human,
Cried, "Oh spare me, I'll assist you,"
And the prince displayed compassion.

So, a slant-eyed hare came quickly;
Saying, "Shoot not, I will help you."
It escaped the threatened arrow.

Pity-touched, the prince went further
Till he saw, near Ocean's waters,
On the sand, a pike expiring.
"Mercy show!" the fish gasped faintly,
"To the sea, good prince transfer me!"

Having saved the pike, John wandered
By the shore, until the ball went
Or a short way, or a long way,
Lastly reached a little cottage
That revolved, or stood on fowls' legs.

John now raised his voice as follows:
"Hut! resume your old position,
Stand as you, at first, were standing;
Turn, forthwith, your back to Ocean!"

Then the cottage faced the speaker
Who, intruding, saw before him,
"Bony legs," great Baba-Yaga
Stretched upon the stove, on nine bricks,
And about her teeth to sharpen.

"Why this visit, eh! young fellow?"
Baba-Yaga asked the tsar's son.

"Ha! before you put the question,
First, old woman! you should feed me.
Give me drink, and heat the bath-house."
After she performed her duties,
John the prince divulged his mission:
He would find his roaming consort,
Vasilissa the sagacious.

"Ah, I know," said Baba-Yaga,
"She was lately taken captive;
Deathless Skeleton has seized her.
You must be both brave and skillful
To o'ercome him and regain her.
In a needle's point his death is,
And that needle in a hare is,
And that hare within a chest is,
High that chest upon an oak is,
And he guards that tree as something
Of a value vast and mighty."
Then the witch, with bony fingers,
Pointed out the tree's position.

John the prince advanced, but knew not
What to do to win the coffer.
Suddenly, from where's no matter,
Out a bear swift rushed and roughly
Tore a tree; its roots uplifted.

Down a chest came tumbling quickly,
Setting free a hare elusive,

But another hare pursuing,
Overtook and tore her piecemeal,
Let escape aloft a duckling.

But a drake uprose to strike her,
And she dropped an egg which, falling,
Reached the surface of the Ocean.

When he witnessed this occurrence,
John the prince with tears lamented;

But a pike swam swiftly shorewards,
And its jaws an egg held firmly.
Taking now the egg, John broke it,
Drew a needle forth, and severed
Point from body. And, thereafter,
Though the skeleton might struggle,
He was destined to be conquered.

Vasilissa, the sagacious,
From his house was quickly rescued.
With her, then the prince went homeward,
Passed a life both long and blissful.

Source: Coxwell, *Siberian and Other Folk-tales*, 712-720.

Princess Miranda and Prince Hero

This is a story from Poland, and Baba Yaga here is called Jandza.

Far away, in the wide ocean there was once a green island where lived the most beautiful princess in the world, named Miranda. She had lived there ever since her birth and was queen of the island. Nobody knew who her parents were, or how she had come there. But she was not alone; for there were twelve beautiful maidens, who had grown up with her on the island, and were her ladies-in-waiting.

But a few strangers had visited the island and spoken of the princess's great beauty. Many more came in time and became her subjects. They built a magnificent city, in which she had a splendid palace of white marble to live in.

And in course of time, a great many young princes came to court her. But she didn't care to marry any of them. If anyone persisted and tried to force her to become his wife, she would turn him and all his soldiers into ice, by merely fixing her eyes upon them.

One day the wicked Kosciey, the king of the Underground realm, came out into the upper world and began to gaze all around it with his telescope. Various empires and kingdoms passed in review before him. At last, he saw the green island and the rich city upon it, and the marble palace in this city, and in this palace the twelve beautiful young ladies-in-waiting. Among them he beheld, lying on a rich couch of swans down, the Princess Miranda asleep. She slept like an innocent child, but she was dreaming of a young knight, wearing a golden helmet, on a gallant horse, and carrying an invisible mace, that fought of itself. And she loved him better than life.

Kosciey looked at her. He was delighted with her beauty. He struck the earth three times and stood upon the green island.

Princess Miranda called together her brave army and led them into the field, to fight the wicked Kosciey. But he, blowing on them with his poisonous breath, put them all fast asleep. He was just about to grab the princess when she, throwing a glance of scorn at him, changed him into a lump of ice and fled to her capital.

Kosciey did not long remain ice. As soon as the princess was away, he freed himself from the power of her glance. Regaining his usual form, he followed her to her city. Then he put all the inhabitants of the island to sleep, among them the princess's twelve faithful damsels.

She was the only one whom he could not injure; but being afraid of her glances, he surrounded the castle—which stood upon a high hill—with an iron rampart, and placed a dragon with twelve heads on guard before the gate, and waited for the princess to give herself up of her own accord.

The days passed by, then weeks, then months, while her kingdom became a desert. All her people were asleep, and her faithful soldiers also lay sleeping on the open fields, their steel armor all rusted, and wild plants were growing over them undisturbed. Her twelve maidens were all asleep in different rooms of the palace, just where they happened to be at the time. She herself, all alone, kept walking sadly to and fro in a little room up in a tower, where she had taken refuge—wringing her white hands, weeping, and her bosom heaving with sighs.

Around her all were silent, as though dead. Only every now and then, Kosciey, not daring to encounter her angry glance, knocked at the door asking her to surrender, promising to make her queen of his Underground realm. But it was all of no use. The princess was silent, and only threatened him with her looks.

Grieving in her lonely prison, Princess Miranda couldn't forget the lover of whom she had been dreaming. She saw him just as he had appeared to her in her dream.

And she looked up with her blue eyes to heaven, and seeing a cloud floating by, she said:

"O cloud! through the bright sky flying!
Stay, and hearken my piteous sighing!
In my sorrow I call upon thee;
Oh! where is my loved one? say!
Oh! where do his footsteps stray?
And does he now think of me?"

"I don't know," the cloud replied. "Ask the wind."
"And she looked out into the wide plain, and seeing how the wind was blowing freely, she said:

"O wind! o'er the wide world flying!
Do thou pity my grief and crying!

Have pity on me!
Oh! where is my loved one? say!
Oh! where do his footsteps stray?
And does he now think of me?"

"Ask the stars," the wind replied. "They know more than I do."
So she cried to the stars:

"O stars! with your bright beams glowing!
Look down on my tears fast flowing!
Have pity, have pity on me!
Oh! where is my loved one? say!
Oh! where do his footsteps stray?
And does he now think of me?"

"Ask the moon," said the stars; "who being nearer to the earth, knows more of what happens there than we do."
So she said to the moon:

"Bright moon, as your watch you keep,
From the starry skies, o'er this land of sleep,
Look down now, and pity me!
Oh! where is my loved one? say!
Where? where do his footsteps stray?
And does he now think of me?"

"I know nothing about your loved one, princess," replied the moon, "but here comes the sun, who will surely be able to tell you."
And the sun rose up in the dawn, and at noontide stood just over the princess's tower, and she said:

"Thou soul of the world! bright sun!
Look on me, in this prison undone!
Have pity on me!
Oh! where is my loved one? say!
Through what lands do his footsteps stray?
And does he now think of me?"

"Princess Miranda," said the sun, "dry your tears, comfort your heart. Your lover is hurrying to you. From the bottom of the deep sea, from under the coral reefs, he has won the enchanted ring. When he puts it on his finger, his army will increase by thousands, regiment after regiment, with horse and foot. The drums are beating, the sabers gleaming, the colors flying, the cannon roaring, they are bearing down on the empire of Kosciey. But he cannot conquer him by force of mortal weapons. I'll teach him a surer way. There is good hope that he will be able to deliver you from Kosciey and save your country. I'll hasten to your prince. Farewell."

The sun stood over a wide country, beyond the deep seas, beyond high mountains, where Prince Hero in a golden helmet, on a gallant horse, was drawing up his army and preparing to march against Kosciey, the besieger of the fair princess. He had seen her three times in a dream, and had heard much about her, for her beauty was famous throughout the world.

"Dismiss your army," said the sun. "No army can conquer Kosciey, no bullet can reach him. You can only free Princess Miranda by killing him, and how you are to do it, you must learn from the old woman Jandza. I can only tell you where you will find the horse that must carry you to her. Go toward the East. You'll come to a green meadow, in which there are three oak trees. Among them you'll find hidden in the ground an iron door, with a brazen padlock. Behind this door you'll find a battle charger and a mace. The rest you'll learn afterwards. Farewell!"

Prince Hero was most surprised, but he took off his enchanted ring and threw it into the sea. With it, all his great army vanished immediately into mist, leaving no trace behind. He turned to the East and traveled onward.

After three days, he came to the green meadow, where he found the three oak trees and the iron door as he had been told. It opened upon a narrow, crooked stairway, going downward, leading into a deep dungeon, where he found another iron door, closed by a heavy iron padlock. Behind this, he heard a horse neighing, so loudly that it made the door fall to the ground. At the same moment, eleven other doors flew open and out came a warhorse, which had been shut up there for ages by a wizard.

The prince whistled to the horse. The horse tugged at his fastenings and broke twelve chains by which he had been fettered. He had eyes like stars, flaming nostrils, and a mane like a thunder-cloud. He was a horse of horses, the wonder of the world.

"Prince Hero!" said the horse, "I have long waited for such a rider as you, and I am ready to serve you forever. Mount on my back, take that mace in your hand, which you see hanging on the saddle. You need not fight with it yourself, because it will strike wherever you command it, and beat a whole army. I know the way everywhere. Tell me where you want to go, and you will presently be there."

The prince told him everything. He took the self-fighting mace in his hand and sprang on his back. The horse reared, snorted, spurned the ground, and they flew over mountains and forests, higher than the flying clouds, over rapid rivers, and deep seas. When they flew along the ground, the charger's light feet never trampled down a blade of grass, nor raised an atom of dust on the sandy soil. Before sunset Prince Hero had reached the primeval forest in which the old woman Jandza lived.

He was amazed at the size and age of the mighty oaks, pine trees and firs, where there reigned a perpetual twilight. And there was absolute silence—not a leaf or a blade of grass stirring; and no living thing, not so much as a bird, or the hum of an insect; only amidst this grave-like stillness the sound of his horse's hoofs.

The prince stopped before a little house, supported on crooked legs, and said:

"Little house, move
On your crooked legs free:
Turn your back to the wood,
And your front to me."

The house turned around, with the door toward him. The prince went in, and the old woman Jandza asked him, "How did you get here, Prince Hero, where no living soul has penetrated until now?"

"Don't ask me, but welcome your guest politely."

So the old woman gave the prince food and drink, made up a soft bed for him, to rest on after his journey, and left him for the night.

The next morning, he told her everything and what he had come for.

"You have undertaken a great and splendid task, prince. I'll tell you how to kill Kosciey. In the Ocean-Sea, on the island of Everlasting Life, there is an old oak tree. Under this tree is buried a chest bound with iron. In this chest is a hare. Under the hare sits a gray duck. This duck carries within her an egg, and in this egg is enclosed the life of Kosciey. When you break the egg, he'll die at once. Now good-bye, prince, and good luck go with you. Your horse will show you the way."

163

The prince got on horseback, and they soon left the forest behind them, and came to the shore of the ocean. On the beach was a fisherman's net, and in the net was a great fish, who when he saw the prince, cried out piteously, "Prince Hero, take me out of the net and throw me back into the sea. I will repay you!"

The prince took the fish out of the net and threw it into the sea. It splashed in the water and vanished. The prince looked over the sea and saw the island in the gray distance, far, far away. But how was he going to get there? He leaned upon his mace, deep in thought.

"What are you thinking of, prince?" asked the horse.

"I'm thinking how I'm to reach the island, when I cannot swim over that breadth of sea."

"Sit on my back, prince, and hold fast."

So the prince sat firmly on the horse's back and held the thick mane tight. A wind arose, and the sea was somewhat rough, but rider and horse pushed on, through the billows, and at last came to shore on the island of Everlasting Life.

The prince took off his horse's bridle and let him loose to feed in a meadow of luxuriant grass. He walked on quickly to a high hill, where the old oak tree grew. Taking it in both hands, he tugged at it. The oak resisted all his efforts, so he tugged again. The oak began to creak and moved a little. He mustered all his strength and tugged again. The oak fell with a crash to the ground, with its roots uppermost. There, where they had stood firmly fixed so many hundred years, was a deep hole.

Looking down, he saw the iron-bound chest. He brought it up, broke open the lock with a stone, raised the lid, picked up the hare lying in it by its ears. At that moment, the duck, which had been sitting under the hare, became alarmed and flew off straight to sea.

The prince fired a shot after her. The bullet hit the duck. She gave one loud quack and fell, but in that same moment, the egg fell from her—down to the bottom of the sea. The prince gave a cry of despair, but just then a great fish came swimming, dove down to the depths of the sea, and coming to the shore, with the egg in its jaws, left it on the sand.

The fish swam away, but the prince, taking up the egg, mounted his horse once more. They swam until they reached Princess Miranda's island, where they saw a great iron wall stretching all around her white marble palace.

There was only one entrance through this iron wall to the palace, and in front of this lay the monstrous dragon with the twelve heads, six of which kept guard alternately, when the one half slept the other six remained awake. If anyone were to approach the gate, he could not escape the horrid jaws. Nobody could hurt the dragon, because he could only suffer death by his own act.

The prince stood on the hill in front of that gate and commanded his self-fighting mace, which also could turn invisible, to go and clear the entrance to the palace.

The invisible, self-fighting mace fell upon the dragon and began to thunder on all his heads with such force, that all his eyes became bloodshot. He began to hiss fiercely. He shook his twelve heads and stretched wide his twelve horrid jaws. He spread out his forest of claws, but this helped him not at all. The mace kept on beating him, moving around so fast, that not a single head escaped, but could only hiss, groan, and shriek wildly!

Now it had been given a thousand blows, the blood gushed from a thousand wounds, and there was no help for the dragon. He raged, writhed about, and shrieked in despair. Finally, as blow followed blow, and he couldn't see who gave them, he gnashed his teeth, belched forth flame, and at length turned his claws upon himself, plunging them deep into his own flesh, struggled, writhed, twisted himself around, in and out. His blood flowed freely from his wounds, and then it was all over with the dragon.

The prince, seeing this, went into the palace courtyard, put his horse into the stable, and went up by a winding stair, toward the tower, where Princess Miranda, having seen him, addressed him, "Welcome, Prince Hero! I saw how you disposed of the dragon, but do be careful, for my enemy, Kosciey, is in this palace. He is most powerful, both through his own strength, and through his sorceries. If he kills you, I can no longer live.

"Princess Miranda, don't worry about me. I have the life of Kosciey in this egg." Then he called out, "Invisible self-fighting mace, go into the palace and beat Kosciey."

The mace roused itself quickly, battered in the iron doors, and set upon Kosciey. It struck him on the neck, until he crouched all together, the sparks flew from his eyes, and there was a noise of so many mills in his ears.

If he had been an ordinary mortal, it would have been all over with him at once. As it was, he was horribly tormented, and puzzled—feeling all these blows and never seeing where they came from. He sprang about, raved, and raged until the whole island resounded with his roaring.

At last, he looked through the window and saw Prince Hero. "Ah! that is all your doing!" he exclaimed.

He sprang out into the courtyard, to rush straight at him, and beat him to a pulp! But the prince held the egg in one hand ready. He squeezed it so hard that the shell cracked and the yolk and the white were all spilled together, and Kosciey fell lifeless!

With the death of the enchanter, all his spells were dissolved at once. All the people in the island who were asleep woke up and began to stir. The soldiers woke from sleep, and the drums began to beat. They formed their ranks, massed themselves in order, and began to march toward the palace.

In the palace there was great joy because Princess Miranda came toward the prince, gave him her white hand, and thanked him warmly. They went to the throne-room, and following the princess's example, her twelve waiting-maids paired off with twelve young officers of the army, and the couples grouped themselves around the throne, on which the prince and princess were sitting.

Then a priest, arrayed in all his vestments, came in at the open door, and the prince and princess exchanged rings and were married. And all the other couples were married at the same time, and after the wedding, there was a feast, dancing, and music, which it is a pleasure to think of. Everywhere there was rejoicing.

Source: Gliński, *Polish Fairy Tales*, 15-28.

Go I Don't Know Where, Bring I Don't Know What

In a land far, far away there lived a tsar, who had never married. He had a shooter in his service, named Andrey. Once Andrey the shooter went hunting. He walked the whole day through the forest, but was not lucky, as he couldn't spot the wild fowl. In the evening, he was going back and feeling down. Suddenly, he saw a turtledove on a tree.

"Let me at least shoot this one."

He fired a shot and wounded her. The turtledove fell from the tree onto mother earth. Andrey picked her up and wanted to twist her neck and put her in a bag.

But the turtledove spoke to him in a human voice, "Don't kill me, Andrey the shooter. Don't chop off my head. Take me alive, bring me home, and put me on the windowsill. And watch. When I get drowsy, hit me with the back of your right hand. You'll receive for yourself a great happiness."

Andrey the shooter was surprised. "What is this? It looks like a bird, but speaks with a human voice." He brought the turtledove home, put her on the windowsill, and started to watch what would happen next.

It wasn't long until the turtledove put her head under her wing and fell into a snooze. Andrey recalled what she told him. He hit her with the back of his right hand. The turtledove fell onto the ground and turned into a maiden, Marya Tsarevna. Her beauty defied all description, beyond the telling of it.

Marya Tsarevna told the shooter, "You managed to take me. Now, you must be able to keep me. Arrange a prolonged feasting for the wedding. I'll be your faithful and cheerful wife."

That's what they agreed. Andrey the shooter married Marya Tsarevna and lived with his young wife and was enjoying his life. In the meantime, he didn't forget about his work: every morning he rose with the sun and went to the forest, shot some game, and brought it to the tsar's kitchen.

After living together for a while, Marya Tsarevna said, "You live in poverty, Andrey."

"Yes, as you can see."

"Get a hundred rubles, buy different sorts of silk with that money, and I'll fix everything."

Andrey did what she said, went to his friends, borrowed some money from them, bought different silk fabrics, and brought it to his wife.

Marya Tsarevna took the silk and said, "Go to bed. The morning is wiser than the evening."

Andrey went to bed, and Marya Tsarevna sat down to weave. She wove all night long and made a carpet, which had never been seen in the whole world: the whole tsardom was painted on it with cities and villages, with forests and crop fields. And there were birds in the sky, and animals on the mountains, and fish species in the sea. The moon and the sun were going around all that.

The next morning, Marya Tsarevna gave the carpet to her husband. "Take it to the merchant court and sell it to the traders. But look, don't set your own price; accept whatever offer they'll give you."

Andrey took the carpet, hung it on his arm, and walked along the rows of shops.

One merchant ran up to him. "Listen, sir, how much do you want for it?"

"You're a trader, so set the price yourself."

The merchant thought hard and couldn't estimate the price of the carpet. Another one jumped up, followed by another. A great crowd of merchants had gathered. They were looking at the carpet and were astonished, but couldn't appraise its value.

At that time, the royal adviser was passing by. He wished to know what the merchants were talking about. He got out of the carriage, barely forced his way through the great crowd, and asked, "Hello, merchants, overseas guests! What are you talking about?"

"So and so, we cannot appraise the price of this carpet."

The royal adviser looked at the carpet and was astonished too. "Shooter, tell me the truth: where did you get such a nice carpet from?"

"So and so, my wife embroidered it."

"How much do you want me to pay for it?"

"I don't know. My wife ordered me not to bargain: I should agree to whatever you offer."

"Well, shooter, here are ten thousand for you."

Andrey took the money, gave him the carpet, and went home. And the royal adviser went to the tsar and showed him the carpet.

The tsar looked at it. His entire tsardom was in full view on the carpet. He gasped in surprise. "Well, you can ask whatever you want, because I won't give you back the carpet!"

The tsar took out twenty thousand rubles and personally handed it to the adviser. He took it and thought, "That's fine. I'll order another one for myself. It'll be even better."

He got back into the carriage and galloped to the settlement. He found the hut where Andrey the shooter lived and knocked on the door. Marya Tsarevna opened the door. The royal adviser lifted one foot over the threshold but didn't move the other one. Then he became silent and forgot about his business: there was such a beauty standing in front of him that he couldn't take his eyes off of her for a century. He could continue to look forever.

Marya Tsarevna waited for an answer, but then turned the royal adviser around by his shoulders and closed the door. He hardly recovered consciousness and unwillingly trudged home. And from that time on, he couldn't properly eat and drink. He continued to imagine the shooter's wife.

The tsar noticed that and began to ask what kind of trouble he had.

The adviser said to the tsar, "Ah, I saw the wife of a shooter. I keep thinking about her! I can't drink, can't eat, and I can't fix the spell with any potion."

The tsar decided to see the shooter's wife himself. He dressed in a simple attire, went to the settlement, found the hut where Andrey the shooter lived, and knocked on the door. Marya Tsarevna opened the door to him. The tsar lifted one foot over the threshold, but didn't move the other one. Then he became completely numb: an indescribable beauty was standing in front of him.

Marya Tsarevna waited for an answer for a while, then turned the tsar around by his shoulders and closed the door.

The tsar was caught up with a romantic passion. He thought, "Why am I still single, not married? I wish I could marry this beauty! She shouldn't be a shooter's wife. She was preordained to be a tsar's wife."

The tsar returned to the palace and conceived an evil plan to win the wife away from her living husband. He called his adviser and said, "Think about how to get rid of Andrey the shooter. I want to marry his wife. If you manage to come up with an idea about how to do it, I'll reward you with cities and villages and a golden treasury. If you can't devise a plot, I'll take your head off of your shoulders!"

The royal adviser began to grow sad, went away, and was feeling down. He couldn't figure out how to exterminate the shooter. Out of grief, he turned into a tavern to drink some wine.

A tavern drinker in a tattered coat ran up to him and asked, "What are you upset about, royal adviser? Why are you feeling down?"

"Go away, you tavern drinker!"

"Don't drive me away. It's better to give me a glass of wine, and I'll give you an idea."

The royal adviser bought him a glass of wine and told him about his trouble.

The tavern drinker said to him, "It's an easy task to get rid of Andrey the shooter. He's straightforward, but his wife is very cunning. Therefore, we'll propose to them such a riddle that she won't be able to manage it. Go back to the tsar and tell him, 'Let him send Andrey the shooter to the tsardom to come to find out how the deceased Father the Tsar is doing. Andrey will leave and will never come back.' "

The royal adviser thanked the tavern drinker and ran to the tsar. "So and so, you can get rid of the shooter." And he told him where to send him and for what. The tsar brightened up, ordered Andrey the shooter to come.

"Well, Andrey, you've served me faithfully. Perform another task for me. Go to the tsardom to come, find out how my father is doing. Otherwise, my sword will cut off your head."

Andrey returned home, sat down on a bench, and hung his head.

Marya Tsarevna asked him, "Why do you look unhappy today? Has some misfortune happened?"

Andrey told her what kind of task the tsar demanded from him.

Marya Tsarevna said, "This is something to worry about! But this isn't a great challenge yet. It's a simple task. The great challenge is still ahead. Go to bed. The morning is wiser than the evening."

Early in the morning, as soon as Andrey woke up, Marya Tsarevna gave him a bag of dry toast and a golden ring. "Go to the tsar and ask for a royal adviser to accompany you. Otherwise, they won't believe that you visited the tsardom to come. And when you go out with the royal advisor on the road, throw this ring in front of you and it will guide you."

Andrey took the bag of dry toast and the ring, said goodbye to his wife, and went to the tsar to ask for a travelling companion. The tsar agreed and ordered his adviser to go with Andrey to the tsardom to come.

They traveled on the road together. Andrey threw the ring, and it began to roll. Andrey followed it through the open country, mossy swamps, rivers and lakes, and the royal adviser trailed along behind Andrey. When they were tired of walking, they ate dried toast and continued to walk. We don't know how far they walked, how long they walked, but eventually they came to a thick deep forest, descended into a deep ravine, and that's where the ring stopped.

Andrey and the royal adviser sat for a while to eat some dry toast. They looked aside and saw that two devils were transporting firewood past them on an old, aged tsar. He pulled a huge cart, and they were urging the tsar on with clubs, one from the right side and the other from the left.

Andrey said, "Have a look: it looks as if this is the deceased Father the Tsar."

"You're right. He's the one carrying the firewood."

Andrey shouted to the devils, "Hey, Mister Devils! Release this dead man for me, at least for a short time. I need to ask him about something."

The devils answered, "We don't have time to wait! Do you want us to carry firewood ourselves or what?"

"Then take from me this fresh man to replace him."

Then the devils unharnessed the old tsar, harnessed the royal adviser to the cart instead of him, and started to urge him on with clubs from both sides. He bent under the strain, but continued to carry the load.

Andrey began to ask the old tsar about his life.

"Ah, Andrey the shooter," the tsar answered, "my life is bad in the tsardom to come! Bow to my son from me and say that I firmly order him not to do injustice to people. Otherwise, the same will happen to him."

As soon as they finished talking, the devils were already returning with an empty cart. Andrey said goodbye to the old tsar, took the royal adviser from the devils, and they hit the return trail. They came back to their tsardom and presented themselves in the palace.

The tsar saw the shooter and in a fit of anger attacked him, "How dare you come back?"

Andrey the shooter answered, "So and so, I was in the tsardom to come and met your deceased parent. His life is bad. He ordered me to bow to you and strongly instructed you not to do injustice to people."

"And how can you prove that you went to the tsardom to come and talked to my parent?"

"I'll prove it because your adviser still has stroke marks on his back. These stroke marks were left by the devils, which urged him on with clubs."

Then the tsar became convinced. He had nothing else to do but to let Andrey go home.

Then he said to the adviser, "Think about how to get rid of the shooter. Otherwise, my sword will cut off your head."

The royal adviser went away and was feeling even more down. He entered a tavern, sat at a table, and asked for some wine.

The tavern drinker ran up to him and said, "Why are you upset, royal adviser? Give me a glass of wine. I'll give you an idea."

The adviser poured him a glass of wine and told him about his trouble.

The tavern drinker said to him, "Go back and tell the tsar to give the shooter the following task. It's not only difficult to perform, it's difficult even to discover. Send him beyond the thrice-nine lands to the thrice-tenth tsardom to get Kot Bayun."

The royal adviser ran to the tsar and told him what task to give to the shooter so that he wouldn't return.

The tsar ordered Andrey to come. "Well, Andrey, you performed your task well, so do another one: go to the thrice-tenth tsardom and get me Kot Bayun. Otherwise, my sword will cut off your head."

Andrey went home, hung his head below his shoulders, and told his wife what kind of task the tsar had given him.

"This is something to be upset about!" Marya Tsarevna said. "But this isn't a burden, just a little burden. The real burden waits for you in the future. Go to bed. The morning is wiser than the evening."

Andrey went to bed, and Marya Tsarevna went to the blacksmith shop and ordered the blacksmiths to forge three iron caps, iron tongs, and three rods: iron, copper, and tin.

Early in the morning Marya Tsarevna woke up Andrey. "Here are three caps, tongs, and three rods. Go beyond the thrice-nine lands into the thrice-tenth tsardom. Three miles before it, you'll start to feel very sleepy. Kot Bayun will be sending drowsiness to you. But don't fall asleep. Put one of your hands on top of the other, drag one of your feet behind the other one, and in some places roll like a roller. And remember: if you fall asleep, Kot Bayun will kill you."

And then Marya Tsarevna taught him what to do and let him go.

Easier said than done. Andrey the shooter came to the thrice-tenth tsardom. Three miles before reaching it, he began to feel sleepy. Andrey placed three iron caps on his head, put one of his hands on top of the other, dragged one of his feet behind the other one. He walked and in some places he rolled like a roller. Somehow, he managed not to fall asleep and found himself near the high post.

Kot Bayun saw Andrey. He began to whir and grumble and jumped from the post onto his head. He broke the first cap and the second one and started to break the third one. Then Andrey the shooter grabbed the cat with tongs, dragged him to the ground, and started to hit him with rods. At first, he whipped him with an iron rod. After it broke, he began to beat him with the copper one. This one also broke, and after that, he began to beat him with the tin one.

The tin rod was bending but not breaking. It was wrapping around his back. Andrey was beating him, and Kot Bayun began to tell fairy tales: about priests, about psalm readers, about priest's daughters. Andrey didn't listen to him. He just kept threshing the cat with the rod.

The cat was at the end of his rope. He saw that he wouldn't fool Andrey with smooth talk, and he started to beg, "Please leave me alone, good man! I'll do everything for you, whatever you need."

"Will you come with me?"

"Yes, I'll go wherever you want to go."

Andrey went back and took the cat with him. When he reached his tsardom, he went with the cat to the palace and said to the tsar, "So and so, I did the task, got you Kot Bayun."

The tsar was surprised and said, "Well, Kot Bayun, show me what's your great passion."

The cat began to sharpen his claws, placed them on the tsar, wanted to tear his white chest and take the heart out.

The tsar got scared. "Andrey the shooter, please stop Kot Bayun!"

Andrey calmed the cat, locked him in a cage, and went home to Marya Tsarevna. He started to live out his days in enjoyment with his young wife.

The tsar was even more sparked by his romantic interest. He called his adviser. "Think up something to get rid of Andrey the shooter. Otherwise, my sword will cut off your head."

The royal adviser went straight to the tavern, found there a tavern drinker in a tattered caftan, and asked him for help, to give him some idea. The tavern drinker drank a glass of wine and wiped his mustache.

He said, "Go to the tsar and say: tell him to send Andrey the shooter to go I know not where and fetch I know not what. Andrey will never accomplish this task and won't return."

The royal adviser ran back to the tsar and reported everything to him. The tsar sent for Andrey.

"You did two tasks for me, so do it a third time: go I know not where and fetch I know not what. If you manage to do it, I'll reward you royally. Otherwise, my sword will cut off your head."

Andrey came home, sat down on a bench, and began to cry.

Marya Tsarevna asked him, "Why are you unhappy, my dear? Has some other misfortune happened?"

He answered, "I bear all these misfortunes because of your beauty! The tsar told me to go I know not where and fetch I know not what."

"Well, this is a really complex task! But it's fine. Go to bed. The morning is wiser than the evening."

Marya Tsarevna waited until nightfall, opened her magic book, read it for a while, then left it and seized her head in her hands: in it nothing was said about the tsar's riddle. Marya Tsarevna went out onto the porch, took out a handkerchief, and started waving it. All kinds of birds flew to her and all kinds of animals came running up to her.

Marya Tsarevna asked them, "Forest animals, sky-high birds, you, animals, roam everywhere, and you, birds, fly everywhere. Have you ever heard how to go I know not where and fetch I know not what?"

The animals and birds answered, "No, Marya Tsarevna, we haven't heard of that."

Marya Tsarevna waved her handkerchief one more time, and the animals and birds disappeared, as if they had never showed up. She waved once more, and two giants appeared in front of her. "What do you need?"

"My faithful servants, take me to the middle of the Ocean-Sea."

The giants picked up Marya Tsarevna, carried her to the Ocean-Sea, and stopped in the middle, over the very abyss. They stood like pillars and held her in their arms. Marya Tsarevna waved her handkerchief, and all the reptiles and sea fishes came swimming to her.

"You, reptiles and sea fishes, you swim everywhere, you visit all the islands: have you ever heard how to go to I know not where and fetch I know not what?"

"No, Marya Tsarevna, we haven't heard about this."

Marya Tsarevna began to grow sad and asked to be carried home. The giants took her up, brought her to Andrey's yard, and placed her near the porch.

Early in the morning Marya Tsarevna prepared Andrey for the journey and gave him a ball of yarn and an embroidered piece of cloth. "Throw the ball in front of yourself and go wherever it rolls. And remember, wherever you go, don't wipe yourself with someone else's piece of cloth. Use mine instead."

Andrey said goodbye to Marya Tsarevna, bowed to the four winds, and went behind the outpost. He threw the ball of yarn in front of him. The ball rolled, and Andrey followed it.

It is tales that are quickly spun; deeds are sooner said than done. Andrey passed through many tsardoms and lands. The ball rolled, and the yarn stretched from it. The ball became small, about the size of a chicken's head. It became so little that it wasn't possible to see it on the road. Andrey reached a forest and saw a little hut perched on chicken legs.

"Little hut, little hut, turn your front to me and back to the forest!"

The hut turned around. Andrey walked in and saw a gray-haired old woman sitting on a bench and spinning.

"Eww, eww, the Russian spirit hasn't been heard, hasn't been seen, but now it has come by itself. I'll roast you in the heating stove, eat you, and ride on your bones."

Andrey answered the old woman, "What are you going to do, old Baba Yaga, eat a traveler?! I'm bony and unclean. You better heat up the steam bath, wash me, steam me, and only then eat."

Baba Yaga heated the bathhouse. Andrey took a steam bath, washed himself, took out his wife's piece of cloth, and began to wipe himself with it.

Baba Yaga asked, "Where did you get this piece of cloth? It was embroidered by my daughter."

"Your daughter is my wife. She gave me this piece of cloth."

"Ah, dear son-in-law, how can I entertain you?"

Then Baba Yaga prepared supper, placed many sorts of foods, wines, and honeys in front of him. Andrey didn't hesitate. He sat at the table and started to eat with zest. Baba Yaga sat next to him. He ate and she asked him how he had married Marya Tsarevna, and if the two of them lived together well.

Andrey told her everything: how he got married and how the tsar sent him to go I know not where and fetch I know not what.

"I wish you could help me, grandma!"

"Ah, son-in-law, even I have never heard of this wonder of wonders. However, one old frog knows about it. She's lived in a swamp for three hundred years. Well, it's fine. Go to bed. The morning is wiser than the evening."

Andrey went to bed, and Baba Yaga took two brooms, flew to the swamp, and began to call out, "Grandmother, jumping frog, are you alive?"

"Alive."

"Come out to me from the swamp."

The old frog came out from the swamp, and Baba Yaga asked her, "Do you know where is I know not what."

"I know."

"Do me a favor and tell me. My son-in-law was assigned a task to go I know not where and fetch I know not what."

The frog replied, "I would have shown him the way, but I'm too old. I won't be able to jump to that place. If your son-in-law will carry me in fresh milk all the way to the River of Fire, then I'll tell you."

Baba Yaga took the jumping frog, flew home, milked some milk into a pot, put the frog in it, and early in the morning woke up Andrey. "Well, my dear son-in-law, get dressed, take this pot of fresh milk. There is a frog in the milk. Sit on my horse. He will take you to the fiery river. Leave the horse there and take the frog out of the pot. She will show you."

Andrey got dressed, took the pot, sat on Baba Yaga's horse. I don't know how long the trip was, but the horse quickly delivered him to the River of Fire. There is no animal that was able to jump over it; no bird was able to fly over it.

When Andrey got off his horse, the frog said to him, "Take me out of the pot, good friend. We need to cross this river."

Andrey took the frog out of the pot and put it on the ground.

"Well, good fellow, now sit on my back."

"But how, grandma? You're so little. I might crush you to death."

"Don't be afraid. You won't. Sit down and hold on tight."

Andrey sat on the jumping frog. She began to inflate herself. She inflated herself to the size of a haystack.

"Are you holding on tight?"

"Tight, grandma."

Again, the frog pouted, pouted, became even bigger, like a haystack.

"Are you holding on tight?"

"Yes, grandma."

She continued to inflate herself and became taller than the dark forest, and then she jumped over the River of Fire, carried Andrey to the other bank, and became small again.

"Go, good friend, along this path, and you'll see a palace. Not a palace, a hut. Not a hut, a barn. Not a barn. Go in it and stand behind the heating stove. There you'll find something I know not what."

Andrey went along the path and saw the old hut, which was not actually a hut, surrounded by a fence, without windows, without a porch. He went in and hid behind the heating stove.

A little later, there was a knock, thunder throughout the forest, and a tiny man with a long beard entered the hut and shouted, "Hey, in-law Naum, I want to eat!"

After he shouted, out of nowhere a table with a lot of food appeared. There were a keg of beer and a baked bull with a sharp knife in its side. The tiny man with a long beard sat down next to the bull, took out a sharp knife, began to cut the meat, dip it in garlic, eat it, and compliment his fare.

He ate the whole bull until the last bone, drank a whole barrel of beer.

"Hey, in-law Naum, clean up the leftovers!"

Suddenly the table disappeared, as though it had never been there, no bones and no keg. Andrey waited for the tiny man to leave, went out from behind the heating stove, got up the nerve to call, "In-law Naum, feed me."

After he called, quite unexpectedly a table appeared. There were various viands, snacks, wines, and honeys on it.

Andrey sat down at the table and said, "In-law Naum, sit down with me, brother. Let's eat and drink together."

An invisible voice answered him, "Thank you, good man! I have been serving here for so many years. I have never received even a burnt crust, and you offered me a seat at the table."

Andrey looked and wondered. No one was visible, but the dishes from the table seemed to be swept away with a whisk, wines and honeys were pouring into the glass by themselves. A glass was jumping here and there.

Andrey asked, "In-law Naum, show yourself to me!"

"No, no one can see me. I'm something, I don't know what."

"In-law Naum, do you want to work for me?"

"Why wouldn't I want to? I see you are a kind person."

They ate. Andrey said, "Well, clean up everything and come with me."

Andrey went out of the hut and looked around. "In-law Naum, are you here?"

"I'm here. Don't be afraid. I won't be slow."

Andrey reached the fiery river. The frog was waiting for him there. "Good friend, did you fetch I know not what?"

"I found it, grandma."

"Get on top of me."

Andrey again sat on the frog. It began to inflate, became swollen, jumped, and carried him across the fiery river.

Then he thanked the jumping frog and went his own way back to his tsardom. He walked for a while and turned around. "In-law Naum, are you here?"

"Here. Don't be afraid. I won't be slow."

Andrey walked. The journey was long. His fast legs got tired, and he lowered his hands. He said, "Oh, how tired I am!"

And the in-law Naum said to him, "Why didn't you tell me before? I can quickly take you to your destination."

A vigorous whirlwind picked Andrey up and carried him away. Mountains and forests, cities and villages flashed below him. Andrey flew over the deep sea, and suddenly he became scared. "In-law Naum, it would be nice to take a break!"

The wind weakened immediately, and Andrey began to descend to the sea. He looked down and saw an island in the middle of the clamorous blue waves. There was a palace with a golden roof and a beautiful garden all around that island.

In-law Naum said to Andrey, "Rest, eat, drink, and look at the sea from time to time. Three merchant ships will sail not far away. Call the merchants. Wine and dine them. They have three wonders. Exchange me for these wonders. Don't be afraid. I'll come back to you."

After a while, three ships were sailing from the western side. The sailors saw an island. There was a palace with a golden roof on it and a beautiful garden all around.

"What kind of wonder is that?" they said. "We've sailed here many times, but saw nothing but the blue sea. Let's go to shore."

The three ships cast anchor, and the three merchant-shipowners boarded a light boat and sailed to the island.

Andrey the shooter met them. "Welcome, dear guests."

The merchant-shipowners were walking and looking around with wonder. The roof of the palace blazed like fire, birds sang on the trees, and wonderful animals jumped along the paths.

"Tell me, good man, who built this wonder of wonders here?"

"My servant, in-law Naum, built it within one night." Andrey led the guests inside the palace. "Hey, in-law Naum, prepare for us something to drink and eat!"

A prepared table appeared out of nowhere. Wine and food were on it, whatever floats your boat. The merchant-shipowners only gasped.

They said, "Come on, good friend, let's swap. Let us have your servant, in-law Naum. You can take any wonder from us in exchange for him."

"Why not swap? What kind of wonders do you have?"

One merchant took out a club from somewhere under his clothes. Just tell this club, "Come on, club, beat this man!" and the club will begin to beat by itself. It'll break the resistance of any strong man."

Another merchant pulled an axe from the front of his coat, turned it with its back edge up. The axe began to chop by itself. A few strikes and a ship appeared; another few strikes, another ship was ready. There were sails, cannons, and brave sailors on it. Ships were sailing, cannons were firing, brave sailors were asking for orders. He turned the axe with its back edge down, and the ships disappeared immediately, as if they had not been there.

The third merchant took a pipe out of his pocket and blew it. An army appeared: both cavalry and infantry, with rifles and cannons. Troops were marching, music was thundering, banners were waving in the breeze, and horsemen were galloping and asking for orders. The merchant blew the pipe from the other end, and everything was suddenly gone.

Andrey the shooter said, "Your wonders are good, but mine is more expensive. If you want to change, give me all three wonders in exchange for my servant, in-law Naum."

"Won't it be too much?"

"It's up to you. Otherwise, I won't swap."

The merchants thought hard. "What do we need a club, an axe, and a pipe for? It's better to swap. With the help of in-law Naum, we'll be full and drunk every day and night."

The merchant-shipowners gave Andrey the club, axe, and pipe and shouted, "Hey, in-law Naum, we'll take you with us! Will you serve us faithfully?"

An invisible voice answered them, "Why wouldn't I serve you? I don't care whom I stay with."

The merchant-shipowners returned to their ships and started to feast. They were drinking, eating, and screaming, "In-law Naum, turn around, give us this one and that one!"

They all got rip-roaring drunk and fell to sleep in the same place where they sat.

Meanwhile the shooter was sitting alone in the palace and felt sad. Oh, he was thinking, "Where is my faithful servant, in-law Naum?"

"I'm here. What do you need?"

Andrey brightened up. "In-law Naum, isn't it time for us to go to our native land, to my young wife? Carry me home."

A whirlwind picked up Andrey again and carried him to his tsardom, to his native land.

The merchants woke up and wanted to take a drink to cure a hangover. "Hey, in-law Naum, prepare for us something to drink and eat. Hurry up!"

No matter how much they called, or screamed, it had no effect. They looked, and the island had disappeared. Only blue waves were making noise in the place where it had been.

The merchant-shipowners grieved for a while. "Oh, an evil-minded person cheated us!"

But there was nothing to be done. They hoisted the sails and navigated to the place where they needed to go.

Andrey the shooter flew to his native land, landed near his house, and saw that instead of it only a scorched chimney was sticking out. He hung his head and went from the city to the shore of the blue sea, to an empty place. He sat on the sand. Suddenly, out of nowhere a grey-blue turtledove flew in, hit the ground, and turned into his young wife, Marya Tsarevna. They hugged, greeted each other, began to ask each other questions and to tell everything.

Marya Tsarevna said, "Since you left home, I have been flying in the form of a grey-blue turtledove through forests and groves. The tsar sent for me three times, but they didn't find me and burned down the house."

Andrey said, "In-law Naum, can we build a palace in this empty place by the blue sea?"

"Why not? It will be done immediately."

They didn't even have time to look around before the palace appeared. It emerged and it looked astonishing, better than the tsar's. There was a green garden around it, birds sang on the trees, and wonderful animals jumped along the paths.

Andrey the shooter and Marya Tsarevna went up to the palace, sat by the window, and talked to each other, admiring each other. They lived well and they didn't experience any distress for three days in a row.

The tsar at that time went hunting along the coast of the blue sea and saw a palace in the place where there had been nothing. "What kind of crude person has decided to build a house on my land without asking me?"

Messengers ran, scouted out everything, and reported to the tsar that the palace was set up by Andrey the shooter and that he lived in it with his young wife, Marya Tsarevna.

The tsar became even more angry and sent messengers to find out if Andrey had gone to I know not where and fetched I know not what.

Messengers ran, scouted out, and reported, "Andrey the shooter went to I know not where and fetched I know not what."

After that, the tsar became angry to the bone, ordered an army to gather and go to the seaside, ruin that palace to the ground, and put Andrey the shooter and Marya Tsarevna to a fierce death.

Andrey saw that a strong army was coming at him. He quickly grabbed the axe, turned it with its back edge up. The axe began to chop by itself: a few strikes and a ship appeared; another few strikes, another ship. He chopped a hundred times, and a hundred ships started to sail across the blue sea.

Andrey took out the pipe and blew it, and suddenly an army appeared: both cavalry and infantry, with cannons and banners. The commanders were jumping, waiting for orders. Andrey ordered them to start the battle. The music began to play, the drums beat, and the regiments started to move. The infantry defeated the royal soldiers; the cavalry galloped and took them prisoner. And cannons from a hundred ships were shelling the capital city.

The tsar saw that his army was fleeing and rushed to the soldiers to stop them. Then Andrey took out his club. "Come on, club, beat this tsar!"

The club itself started to move like a wheel. It flipped from one end to another across the open field. It overtook the tsar and killed him by hitting him in the forehead. After that, the battle ended. The people poured out of the city and began to ask Andrey the shooter to take the whole state into his hands.

Andrey didn't argue. He arranged a sumptuous feast and ruled this tsardom together with Marya Tsarevna until his old age.

Source: Nukadeti.ru, "Поди туда не знаю куда, принеси то не знаю что." Translated from the Russian by Vadym Grebniev.

The Nobleman Zaoleshanin

This story is said to be the first narrative account of Baba Yaga. It appears in a collection of literary fairy tales in Russkie skazki *[Russian Fairy Tales] that depict the exploits of various heroes. One story leads into the other, but in this one, the hero encounters Baba Yaga. The book was originally published in 1780 by Vasilii Levshin.*

The end of Gromoboy's and Milana's adventure and the beginning of nobleman Zaoleshanin's own story.

The life of the newly married couple flowed in perfect prosperity, their love toward one another was increasing, and they had nothing else to desire but to love each other forever. Milana was only worried about not getting pregnant during the prefeast of Didilia because she wanted to raise her little son with her breast, and she swore that she would not give away someone who should look like Gromoboy.

Milana often asked the priest when the festivity of Didilia would be celebrated. He announced it; however, she forgot about that in the evening, and on the day of this feast Dobrada showed up to wish them a good morning.

"You forgot the prediction," she told them. "But what should happen, will happen. Gromoboy, you will become the father of a glorious bogatyr, who will fill the whole world with the sound of his great deeds. I know that this is flattering for you, but I didn't come to congratulate you," she said with a friendly smile. "I came to comfort Milana and prepare her in advance for the separation from her son, whom she will not see from his birthday until he turns thirty. I hope that you, my daughter," she said to Milana, "will honorably bear this twist of fate. Don't worry about his upbringing. I will take care of that myself. Goodbye, Milana! Don't cry because you won't play with a baby, but be glad that you will become the mother of a great man who will adorn your name with glory and honor."

She disappeared after saying that. Milana began to cry, but Gromoboy knew how to comfort her and prepare her for handing over their son to Dobrada after nine months. This time passed, and as soon as they kissed their beautiful baby, the sorceress showed up, took the boy from their hands, and carried him away beyond the Klyazma forests. That's why this bogatyr was nicknamed "the nobleman Zaoleshanin," although, however, his first name was Zvenislav.

Now let's leave his parents because, during thirty years, in which they did not see their son, nothing bad happened to them. They pursued a calm and pleasant lifestyle, and Gromoboy soon managed to make his dear wife forget that she would not bring up their son herself.

Dobrada brought the baby to the magical castle, handed him over to the rusalki of those forests, commanded them to guard him, and assigned the lioness to be his foster mother. This wild animal handled her duties with great diligence, and the child grew beyond his years. The lovely maidens of the woods kept their eyes on him, and they enjoyed looking at his beauty.

At the age of six, Zvenislav was already as tall as an average man and was so strong that he was able to knock down with his fist a big oak tree out of its roots. His intelligence corresponded to his height; it evolved ahead of time and made him capable of accepting instructions.

Dobrada tried her best to spruce up his talents with knowledge of sciences. She came, rewarded the lioness for her labor with wings, and took Zvenislav away to the great regret of the forest nymphs. The rusalki of these forests were so upset by this loss that since that time they no longer braid their green hair. They are sometimes seen running with disheveled hair or swinging on birch branches and uttering complaints.

Zvenislav was transferred to the chambers of the twelve wise men, which are located in the East, on the barely accessible mountain of truth. Scientists traveled to these chambers, but only a few of them succeeded in reaching that place after overcoming the struggle. The wise men accepted Zvenislav as their own son at the request of Dobrada. For as long as ten years they provided him foundational knowledge, taught sciences and exercises of the body, and by the end of this time, he was an example of erudition, good manners, courage, and heroic qualities. The sorceress showed up again and thanked the wise men for their work, picked up the bogatyr, and led him to the bottom of the mountain along a golden staircase decorated with multi-colored carpets.

She stopped in a spacious valley and said to him, "My dear son! I can call you by this name because your parents gave you only your life, and I made you capable of living it out in glory and virtue. Your fate is not the best one, because you will not have peace of mind until you turn thirty. You will not know and see your parents until you reach this age. Troubles and dangers will accompany your deeds, and righteousness will be your only helper. I am the sorceress Dobrada, whom you consider to be your mother. Although I have great power and am able to set the world on fire, do not expect protection from me. Even though I love you so much, I have no power to help you. Your courage and magnanimity should be your defense against all misfortunes. Endure all ups and downs, be vivacious in troubles and moderate in happiness. Don't forget about justice. Always keep your promise, and don't do unto others what you would not have done unto you. Protect the oppressed, respect the female kind, choose from them a worthy one for yourself, so that she will make happy the last days of your life, but do not overindulge yourself and do not become a slave to their assets. When you turn thirty, and I see that you did not turn away from virtue, I will commend your courage and return you to your parents. Don't ask me anything and go wherever you want. From now on you will begin to be a bogatyr, because I initiate you into this title."

Having said this, she put armor on him, belted on a sword, handed him a spear, and ordered him to get himself a mighty horse. Then she blew on him and disappeared from his sight, and Zvenislav found himself in a terrible desert.

The bogatyr thought while sitting under the shade of a tree that was growing there, "What will I start with? Where can I go? I don't know where I am or where my homeland is. I'm not allowed to see my parents, and I don't even know where they are. My kind-hearted sorceress left me to my own fate. I am a bogatyr and must go on travels, but do I look like a bogatyr without having a horse? Is it possible to find him in the desert, where I, most likely, will starve to death? However, Dobrada told me to be patient, and I'm starting my new title very poorly because I show such cowardice in myself."

After this discourse, he cheered up and began to admire his weapon and examine it. Its high quality amused him and reminded him again about the horse. "Ah, if I were not in the desert, the first bogatyr that met me would have provided me with it; but here I have no hope of testing my courage."

He would have continued to think like that, but a heavy sigh that had spilt to his ears stopped it. Zvenislav looked around in all directions to figure out where it had come from, but he could not see anyone. He was surprised because there was nothing anyone could hide behind except the tree under which he was sitting.

He could not restrain himself from shouting, "Unfortunate person! Whoever you are, don't hide from me. You should not be afraid to show yourself to a hero, who will consider it a pleasure to protect you if you endure oppression."

A voice answered him, "Ah, a virtuous bogatyr. What thanks the unfortunate Lyubana would owe you if it was in your power to return her first appearance."

The bogatyr said with amazement, "Where are you? Do not be afraid to appear to the person who is obliged to maintain respect for your gender."

The voice answered, "You are near me. The tree, which gave you protection from the sun's rays, is looking for your protection. This is me, the unfortunate. I was brought to this state by the anger of Baba

Yaga. It was not enough for her to deprive me of my beloved prince, she also turned me into this tree. If you find in yourself enough humanity to help me, and enough courage to kill the winged serpent that dwells in this desert, then do not hesitate to return to me my human appearance by anointing me with the bile of this serpent."

The tree couldn't continue to speak. Her sobs stopped his speech, but this was enough to inflame the knight to the accomplishment of this glorious feat. He said, "Lyubana, be sure that I will perish or I will bring you the bile that you need." He said so and went to look for the monster.

Zvenislav spent the whole day climbing the steep cliffs of stone mountains, crossing rapids and dangerous abysses but did not meet a single living creature. He felt exhausted when he reached a pleasant meadow. He saw a river that was flowing through it. The transparent stream urged him to quench his thirst. As he was drinking, thinking about the serpent, he felt annoyed that he had not found the creature. Suddenly, he saw a girl who was driving a herd of sheep to the place where he was sitting. The beauty of this girl was so great that the bogatyr could not protect himself from the movements that happened in his heart. He jumped up and knelt before her full of amazement.

He said, "I don't know whether you are a divine being or a mortal one. In any case, I am happy to see you."

The girl answered while feeling embarrassed, "Don't lower your standards, knight. I am not worthy of your flattery. Baba Yaga's bondmaid does not deserve such respect."

Zvenislav said, "This does not prevent me from giving you justice and offering you my services. You just have to command, and I will force Baba Yaga to return your freedom to you." He was even more captivated by her modesty.

The girl seemed to be touched by that. She approached the bogatyr, lifted his face, and answered, "I am way too thankful for your generosity, brave bogatyr, and I don't want to endanger your precious life for my freedom. I know the power of Baba Yaga, which is supported by the strongest witchcraft. To avoid it, please leave quickly. I would be very sorry if you paid with your life because of meeting with me."

Her sheep satisfied their thirst, and she drove them away.

Zvenislav couldn't stop her, and begging her to show him Baba Yaga's dwelling had no effect. The beauty retreated, and the bogatyr remained behind greatly confused. He asked his heart what effect this meeting had produced in him, and found out that it was captivated to the extreme by the qualities of this bondmaid. He was wondering whether he should follow his temptation and whether it would not contradict his title to fall in love with a simple serf. His heart got the better of him, took advantage of the situation, and made him forget to look for the serpent.

Zvenislav stopped and waited for the morning on the bank of the river and hoped that in the morning he would again see the girl driving her herd. Some herbs helped him to fill up his stomach, but sleep escaped from his eyes. He was filled with thought of the one who had stolen his peace.

He thought, "Gods! It makes no sense for my soul to have feelings of love, which I have never known before, just so I love without hope. This beauty didn't want to stay with me. My fascination with her didn't keep her here. Oh! She didn't find anything to attract her to me."

After these passionate thoughts, he asked himself, "What do I want? I wish to be loved by a girl who doesn't know who I am, and to whom I cannot tell about myself. How can I convince her to love me back? Do my situation and the troubles, which were promised to me for another fourteen years, allow me to offer her decent conditions of life? No, a travelling bogatyr must not have a wife, but even if it was possible, why should I endanger her. Forget, Zvenislav, about your indecent temptation and think only of your glory."

But his heart had other ideas. It said, "Zvenislav, look for a way to please this girl. She is the one who, according to Dobrada, will make your upcoming days happy. Look for a way to make her feel obligated to you by releasing her from slavery. Conquer her heart by doing that, return her to her fatherland, and then she won't be indifferent to your actions."

So, he decided to follow the power of love. The morning again led his beloved shepherdess to the river banks. She didn't think that the knight would dare spend the night near such a dangerous place. Because of that, she began to wash her feet without noticing him.

The happy bogatyr didn't dare breathe and thought that only a goddess could have such well-shaped, white legs. Their loveliness made Zvenislav vow not to love anyone else in the world if she would not love him.

The girl sat down and, thinking that she was alone, sighed and said, "Can anyone be more unhappy than me? Oh, my cruel fate! Is it not enough for you that you have separated me from my fatherland and made me the last servant of Baba Yaga out of the prince's daughters? And you decided to subject me to cruel feelings of hopeless love before I could control my mind."

Zvenislav said, "She already loves me," and his heart began to tremble.

But the girl brought him out of his nervousness and was ready to plunge him into jealousy by continuing her complaint, "Oh handsome knight! If only you hadn't met me so I wouldn't know who you are. If only I didn't have a hope of ever seeing you. Why should you contaminate my soul in this very place? If you showed up at the court of my father, there, maybe, I would manage to hold you. In that place, maybe it would be more convenient for me to reward you not only with my heart but also with the crown. But you have already gone, gallant knight. I have no hope of seeing you again. Ah, it's my fault. He did try to persuade me yesterday not to go away that fast. He didn't have feeling toward me and…"

"Gods! You love me, beautiful princess!" screamed Zvenislav and with the last word was already at her feet.

He couldn't speak anymore. The princess also became speechless because of confusion and a sense of shame that someone got to know her secret feelings.

But Zvenislav soon came to his senses. Joy and love made him eloquent. He said, "So, fair princess, is it possible to be mindless after having a good fortune to see you? You would have seen me dying in this place if I had not found out that I am the happiest man alive. The loveliest of your kind, don't regret that I accidentally found out about something that, perhaps, you wanted forever buried in your soul. If you reward the most passionate person with your love, then believe that he is also most respectful one and would agree to pass the sword through his breast a thousand times, rather than make you regret your love."

"Oh, great goddess Lada!" said the princess. "It couldn't have let you find out better about my secret feelings if I had purposefully arranged it. Don't let me waste the opportunity, so I can make happy the one who will create my own happiness. It's too late for me to hide, dear knight since you found out what is happening in my soul. I admit that I would be always unhappy if you didn't find out about this, or if you had been indifferent when you parted with me yesterday. I was overcome by your perfection since I first glanced at you. I thought I would sigh forever, having no hope of seeing you again, and decided that I wouldn't belong to anyone. Not to see you! My soul couldn't bear the pain! I couldn't fall asleep. I would have gone to look for you in this desert, if only my tormentor didn't lock me up every night in the storage closet and if I didn't fear I'd betray you into her hands. But do you believe, Zvenislav, that the gods will bless our love?"

"How do you know my name?" screamed the bogatyr while kissing her hands incessantly.

"I know more about you than you know about yourself. Listen, when I was hopeless to see you again and fell asleep before sunrise. A magnificent woman in a white dress appeared to me. She said, 'My daughter! Don't be ashamed of the feelings that an unknown bogatyr triggered in you. These feelings are blessed by the heavens because he has been appointed to be your savior and future husband. But before you get married, you'll have to endure many obstacles.' After that, she told me who you were but forbade me to tell you any of this if I saw you. She became invisible, and I woke up. To my greatest pleasure, I came to this place again."

Zvenislav's joy about this happy news was unspeakable. The princess, in return, didn't consider it a crime to accept her lover's tenderness and responded to him with mutual affection. They pledged eternal allegiance to one another. After their initial pleasures were over, Zvenislav was curious about his lover and what disaster had occurred that made her fall under the power of Baba Yaga.

The princess answered him, "My adventures are insignificant. My name is Alzana. I'm the daughter of Kotaged, the prince who rules over the strong tribe Obry, which live on the great river Danube. My father was a great fan of hunting. He often took my mother to the woods. I was only ten years old when my mother was invited on such a hunt, and she took me with her. The traps were set and the animal chase began. Since I've been an infant, I had practiced handling arms along with my brother Tarbels. I was permitted to try my luck with arrows in a chase. First, I chased foxes, then a wild goat, and then I trudged away from my parents. Suddenly, a great whirlwind arose, the trees were bending on both sides, and I saw Baba Yaga hopping on a mortar, which she was driving with an iron pestle like a horse. She was so scary that when I saw her, I trembled. Who wouldn't be frightened?

"Imagine a skinny woman with dark skin, about 16 feet tall, whose teeth protruded on both sides like those of a wild pig. Her teeth were three feet long. Moreover, her hands were bear claws. She rushed forward, grabbed me, and took me away with her. And even though my bodyguards shot a rain of arrows at her, they didn't harm her. I was terrified and heard only my parents' pitiful groans. Since then, I haven't seen them. At two o'clock, Baba Yaga brought me on her mortar to her nearby dwelling. Taking into account our speed, I think we covered at least two thousand miles. I cried disconsolately and felt even worse when I saw that Baba Yaga was getting ready for dinner and took out a fried boy of about six years old from the heating stove. I expected that I too would satisfy the hunger of my kidnapper. However, Baba Yaga reassured me that she in respect for my origins would accept me as her daughter and entrust her herd to me. I regarded my fate as a happy one. I think anyone would have the same thoughts in my situation because it is better for a prince's daughter to be Baba Yaga's shepherd girl than to become roast meat on her table.

"I've been living like this for three years. I'm starting to get used to my fate, although I regret seeing the death of innocent children, whom my witch steals and devours. Every day, as soon as the sun rises, she goes to catch her prey and usually returns by noon. She entrusts me the use of her house and doesn't allow me to enter only one garden. There, she keeps safe a winged serpent. She visits him every day and returns from him sometimes in tears, and sometimes in great anger, which always ends with her sighing. I think this serpent is her lover. Even though he is a monster, he doesn't seem to want to respond to her passion."

Zvenislav exclaimed, "Ah, princess, I think this very snake is the one I'm looking for and from which I must take out bile to free an enchanted tree."

Suddenly Alzana screamed, "Gods!"

Zvenislav saw at that moment a winged, ghastly serpent attacking her. Before he managed to draw his sword to protect her, the monster swallowed his beloved one and flew off the ground. His heart turned into stone. Zvenislav couldn't grieve, but despair prompted him to run after and tear the monster to pieces. As he was chasing the serpent, it seemed that it couldn't fly for a long distance. From time to time, it came down to the ground, so Zvenislav ran faster.

He almost managed to reach the serpent, and blows from his sword had already dinged its long tail, but the serpent hit the cliff of the stone mountain. It opened wide, hid the snake inside, and closed again.

Zvenislav didn't see how he could either get revenge or perish, so he fell to the ground, shed tears, and screamed in despair, "Alas! I was born under an ill-fated constellation of stars! Why did I receive this unbearable defeat? Why have you shown me this most perfect princess, whom I felt the cruelest love for, and later on deprive me of her forever? Oh, I can't overcome my sorrow, nor can I continue to live."

He was ready to impale himself on his sword, but then the words of the kind-hearted sorceress entered into his thoughts. He lowered his desperate hand and blamed his weakness.

He said, "Will patience build my character and lead me to glory? I won't be able to return you, beauteous Alzana, but should I leave your death unavenged?"

He said this, and his heart filled with bogatyr rage. He got up, went to this mountain, which prevented him from catching up with the monster, and in anger struck it with a sword. He stopped in surprise and saw that the mountain had disappeared. He found himself standing at the gates of a castle, surrounded by iron poles instead of walls, on which human heads stuck out.

He exclaimed, "This is the dwelling of Baba Yaga; a monster dwells here."

After saying that, he put his hands between the poles and tore the wall apart. But what a view awaited him inside the courtyard! The serpent was vomiting up the body of his beloved Alzana. He began to boil with a vengeance and rushed with the sword toward the monster. After seeing him, the snake left the body, which it was preparing to crush with its poisonous teeth, and rose to its hind legs to tear Zvenislav apart with its front claws. It opened its mouth and displayed a fiery tongue and two rows of razor-like teeth.

The knight wasn't scared and plunged his sword into the snake's throat, but the serpent swallowed the sword without causing the monster any harm. Zvenislav's only hope was a spear. He struck it in the chest of the monster and broke it over its hard scales. What was left for Zvenislav? Only his fearlessness, and he used it instead of weapons. He attacked the serpent, grabbed its neck with one hand, caught its front legs with the other, and tore the monster into pieces.

After satisfying his anger, Zvenislav remembered he had promised to get the serpent's bile to help the transformed tree. He examined the snake's intestines, found what he wanted, pulled out the gall bladder, and at that moment thick smoke covered the monster's corpse. The bogatyr stepped away in amazement. The smoke rose into the air, and the corpse disappeared. Even more surprising, Zvenislav saw a handsome warrior standing in that place. Being prepared for other enchantments in Baba Yaga's dwelling, he was expecting a new attack.

But the warrior rushed to him to embrace him. "My savior!" he exclaimed. "You're my relative, because the divine oracle cannot lie. You are my sister's appointed protector and her future husband, because none other than the brave Zvenislav would have dared to come to these deathly lands."

Zvenislav exclaimed, "You are Tarbels! You are the brother of my beloved Alzana," and embraced him in his arms.

"Yes, it's true, fearless knight," the warrior answered.

"But let's put the pleasantries aside, dear Tarbels," said Zvenislav and shed tears. "I'm destined only to seek your friendship. I cannot be your brother-in-law. Look at the mournful object of my eternal despair." He pointed to the body of Tarbel's sister.

"The gods cannot lie," said Tarbels. "I won't despair yet."

A terrible whirlwind interrupted his speech.

"Let's get ready to die or win," Tarbels said to Zvenislav. "That whirlwind announces Baba Yaga's return."

"We'll die when it's destined," answered Zvenislav, "but the witch won't get much. She'll pay a high price for my life."

Then the bogatyr, deprived of weapons, picked up an iron pole from the fence, which he had broken, and Tarbels drew his sword.

The sky darkened because a great number of ravens, vultures, big and small owls had flown in. They hovered over Baba Yaga's courtyard, emitting a vile cry, which should have horrified the warriors before the witch's arrival. However, she didn't give the bogatyrs time to think and appeared on her mortar, urging on her chariot with the blows of her pestle. Her eyes looked like red-hot coals, bloody foam was pouring from her mouth, and her fangs were gnashing with a terrible sound. She roared, jumping off her mortar and throwing down the pestle.

"Wow! Finally, you're here, Zvenislav! Today my meal will be delicious. You have come to deprive me of my precious prey, and you're right on time. I'm very hungry."

After saying this, she extended her terrible claws and stretched out her hands to rip the hero to pieces. Zvenislav prevented this by hitting both the witch's hands with a fierce blow. The iron pole fell to pieces, and the witch grunted. Sparks shot out from her hands from the blow, but they didn't break. Baba Yaga pulled them back and began to blow on them. Meanwhile, Zvenislav grabbed the saber from Tarbels' hands and began to chop the witch down. The witch defended herself with her hands. She also used her fangs and inflicted intense blows on Zvenislav through the impenetrable armor.

The battle was intense. The bogatyr did not have mercy upon the witch, and she lost all her fingers and claws. However, the saber became stuck and useless. The knight was left without a weapon, and the witch still had her terrible fangs. She made a deep indent on Zvenislav's helmet.

Then Tarbels, surprised by the fearlessness and agility of the knight, saw that he needed to help, because although Zvenislav was incessantly beating Baba Yaga's cheeks until they turned purple and became swollen, her fangs badly scratched his hands. Tarbels rushed forward and grabbed her fangs so that he grasped the top one with one hand and the bottom one with the other. He stretched open her mouth and allowed his companion to grab another iron pole.

Baba Yaga was moving away from Tarbels, and Zvenislav couldn't hit her in the head, but he had a chance to crush her legs. He landed a thousand blows, each of which would have crushed down an oak, on the witch's bony legs. Twenty-seven iron poles broke in his hands, but her legs consisted of such a strong bone that only small chips broke off of them. However, they became very thin. The witch roared and wanted to speak magic, but only managed to poke out her tongue.

Then Tarbels, who was holding her by her fangs, bit her with his teeth. Zvenislav was ready. He grabbed the witch's tongue and pulled it out. Blood poured over Alzana's brother from his head to his feet.

Nevertheless, it was still dangerous for him to let go of her fangs, and he had to completely beat off her legs. Fortunately, a copper pillar was dug in the middle of the courtyard. Baba Yaga had tied her mortar to it like a horse, and Zvenislav pulled this pillar out. Her fate was contained within this copper pillar, because after that her bony legs broke off at the ball-and-socket joints.

Tarbels saw that victory was close and let go of the witch, but she continued to jump even without legs while babbling barbaric words. However, she could not pronounce them intelligibly without a tongue, and her witchcraft didn't work. Desperate, Baba Yaga began to roar so fiercely that Tarbels barely managed to keep his balance. She threw herself at Zvenislav's feet, and he landed a blow to the head so it flattened out. Baba Yaga's mean soul left its vile chamber and crashed down to hell. Birds of prey, which were hovering until then over the place of the bloody battle, intensified their screech, flew down to the witch's corpse, pecked it up in a twinkle of an eye so that there was no bone scrap left, and flew away.

Tarbels started to congratulate his savior on the victory, but Zvenislav after getting free, ran to shed tears over the body of his beloved princess. But he almost fainted from joy when he saw that Alzana got up, ran to him, and hugged him.

"You're alive, dearly beloved Alzana!" He couldn't say anything else.

The princess said, "Yes, my rescuer, dear Zvenislav! I'm alive, and only your fearlessness has freed your Alzana from all disasters."

Tarbels came closer and added to his sister's joy, because she hadn't expected this happy meeting. Hugs, gentle exclamations, numerous questions and answers followed.

In the end, Alzana said, "I didn't expect to find you in these chambers of horrors, dear brother!"

Tarbels replied, "I admit, my dear sister, that it's difficult to imagine how I managed to come here. It's only because of your brother's tender love for you."

Zvenislav was delighted and pleased to see how important the brother of his beloved was. Tarbels expressed his gratitude that Zvenislav didn't forget to take the bile from the killed serpent.

"Ah, my dear Zvenislav!" he said. "I am obliged to you: my own rescue is not that important, because you freed my sister from the tyrannical hands of Baba Yaga, but this bile will bring back to her former image the person who means the world to me."

Zvenislav said, "Of course, you mean that enchanted tree that stands in this desert, my dear friend. I promised Lyubana to help, but we're wasting time. Let's go!"

Tarbels couldn't say anything, but hugged Zvenislav and pulled him to his chest. Then they began to walk.

Alzana, whom Zvenislav was leading by the hand, stopped them. She said, "We can make it faster if we take the horses. Baba Yaga has three excellent mighty horses, which cost the lives of many brave bogatyrs, who wanted to get them. The fierce witch gobbled them up, tearing them apart with her sharp claws. I know the secret stable where they stand, and although they are locked with thirty locks behind the same number of doors, maybe we'll find the keys. Baba Yaga loved me and revealed that one of these horses belonged to the glorious bogatyr Tugorkan. There's a saber tied to its saddle, and no charm is efficient against it. This Tugorkan was invincible as long as he owned this horse, which was called Zlatokopyt, and this saber, no one dared to stand against him. Baba Yaga didn't dare attack him openly. She stole the horse and the saber from him, which made the unfortunate bogatyr become so depressed that he lived no more than a week after that."

"Ah, my dear lady!" exclaimed Zvenislav with joy. "You provided me with an invaluable piece of news. I have heard a lot from one of my teachers about Tugorkan, his horse and saber, or, better to say, a sword called Samosek. This Tugorkan was the right-hand man of the Old Slavonic prince Asan and conquered thirty different states for him. Asan loved him very much and erected an eternal sign over his grave. He has raised a tall burial mound in that place, which was nicknamed Bronnitsa because, even though it was so large, it was all covered with armor collected by Tugorkan from the bogatyrs whom he defeated. Ah, my good lady, please show the place where this priceless treasure is kept!"

Alzana went to the garden. Zvenislav, who wanted to acquire a nice horse and sword, did not walk, but flew. And Tarbels, although he would rather have preferred to reach his beloved tree like an arrow from a bow, could not refuse to help his rescuer obtain Zlatokopyt and Samosek.

They used the ring to lift the copper door, which Alzana had pointed out to them, went down a hundred steps to the first door of the stable. It was locked with such a huge lock that its shackle was as thick as a waist. Alzana wanted to look for keys, but Zvenislav prevented her. With one blow of his fist, he knocked down the lock and the door from the hinges.

The mighty horse realized he was about to be of use again and fall into the hands of a bogatyr similar to his former master. He began to neigh so eagerly that the arches of the underground passage shook, and he began to beat the doors with his hooves. Soon there was no obstacle left. The doors were knocked down, and they saw a horse, which kneeled before Zvenislav.

The bogatyr happily hugged him, like he was his friend, kissed him on the forehead, and caressed him. Zlatokopyt became so sensitive that tears came to his eyes as a sign of true recognition. Tarbels also found a horse and, what was most pleasant for him, a saber and a spear were tied at the saddle. He brought the horse out of the cellar. Zvenislav found the third horse and handed it over to Alzana.

After doing that, he started to walk and expected that Zlatokopyt, like a mighty horse, would voluntarily follow his rider, and it happened. Before Zvenislav sat down, he took the undefeatable sword Samosek, stuck it into the ground and kneeling, swore to Zlatokopyt in accordance to bogatyr tradition: "I swear to you, tireless horse, with this glorious weapon that until at least a drop of blood remains in my body, you will be my friend and a participant in my glory and misfortune."

After that, he drew his sword, kissed the end of it, sheathed it, and girded himself. The horse, as a sign of his loyalty and obedience, again fell to his knees, because he was not able to speak, but had a sharp mind. After the bogatyr sat on his horse, it began to jump so beautifully that it was impossible to look at this without admiration. Tarbels interrupted Zvenislav's joy, which was constantly busy with the beauty of his horse, and reminded him about his promise to Lyubana.

They started on their way through valleys and mountains, and after a few minutes got off their horses near the enchanted tree.

After seeing the tree, Tarbels shed tears. He rushed to it and hugged it. The tree swung its branches lower to the neck of Alzana's brother. Alzana couldn't understand the reason for her brother's great affection toward the soulless plant. However, Zvenislav immediately stopped her wondering or, better to say, he increased it by anointing the stub of this tree with the serpent's bile.

At that moment, the branches and bark disappeared, and a maiden appeared in its place. Her beauty could compete with the goddess of pleasures. She ran to Alzana's brother and hugged him, and he hugged her back.

They couldn't say anything else except their names: "Ah, Tarbels!" "Ah, Lyubana!" and shed joyful tears.

Zvenislav didn't miss this moment. He kissed the hands of his princess and spoke to her a thousand tender words. After that, they came to their senses, and Lyubana first freed herself from her lover's embrace in order to express her gratefulness to her savior.

Tarbels introduced her to his sister, and Alzana, understanding how much Lyubana meant to her brother, showed her true affection.

"Now, dearest Zvenislav," said prince Obrsky, "I must tell you and my sister about my and this lovely princess' adventures. By doing this, it should satisfy your curiosity, which I noticed in your eyes."

They all sat on the ground, and Tarbels started to tell his story.

Source: Levshin, *Русские сказки*. Translated from the Russian by Vadym Grebniev.

On the Origins of Baba Yaga

This is another story from Vasilii Levshin's Russkie skazki *[Russian Fairy Tales].*

The main devil, or the devil of devils, was a great chemist. He was boiling twelve evil wives in a cauldron and was hoping to extract from them the most perfect essence of evil, which would surpass even his own nature. According to his knowledge in physics, he knew that there was no substance more evil than the one he had chosen. After he conducted mathematical calculations, he found out that each evil woman contained inside herself an evil alcohol in the ratio of 7 to 22, comparing to an ordinary devil, and comparing to him exactly 1/11 part. For this reason, he was cooking twelve of them. But since the retorts had not yet been invented, he was catching particles of alcohol ascending in vapor with his mouth.

His work was nearly done. At the end there was only *caput martuum*, but he forgot and spat into the cauldron. All the alcohol mixed with his saliva and fell into this *caput mortuum*, and the devil, beyond his expectations, saw Baba Yaga arise from it. He decided that she was the most perfect evil. For this, he placed her into a glass jar, intending to extract from her by boiling a dozen more Baba Yagas, and to produce the best evil from them. But in the meantime, he determined how much evil there was in this ready-made one, and compared it with some society women. To his annoyance, he saw that they were not inferior to her in evil temper without any boiling. This made him so angry that out of frustration, he hit the jar onto the floor. It crumbled, and Baba Yaga's legs bounced off.

After he realized that by doing so, he freed the world from a fairly large amount of evil, he changed his mind and attached bony legs to Baba Yaga. He breathed a knowledge of sorcery into her, and when she left hell, instead of a carriage, he gave her a mortar, on which she still jumps around the world, creating various nasty tricks.

The following was written at the end of this story: *this news is communicated to you, curious reader, from a person who patronizes your savior. But as it has already been introduced, in order to punish the secret that was revealed against the will of a woman, then you also should be transformed for your disobedience toward Baba Yaga.*

I didn't expect that what I read was true, but as soon as I went outside the door, in the twinkling of an eye, I turned into that serpent, which you, Zvenislav, killed later on. I was horrified and fell senseless to the ground. Baba Yaga, after returning and seeing me in this state, began to roar and tear her hair out. Although she was also Yaga, she no longer found in the serpent anything to attract her to a man. She reproached me for being disobedient, mourned over my fate, and swore that she would bring me back to my former self against the will of her enemy, the sorceress Dobrada. It was she who had arranged this abusive inscription, which she could not wipe out with her sorcery and which had the power to turn me into a serpent.

After that, Baba Yaga left me, brought a cauldron, placed herbs, snakes, toads, and various poisons into it, cooked this stew for several days, stirring it with her teeth and pronouncing barbaric words unknown to me, but she couldn't fulfill her purpose. She repeated the spell a long time by various means, but I didn't feel even the slightest changes in myself. Sometimes she left me with great anger, and sometimes with tears and sighs.

At last, after losing hope of making me her lover and getting bored of keeping me without any use, she said to me, "Tarbels! My enemy Dobrada deprives me of your pleasures. She's made it a condition that if someone kills you, only then you will be restored to your former appearance. This thing alone destroys my passion for you. After finding out about this, I'll resist with all my might doing what my enemy desires. If I can no longer kill you myself, I'll make you devour everyone who can do this. I'll put bile inside of you, which can bring back my rival Lyubana to her former appearance, but this will ensure she remains forever as a tree, because no one will be able to kill you: my sorcery will protect you."

After saying this, she struck me with her magic poker, with the result that I started to feel such malice that I wanted nothing more than to swallow up and torture everyone. Even the witch had trouble defending herself from me, because I craved to please myself with her flesh. Whenever someone appeared in this desert, I had the freedom to fly out of the garden, descend, and consume him or her. However, after returning to Baba Yaga's yard (to which a force, unknown to me, dragged me), I felt such nausea that I vomited up those engorged victims. After that, I recalled everything, feeling disgusted toward myself and hiding in my garden. I don't know where those bodies disappeared, but I think they served as a meal for Baba Yaga. I only know that my anger took the life of my beloved Miroslav. I consumed him after finding him in this desert, then vomited him out, and left him in the yard.

Yet still, I believed the divine voice of the Golden Baba, but I hoped that, perhaps, he appeared dead to me only because I was spell-bound. I remember that once I saw the tree into which my Lyubana had been turned. I rushed to it in order to hug it. However, suddenly I heard a pitiful cry that came from it. This touched me so much that I jumped away and fell to the ground. I realized that Lyubana had feelings and that she didn't recognize me and was horrified. I wanted to reveal myself, but the spell didn't allow my snake tongue to utter anything but a vile whistle and wheezing. This condition struck me so much that I wanted to pull apart my belly, especially when I recalled that there was bile in me that could restore my beloved's former appearance. But my claws had no effect on me, and I returned to my dwelling with dismay. Since that time, I haven't seen her, and I never thought of her anymore, as well as of my sister.

The last time, when it was almost time for my destruction, I felt the urge to fly. I saw you, brave Zvenislav, with my sister, but I didn't know that it was her. I wanted to open my jaws at you, but you seemed so scary to me that I contented myself to devour Alzana. I felt all the horror of death when you were chasing me. But when you were fighting against me, I no longer had a memory. I felt as if I had just woken from a deep sleep. I woke up when you tore the serpent apart. Then human feelings returned to me, and, after looking at you, I thought that you must be the brave Zvenislav, the rescuer of my sister, appointed by the Gods. I understood from the words of Baba Yaga that no one else could enter her yard.

Source: Levshin, *Русские сказки*. Translated from the Russian by Vadym Grebniev.

About the Author

Ronesa Aveela is "the creative power of two." Two authors that is. Nelly, the main force behind the work, the creative genius, was born in Bulgaria and moved to the US in the 1990s. She grew up with stories of wild Samodivi, Kikimora, the dragons Zmey and Lamia, Baba Yaga, and much more. She's a freelance artist and writer. She likes writing mystery romance inspired by legends and tales. In her free time, she paints. Her artistic interests include the female figure, Greek and Thracian mythology, folklore tales, and the natural world interpreted through her eyes. She is married and has two children.

Rebecca, her writing partner was born and raised in the New England area. She has a background in writing and editing, as well as having a love of all things from different cultures. She's learned so much about Bulgarian culture, folklore, and rituals, and writes to share that knowledge with others.

Connect with us at www.ronesaaveela.com!

Artist Profiles

Alexander Petkov calls his work as an artist "the once upon a time syndrome." It is influenced by the richly told and illustrated tales in books he read as a child and the stories his grandparents shared with him. It is soaked with the visuals of his childhood experiences – the magic of sunlight bursting through the cool, mysterious shadows of the woods, the never ending up-and-down intriguing line of a mountain silhouette over the horizon… About 1,000 years later, all those experiences still play with his imagination giving him the joy to find a wink and a giggle even in the darkest grays.

He is a freelance artist-illustrator based in the Chicago, IL, area, for the last several years creating mostly digitally. He's worked on numerous illustration projects directly with individual writers, Parnas Press, and Fantasy Flight Games.

You can see most of his recent works and join him on his visual adventures at:

artstation.com/alexpart
society6.com/alexpart
instagram.com/alexpdreams
facebook.com/alexander.petkov1
Contact: alexpartcomm@gmail.com

Nelinda is the artistic side of Ronesa. Not only does she have thousands of ideas for stories about her Bulgarian heritage, but she is a talented artist. You can see more of her work at www.nelindaart.com.

Bibliography

Abramov, Mikhail. "Поседел от встречи с Бабой Ягой." [Turned gray from meeting Baba Yaga.] March 16, 2010. http://bio-lnter.net/?q=node/80.

Adonyeva, Svetlana and Laura J. Olson. "Interpreting the Past, Postulating the Future: Memorate as Plot and Script among Rural Russian Women." *Journal of Folklore Research* 48, no. 2 (2011): 133-166. https://www.academia.edu/6922022/_Legend_Dialogue_and_Identity_The_Russian_Case.

Afanas'ev, Aleksandr Nikolaevich. *Russian folk-tales*. New York: E.P. Dutton, 1916. https://hdl.handle.net/2027/inu.30000007718400.

Ancient_daos. "В гости к бабе яге, 3: Лютая язва." [On a visit to Baba Yaga, 3: Fierce ulcer.] February 26, 2011. https://drevniy-daos.livejournal.com/291628.html.

Andrievskikh, Natalia. "Food Symbolism, Sexuality, and Gender Identity in Fairy Tales and Modern Women's Bestsellers." *Studies in Popular Culture* 37, no. 1 (2014): 137-53. Accessed May 20, 2021. http://www.jstor.org/stable/24332704.

Arsenov, Dmitry. "Баба Яга." [Baba Yaga.] https://pandia.ru/text/80/571/54370.php.

Borrow, George. *The Works of George Borrow*, v.2. London: Printed for private circulation, 1913-1914. https://hdl.handle.net/2027/dul1.ark:/13960/t2w38qb52.

Bouthillette, K.S. "Learning to philosophize with Russian folk tales." https://www.academia.edu/37057998/Learning_to_philosophize_with_Russian_folk_tales.

Cagnolati, Antonella, ed. *The Borders of Fantasia*. Salamanca: FahrenHouse, 2015. https://www.academia.edu/65191165/The_borders_of_Fantasia.

Catherine. "Баба-Яга – загадочный гость из тридевятого царства." [Baba Yaga – a mysterious guest from a distant kingdom.] May 14, 2021. https://history.eco/baba-yaga-zagadochnyj-gost-tridevyatogo-czarstva/.

Ciepielak, Ivonka. "Divine Siblings? The Pre-Christian Ancestry of Baba Yaga and the Black Madonna of Czestochowa." 2018. https://www.academia.edu/38960957/Divine_Siblings_The_Pre_Christian_Ancestry_of_Baba_Yaga_and_the_Black_Madonna_of_Czestochowa.

Cigán, Michal. *Priest-King of the Warriors and Witch-Queen of the Others*. Masaryk University, 2019. https://www.academia.edu/43059187/Priest_King_of_the_Warriors_and_Witch_Queen_of_the_Others.

Clarke, Natalia. *Pagan Portals: Baba Yaga Slavic Earth Goddess*. Washington: Moon Books, 2021.

Clifford, Marissa. "The Enduring Allure of Baba Yaga, an Ancient Swamp Witch Who Loves to Eat People." November 3, 2017. https://www.vice.com/en/article/evbbjj/the-enduring-allure-of-baba-yaga-an-ancient-swamp-witch-who-loves-to-eat-people.

Conway, D. J. *Maiden, Mother, Crone: The Myth & Reality of the Triple Goddess*. St. Paul, Minn.: Llwellyn Publications, 1994.

Cooper, Brian. "Baba-Yaga, the Bony-Legged: A Short Note on the Witch and Her Name." *New Zealand Slavonic Journal*, 1997, 82-88. Accessed May 20, 2021. http://www.jstor.org/stable/23806796.

Coxwell, C. Fillingham ed. *Siberian and Other Folk-tales; Primitive Literature of the Empire of the Tsars, Collected and Translated, with an Introduction and Notes*. London: The C. W. Daniel Company [1925]. https://hdl.handle.net/2027/mdp.39015008173604.

Curtin, Jeremiah. *Fairy Tales of Eastern Europe*. New York: R. M. McBride, 1931. https://hdl.handle.net/2027/uc1.$b41194.

Damaschin, Liliana. "Slavic Mythology." https://www.academia.edu/10255821/Slavic_mythology.

De Beer, Welma. "Honouring the Life Stage of the Crone: Self-Revelatory Performance as Rite of Passage." Research report from Wits School of Arts, March 2016. https://www.academia.edu/ 64087240/Honouring_the_life_stage_of_the_crone_self_revelatory_performance_as_rite_of_ passage.

Debicady13. "Cat Bayun." October 28, 2020. https://lukomoryefolklore.wordpress.com/2020/10/29/ cat-bayun/.

Detelić, Mirjana. "Flesh and Bones: On Literary and Real Codes in Fairy Tales." Balcanica 29, Institute for Balkan Studies, Belgrade 1998. https://www.academia.edu/1469721/Flesh_and_ Bones_On_Literary_and_Real_Codes_in_Fairy_Tales.

Dexter, Miriam Robbins. "Neolithic Female Figures and their Evolution into groups of Ferocious and Beneficent Historic-Age Goddesses, Fairies, and Witches." https://www.academia.edu/39228397/ Neolithic_Female_Figures_and_their_Evolution_into_groups_of_Ferocious_and_Beneficent_ Historic_Age_Goddesses_Fairies_and_Witches.

Dexter, Miriam Robbins. Whence the Goddesses: A Source Book. New York: Teachers College Press, 1990. https://www.academia.edu/43589631/Whence_the_Goddesses_A_Source_Book.

Dubhrós, Jeremy. "Cultural Translation and the Iconography of the Master and Mistress of the Animals." The Research annual of The UTA Honors College 1, no 1 (2018): 33-59. doi:10.32855/honorscollegeuta.2018.002. https://www.academia.edu/39558232/ CULTURAL_TRANSLATION_AND_THE_ICONOGRAPHY_OF_THE_MASTER_AND_ MISTRESS_OF_THE_ANIMALS.

Dugan, Frank. "Baba Yaga and the Mushrooms." Fungi 10, no. 2 (Summer2017): 6-18. https://www.researchgate.net/publication/319162721_Baba_Yaga_and_the_Mushrooms.

Elder Mountain Dreaming. "Sun Cults." December 29, 2018. https://www.facebook.com/ElderMountainDreaming/posts/pfbid0R6ZfcSGwsbHr4ip3JAhaer9pzn XiPt25qaGvjSPhdvVuRfmW54LpviQJJpmktV9Jl.

Elderly Attribute. "Реальная встреча с бабой ягой?" [A real meeting with Baba Yaga?] June 10, 2019. https://zen.yandex.ru/media/id/5cb1e72293828900b32eb9c3/realnaia-vstrecha-s-baboi-iagoi- 5cfe2ddce24ab100bce1eb01.

Engela, Wendy K. "Baba Yaga: A Demon or A Goddess?" September 26, 2019. https://witchswell.wordpress.com/2019/09/26/baba-yaga-a-demon-or-a-goddess/.

Ferre, Lux. "Tabiti." November 13, 2017. https://occult-world.com/tabiti/.

Fiske, John. Essays Historical and Literary. New York: The MacMillan Company, 1902. https://hdl.handle.net/2027/hvd.hwjtkp.

Forrester, Sibelan, trans. Baba Yaga: The Wild Witch of the East in Russian Fairy Tales. Jackson: University Press of Mississippi, 2013.

Ganeva, Dr. Radoslava. "Bulgarian Folk Costumes – Symbols and Traditions." Bulgarian Diplomatic Review, Supplement to Issue 3/2003, Year 3.

Gilbert, Paul T., et. al., eds. "On the Treatment of the Scourge." The Yale Literary Magazine 66, no. 6 (March 1901). https://hdl.handle.net/2027/hvd.hxt9by.

Gimbutas, Marija. The Living Goddesses. Berkeley and Los Angeles, California: University of California Press, 1999.

Gliński, Antoni Józef. Polish Fairy Tales. London: John Lane, 1920. https://hdl.handle.net/2027/ mdp.39015012429364.

Goriaeva, Lioubov V. "The character of the old woman-mediatrix in Malay and Russian narrative tradition." Malay-Indonesian Studies 15 (2002): 92-101. https://www.academia.edu/2762323/ _The_character_of_the_old_woman_mediatrix_in_Malay_and_Russian_narrative_tradition_Nenek _Kebayan_and_Baba_Yaga_Malay_Indonesian_studies_issue_XV_Moscow_2002_pp_92_101.

Gradinaru, Olga. "Myth and Rationality in Russian Popular Fairy Tales." https://www.academia.edu/9879430/Myth_and_Rationality_in_Russian_Popular_Fairy_Tales.

Gregor, Pearl E. "The Apple and the Talking Snake: Feminist Dream Readings and the Subjunctive Curriculum." Thesis for The University of British Columbia (Vancouver), September 2008. https://www.academia.edu/26597173/THE_APPLE_AND_THE_TALKING_SNAKE_FEMINIST_DREAM_READINGS_AND_THE_SUBJUNCTIVE_CURRICULUM.

Heath, Catherine. "Out of the Waters Beneath the Tree: One Potential Origin of the Seiðrworker." https://www.academia.edu/35266825/OUT_OF_THE_WATERS_BENEATH_THE_TREE_One_Potential_Origin_of_the_Seiðrworker.

Howard-Hobson, Juleigh. "All Cats are Grey in Russian Folklore." https://manticore.press/all-cats-are-grey-in-russian-folklore/.

Hubbs, Joanna. *Mother Russia: The Feminine Myth in Russian Culture*. Bloomington and Indianapolis: Indiana University Press, 1988.

Hvorostov, Yury. "Откуда взялась Баба-яга и Кощей Бессмертный в русских сказках и почему их сравнивают с пришельцами." [Where did Baba Yaga and Koschey the Deathless come from in Russian fairy tales and why are they compared to aliens.] October 25, 2021. https://kulturologia.ru/blogs/251021/51510/.

Ivanova, Evgenia V. "The Problem of Mysteriousness of Baba Yaga Character in Religious Mythology." *Journal of Siberian Federal University. Humanities & Social Sciences* 12 (2013 6) 1857-1866. http://elib.sfu-kras.ru/bitstream/handle/2311/10124/12_Ivanova.pdf; jsessionid=9E696C8398076433412125E8B30DC10E.

Japanese Mythology & Folklore. "Discovering the universality of Baba yaga and Yama-uba, the old mountain crone." November 28, 2013. https://japanesemythology.wordpress.com/comparing-japanese-mountain-crones-or-hags-yamaumba-jigoku-no-baba-datsueba-and-the-universal-mountain-crone-at-the-edge-of-river-of-death-and-the-underworld/.

Järv, Risto. "Characters and Their Combinations in Fairy Tale Jokes and Parodies." *Journal of Ethnology and Folkloristics* 13, no. 1 (2019): 9–28, DOI: 10.2478/jef-2019-0002, https://www.academia.edu/81779047/The_Goldfish_and_Little_Red_Riding_Hood_Characters_and_their_Combinations_in_Fairy_Tale_Jokes_and_Parodies.

Johns, Andreas. "Baba Iaga and the Russian Mother." *The Slavic and East European Journal* 42, no. 1 (1998): 21-36. doi:10.2307/310050. http://www.jstor.org/stable/310050.

Johns, Andreas. *Baba Yaga: the Ambiguous Mother and Witch of the Russian Folktale*. New York: Peter Lang, 2004.

Johnson, JoAnna Kate Ruth. "Baba Yaga: The Judicious Magistrate of Russian Folklore." A thesis presented to the Honor's College of Middle Tennessee State University in partial fulfillment of the requirements for graduation from the University Honors College. Fall 2016. https://jewlscholar.mtsu.edu/items/b6b16107-17ab-4a3f-8d6b-6204adf3fd8e.

Kazakova, Tamara A. "Relativity as a Translation Tool for Mythology-based Texts." *Journal of Siberian Federal University. Humanities & Social Sciences* 2 (2014 7): 238-243. https://www.academia.edu/64222564/Relativity_as_a_Translation_Tool_for_Mythology_based_Texts.

Koptev, Aleksandr. "Mythological triadism as the paradigm of princely succession in early Rus' according to the Primary Chronicle." In *New researches on the religion and mythology of the Pagan Slavs*, Edited by Patrice Lajoye, Paris: Lingva, 2019, p. 127-164. https://www.academia.edu/39626623/Mythological_triadism_as_the_paradigm_of_princely_succession_in_early_Rus_according_to_the_Primary_Chronicle_in_New_researches_on_the_religion_and_mythology_of_the_Pagan_Slavs_Edited_by_Patrice_Lajoye_Paris_Lingva_2019_p_127_164.

Kraus Reprint. "Folk-tales." *The Church Quarterly Review* 16 (April 1883): 31-46. https://hdl.handle.net/2027/uc1.$b621091.

Kuzina, Svetlana. "Баба Яга была инопланетянкой." [Baba Yaga was an alien.] December 18, 2005. https://www.kp.ru/daily/23630.5/48088/.

Lajoye, Patrice, ed. "Slavic deities of death. Looking for a needle in the haystack." In *New Researches on the religion and mythology of the Pagan Slavs*. Lisieux, France: Lingva, 2019: 69-97. https://www.academia.edu/39780238/Slavic_deities_of_death_Looking_for_a_needle_in_the_haystack.

Lamus dworski. "Suida Baba." March 26, 2016. https://lamus-dworski.tumblr.com/post/141736987062/siuda-baba-is-a-rural-custom-of-pagan-origins.

Levchin, Sergey, trans. *Russian Folktales from the Collection of A. Afanasyev*. Mineola, New York: Dover Publications, 2014.

Levshin, Vasilii. *Русские сказки* [Russian Fairy Tales]. University print shop: Moscow, 1783. https://hdl.handle.net/2027/nyp.33433067031488.

Live Journal. "Фото кота баюна из сказки: Мистический Кот Баюн — Все интересное в искусстве и не только. — LiveJournal." [Photo of the cat Bayun from the fairy tale: Mystical Cat Bayun — Everything interesting from the arts and more. — LiveJournal.] https://xn--b1abojhpfasr.xn--p1ai/raznoe/foto-kota-bayuna-iz-skazki-misticheskij-kot-bayun-vse-interesnoe-v-iskusstve-i-ne-tolko-livejournal.html.

Magic_design. "Баба-Яга." [Baba Yaga.] July 22, 2019. https://magic-design.livejournal.com/180122.html. From original source: Valentina Ponomareva, https://www.perunica.ru/etnos/7615-obryad-perepekaniya-rebenka-na-lopatu-iv-pech.html.

Matthews, Yeshe. "Baba Yaga Part I." Oct 27, 2017. https://medium.com/@yeshematthews/baba-yaga-part-i-826c23fab8a9.

McNeil, Oliver. "Who is Baba Yaga?" August 1, 2021. https://www.storymasterstales.com/post/who-is-baba-yaga.

Meet Russia. "Baba Yaga in Russian fairy tales." March 25, 2019. https://meetrussia.online/baba-yaga-in-russian-fairy-tales/.

Mencej, Mirjam. "Connecting Threads." *Electronic Journal of Folklore* 48 (2011): 55-84. https://www.folklore.ee/folklore/vol48/download.php.

Mendis, Michael. "The Role of Women in Russian Fairy Tales." 2009. https://www.academia.edu/33506425/THE_ROLE_OF_WOMEN_IN_RUSSIAN_FAIRY_TALES.

Merisante, Margaret. "Aloft into the Shining Skies: The Mythic Intersections of Celestial Mare Goddesses and Swan Maidens." American Academy of Religion, Society of Biblical Literature & The American Schools of Oriental Research, March 28, 2015.

Mirdinara.com. "The History of Baba Yaga." October 29, 2021. https://www.mirdinara.com/stories/2021/10/29/the-history-of-baba-yaga.

Mitlenko, Svetlana. "Баба-Яга, кто она такая?" [Baba Yaga, who is she?] April 24, 2018. https://zhiznteatr.mirtesen.ru/blog/43080850411/Baba-YAga,-kto-ona-takaya.

Mythos The Historian. "Baba Yaga – The Ugly Evil Witch of Slavic Folklore." October 28, 2021. https://www.youtube.com/watch?v=HSCkdWREr7k.New World Encyclopedia contributors, "Baba Yaga," *New World Encyclopedia*. https://www.newworldencyclopedia.org/p/index.php?title=Baba_Yaga&oldid=985081 (accessed June 1, 2022).

Mythoslavic. "S02E01 The Secret of Baba Yaga." January 11, 2022. https://mythoslavic.buzzsprout.com/1865145/9866150.

Naumovska, O. V., Rudakova, N. I., and Naumovska, N. I. (2021). "The 'Life/Death' Binary Opposition in Folk Prose Narratives." *Linguistics and Culture Review* 5(S4): 540-558.

https://doi.org/10.21744/lingcure.v5nS4.1589. https://www.academia.edu/62799985/
_Life_Death_Binary_Opposition_in_Folk_Prose_Narratives.

Nikitina, Maia. "Baba Yaga." Dialog 4. https://wheretheleavesfall.com/explore/article-index/baba-yaga/.

Nikitina, Maia. "Russian Folklore: Baba Yaga as a Symbol of Mother Nature." Updated July 26, 2019. https://www.thoughtco.com/russian-folklore-4589898.

Nikolskaya, Natalya. "Baba Yaga the Bony-Legged, the Ancient Dark Forest Mother of Slavic Myth." May 20, 2019. https://vk.com/@shellir-baba-yaga-the-bony-legged-the-ancient-dark-forest-mother-of.

Nuernberger, Kathryn. "The Invention of Childhood." *Prairie Schooner* 90, no. 2 (2016): 155-56. Accessed May 20, 2021. http://www.jstor.org/stable/44985053.

Nukadeti.ru. "Баба яга и ягоды читать." [Baba Yaga and the strawberries.] https://nukadeti.ru/skazki/baba_yaga_i_yagody.

Nukadeti.ru. "Поди туда не знаю куда, принеси то не знаю что." [Go I don't know where, bring I don't know what.] https://nukadeti.ru/skazki/uspenskij-podi-tuda-ne-znayu-kuda-prinesi-to-ne-znayu-chto.

Önal, Leyla. "The Discursive Suppression of Women: Female Evils as the Villains of the Motherhood Narrative." *Electronic Journal of Folklore* 48 (2011): 84-116. https://www.folklore.ee/folklore/vol48/download.php.

Pamita, Madame. *Baba Yaga's Book of Witchcraft*. Woodbury, MN: Llewellyn Publications, 2022.

Pamita, Madame. "Baba Yaga's Cottage: Meeting the Goddess of Death and Rebirth." March 17, 2020. https://www.patheos.com/blogs/babayagascottage/2020/03/baba-yagas-cottage-meeting-goddess-death-rebirth/.

Peskiadmin.ru. "Баба яга – мифический персонаж или реальная женщина. Происхождение бабы яги." [Baba Yaga – a mythical character or a real woman. Origin of Baba Yaga.] https://peskiadmin.ru/baba-yaga---mificheskii-personazh-ili-realnaya-zhenshchina-proishozhdenie-baby.html.

Petrova, Elka. "Нов прочит на образа на Баба Яга." [A new reading of the image of Baba Yaga.] Anniversary scientific conference with international participation – 2016. http://research.bfu.bg:8080/jspui/bitstream/123456789/846/1/434_PDFsam_Sbornik-BFU-TOM1.pdf.

Phoenix, Elder Mountain Dreaming, interview on September 2, 2022.

PianoCzarX. "Richter destroys the piano – The Hut on Fowl's Legs // MUSSORGSKY." Jan 16, 2018. https://youtu.be/03Vjclg6mxo.

Polevoĭ, Petr. *Russian Fairy Tales from the Skazki of Polevoi*. London: A. H. Bullen, 1901. https://hdl.handle.net/2027/njp.32101068186160.

Popławska, Marta. "The Female Self as Presented by Clarissa Pinkola Estés in *Women Who Run with the Wolves. The Stories of Female Initiation, Intuition and Instincts.*" *Rozprawy Społeczne* 12, no. 3 (2018): 14-19. https://www.academia.edu/73108313/The_Female_Self_as_Presented_by_Clarissa_Pinkola_Est%C3%A9s_in_Women_Who_Run_with_the_Wolves_The_Stories_of_Female_Initiation_Intuition_and_Instincts.

Propp, Vladimir. *Theory and History of Folklore*. Minneapolis: University of Minnesota Press, 1984.

Pyle, Katharine. *Wonder Tales from Many Lands*. London: G.G. Harrap, 1920. https://hdl.handle.net/2027/uc1.b3331854.

Ralston, William Ralston Shedden. *Russian Folk-tales*. London: Smith, Elder, & Co., 1873. https://hdl.handle.net/2027/uc1.31158010565728.Russiapedia. "Of Russian origin: Baba Yaga." https://russiapedia.rt.com/of-russian-origin/baba-yaga/.

Ralston, William Ralston Shedden. *The Songs of the Russian People, as Illustrative of Slavonic Mythology and Russian Social Life*. London: Ellis & Green, 1872. https://hdl.handle.net/2027/hvd.hwfh5m.

Rancour-Laferriere, Daniel. "Is the Slave Soul of Russia a Gendered Object?" In *The Slave Soul of Russia: Moral Masochism and the Cult of Suffering*, 134-80. New York; London: NYU Press, 1995. Accessed May 20, 2021. http://www.jstor.org/stable/j.ctt9qg1cj.10.

Rouhier-Willoughby, Jeanmarie. 2021. "Review: Andreas Johns. *Baba Yaga. The Ambiguous Mother and Witch of the Russian Folktale*." *FOLKLORICA - Journal of the Slavic, East European, and Eurasian Folklore Association* 10 (1). https://doi.org/10.17161/folklorica.v10i1.3759.

Rountree, Kathryn. "The Politics of the Goddess: Feminist Spirituality and the Essentialism Debate." *Social Analysis: The International Journal of Social and Cultural Practice* 43, no. 2 (1999): 138-65. Accessed May 20, 2021. http://www.jstor.org/stable/23166525.

Ryan, W. F. *The Bathhouse at Midnight: An Historical Survey of Magic and Divination in Russia*. University Park, PA: The Pennsylvania State University Press, 1999.

Scielzo, Caroline. "Notes on Translating Russian Fairytales." *Folklore Forum* 20, no. 1/2 (1987): 119-127. https://scholarworks.iu.edu/dspace/bitstream/handle/2022/1988/20(1,2)%20119-127.pdf;sequence=1.

Sieff, Daniela. "Confronting Death Mother: An Interview with Marion Woodman." *The Psychology of Violence: A Journal of Archetype and Culture* (Spring 1981): 177-200. https://www.academia.edu/1188306/Sieff_D_F_2009_Confronting_Death_Mother_An_interview_with_Marion_Woodman.

Simley, Anne. "The Baba Yaga." In *A Collection of Folk Tales, Legends, and Myths*, v.2. Minneapolis, Burgess Pub. Co., 1962, pp. 57-60.

Slavic Spirituality. "Baba Yaga's Companion – Cat." October 6, 2021. From *Slavonica Antiqua*. https://www.facebook.com/SlavicSpirituality/posts/1478008205705367.

Snider, Amber, C., interviewer. "Who Is Baba Yaga? An Interview with Madame Pamita." April 22, 2022. http://www.enchantmentsnyc.com/stories/who-is-baba-yaga-an-interview-with-madame-pamita.

Stahl, Henrieke. "Releasing the Creative Self in Transcultural Neo-Tales. Baba Yaga in Jane Yolen's 'Finding Baba Yaga' and Lana Hechtman Ayers' 'Red Riding Hood's Real Life.' " Journal of European Languages and Literatures 10 (Autumn 2019): 43-57, DOI: 10.6667/interface.10.2019.99, https://www.academia.edu/79202968/Releasing_the_Creative_Self_in_Transcultural_Neo_Tales_Baba_Yaga_in_Jane_Yolen_s_Finding_Baba_Yaga_and_Lana_Hechtman_Ayers_Red_Riding_Hoods_Real_Life_.

Staines, Rima. "Drawing the Old Woman in the Woods." *Marvels & Tales* 24, no. 2 (2010): 336-40. Accessed May 20, 2021. http://www.jstor.org/stable/41388960.

Storied. "Baba Yaga: The Ancient Origins of the Famous 'Witch' | Monstrum." January 14, 2021. https://www.youtube.com/watch?v=aS4VCxMeWQM.

Studebaker, Jeri. " 'Dolls', Fairy Tales, and Ancient Goddess Figurine." https://www.academia.edu/5767605/Dolls_Fairy_Tales_and_Ancient_Goddess_Figurines.

Tale Foundry. "6 Slavic Mythology Creatures – Slavic Folklore Series." June 1, 2018. https://www.youtube.com/watch?v=Gfh5yYTNIjM.

TopMovieHeroes. "Polish Legends. Jaga film. Allegro (2016) [English Subtitles]." March 13, 2021. https://www.youtube.com/watch?v=9Oc1u4bhTPA.

Ulasevich, Tina Vasilievna. "Баба- Яга: в сказках и в жизни." [Baba-Yaga in fairy tales and in life.] June 25, 2012. https://www.b17.ru/article/6550/.

Ustinova, Daria. "Загадочная повелительница ступы." [Mysterious lady of the stupa.] Novosibirsk 2015. https://153nsk.ru/wp-content/uploads/2016/12/baba_yaga.pdf.

Varga, Éva Katalin. "Метаморфоза образа Бабы-Яги." [Metamorphosis of the Image of Baba Yaga.] May 27, 2017. https://www.academia.edu/38121210/Метаморфоза_образа_Бабы_Яги_The_metamorphosis_of_Baba_Yagas_figure_.

Warner, Elizabeth. *Russian Myths*. Austin: University of Texas Press, 2002.

Western Folklore. "Russian Fairy Tale." *Western Folklore* 7, no. 2 (1948): 188. Accessed May 20, 2021. doi:10.2307/1497406. https://www.jstor.org/stable/1497406.

Wheeler, Joseph Trank. *The Zonal-belt Hypothesis; a New Explanation of the Cause of the Ice Ages*. Philadelphia: J.B. Lippincott, 1908. https://hdl.handle.net/2027/uc1.b4175758.

Wilson, Richard. *The Russian Story Book*. London: Macmillan, 1916. https://hdl.handle.net/2027/mdp.39015002199639.

Winters, Riley. "Baba Yaga: The Wicked Witch of Slavic Folklore." Updated March 10, 2019. https://www.ancient-origins.net/myths-legends-europe/baba-yaga-confounding-crone-slavic-folklore-002836.

Woodruff, Patricia Robin. "The Triple God of Old Europe." 2020. https://www.academia.edu/43812007/The_Triple_God_of_Old_Europe.

Zeitlin, Ida. *Skazki; Tales and Legends of Old Russia*. New York: George H. Doran Company, [c1926]. https://hdl.handle.net/2027/mdp.39015008264445.

Zipes, Jack. *The Irresistible Fairy Tale: The Cultural and Social History of a Genre*. Princeton and Oxford: Princeton University Press, 2012.

End Notes

[1] See Johns, *The Ambiguous Mother*, 8-9, for numerous other name variations.

[2] Wilson, *The Russian Story Book*, 285.

[3] Nikolskaya, "Baba Yaga the Bony-Legged."

[4] Andrievskikh, "Food Symbolism," 148. Referencing Snyder, Midori. "In Praise of the Cook." 2005. In the *Labryinth*. Web. 7 Nov. 2012, page 2.

[5] Mythos The Historian, "Baba Yaga – The Ugly Evil Witch of Slavic Folklore."

[6] Gimbutas, *The Living Goddesses*, 28.

[7] Gimbutas, *The Living Goddesses*, 28.

[8] Forrester, *Baba Yaga: The Wild Witch of the East*, 134.

[9] Warner, *Russian Myths*, 28.

[10] Scielzo, "Notes on Translating Russian Fairytales," 123.

[11] Afanas'ev, *Russian folk-tales*, 328. From "The Legless Knight and the Blind Knight."

[12] We discuss Hala in our book *A Study of Dragons of Eastern Europe*.

[13] Hubbs, *Mother Russia*, 45.

[14] Naumovska, "The 'Life/Death' Binary Opposition," 549-550.

[15] Afanas'ev, *Russian folk-tales*, 198. From "Márya Moryévna."

[16] Afanas'ev, *Russian folk-tales*, 329-330. From "The Legless Knight and the Blind Knight."

[17] Nikolskaya, "Baba Yaga the Bony-Legged."

[18] Arsenov, "Баба Яга."

[19] Ralston, *The Songs of the Russian People*, 163.

[20] Fiske, *Essays Historical and Literary*, 302.

[21] Arsenov, "Баба Яга."

[22] Ralston, *Russian Folk-tales*, 147.

[23] Popławska, "The Female Self," 17. Referencing Tatar, M. (ed.) (2002). *The Annotated Classic Fairy Tales*. New York: W. W. Norton & Company, Inc., p. 334.

[24] Ralston, *The Songs of the Russian People*, 166.

[25] Elder Mountain Dreaming, "Sun Cults."

[26] Interview with shaman Baba Phoenix on September 2, 2022.

[27] Ancient_daos, "В гости к бабе яге."

[28] Ciepielak, "Divine Siblings?" 24.

[29] Rountree, "The Politics of the Goddess," 138.

[30] Dexter, *Whence the Goddesses*, 146.

[31] Rountree, "The Politics of the Goddess," 147.

[32] Dexter, *Whence the Goddesses*, 4.

[33] Dexter, *Whence the Goddesses*, 4.

[34] Forrester, *Baba Yaga: The Wild Witch of the East*, xxxiii.

[35] Ralston, *The Songs of the Russian People*, 164.

[36] Johns, *The Ambiguous Mother*, 58.

[37] Arsenov, "Баба Яга."

[38] Dubhrós, "Iconography of the Master and Mistress of the Animals," 34.

[39] Ivanova, "The Problem of Mysteriousness of Baba Yaga," 1861.

[40] Dexter, *Whence the Goddesses*, 5.

[41] Ivanova, "The Problem of Mysteriousness of Baba Yaga," 1863.

[42] Johns, *The Ambiguous Mother*, 16. Quoting Chulkov, Mikhail D. *Slovar' ruskikh sueverii*. St. Petersburg, 1782: 270.

[43] Nikolskaya, "Baba Yaga the Bony-Legged."

[44] Meet Russia, "Baba Yaga in Russian fairy tales."

[45] Mitlenko, "Баба-Яга, кто она такая?"

[46] Peskiadmin.ru, "Баба яга."

[47] Ivanova, "The Problem of Mysteriousness of Baba Yaga," 1858-1859.

[48] Lamus dworski, "Suida Baba."

[49] Ivanova, "The Problem of Mysteriousness of Baba Yaga," 1865.

[50] Peskiadmin.ru, "Баба яга."

[51] Meet Russia, "Baba Yaga in Russian fairy tales."

[52] Ustinova, "Загадочная повелительница ступы," 5.

[53] Interview with shaman Baba Phoenix on September 2, 2022.

[54] Hubbs, *Mother Russia*, 38.

[55] Ferre, "Tabiti."

[56] Ivanova, "The Problem of Mysteriousness of Baba Yaga," 1862-1863.

[57] Ustinova, "Загадочная повелительница ступы," 5.

[58] Peskiadmin.ru, "Баба яга."

[59] Hvorostov, "Откуда взялась Баба-яга и Кощей Бессмертный."

[60] Peskiadmin.ru, "Баба яга."

[61] Hvorostov, "Откуда взялась Баба-яга и Кощей Бессмертный."

[62] Catherine, "Баба-Яга."

[63] Johns, *The Ambiguous Mother*, 163. Referencing Sanarov, Valerii I. 1981. "On the Nature and Origin of Flying Saucers and Little Green Men." *Current Anthropology* 22 (2): 163-167, p. 165.

[64] Hvorostov, "Откуда взялась Баба-яга и Кощей Бессмертный."

[65] Kuzina, "Баба Яга была инопланетянкой."

[66] Forrester, *Baba Yaga: The Wild Witch of the East*, xxxiv.

[67] Peskiadmin.ru, "Баба яга."

[68] Petrova, "Нов прочит на образа на Баба Яга," 435.

[69] Dexter, *Whence the Goddesses*, 178.

[70] Dexter, *Whence the Goddesses*, 182.

[71] Johns, *The Ambiguous Mother*, 14.

[72] Johns, *The Ambiguous Mother*, 255. From Bandarchyk 1978 no. 65 (AT 707).

[73] Nikolskaya, "Baba Yaga the Bony-Legged." Quoted from *Charadzejnyja Kazki. Chastka II* [Fairytales. Part II]. No. 1, p. 28.

[74] Clifford, "The Enduring Allure of Baba Yaga."

[75] Ivanova, "The Problem of Mysteriousness of Baba Yaga," 1860. Quoting from Laushkin, K.D. (1970) "Baba Yaga and one-legged gods: revisited origin of the character." *Folklore and ethnography*, p. 181.

[76] Ivanova, "The Problem of Mysteriousness of Baba Yaga," 1860.

[77] Johns, *The Ambiguous Mother*, 23. Referencing Propp, Vladimir Ia. 1946. *Istoricheskie korni volshebnoi skazki*. Leningrad: LGU, p. 59.

[78] Johns, *The Ambiguous Mother*, 156, footnote 3.

[79] Coxwell, *Siberian and Other Folk-tale*, 554.

[80] Johns, *The Ambiguous Mother*, 29.

[81] Petrova, "Нов прочит на образа на Баба Яга," 439.

[82] Peskiadmin.ru, "Баба яга."

[83] Andrievskikh, "Food Symbolism," 137.

[84] Detelić, "Flesh and Bones," 287.

[85] Detelić, "Flesh and Bones," 289.

[86] Dexter, *Whence the Goddesses*, 182.

[87] Detelić, "Flesh and Bones," 285.

[88] Detelić, "Flesh and Bones," 285.

[89] Nikolskaya, "Baba Yaga the Bony-Legged."

[90] Ivanova, "The Problem of Mysteriousness of Baba Yaga," 1863.

[91] Johns, *The Ambiguous Mother*, 102.

[92] Arsenov, "Баба Яга."

[93] Damaschin, "Slavic Mythology," 3.

[94] Polevoĭ, *Russian Fairy Tales from the Skazki of Polevoi*, 99. (From "The Tsarevna Loveliness-Inexhaustible.")

[95] Bouthillette, "Learning to philosophize with Russian folk tales," 39.

[96] Ivanova, "The Problem of Mysteriousness of Baba Yaga," 1862.

[97] Ustinova, "Загадочная повелительница ступы," 4.

[98] Andrievskikh, "Food Symbolism," 140.

[99] Scielzo, "Notes on Translating Russian Fairytales," 124.

[100] Afanas'ev, *Russian folk-tales*, 338.

[101] Engela, "Baba Yaga: A Demon or A Goddess?"

[102] Forrester, *Baba Yaga: The Wild Witch of the East*, 6.

[103] Johns, *The Ambiguous Mother*, 162-163. Referencing Eleonskaia, Elena N. 1994. *Skazka, zagovor I koldovstvo v Rossii. Sb. Trudov*. Moscow: Indrik, p. 58.

[104] Clarke, *Baba Yaga Slavic Earth Goddess*, 65-66.

[105] Magic_design, "Баба-Яга."

[106] Kazakova, "Relativity as a Translation Tool for Mythology-based Texts," 241.

[107] Arsenov, "Баба Яга."

[108] Bouthillette, "Learning to philosophize with Russian folk tales," 39.

[109] Petrova, "Нов прочит на образа на Баба Яга," 440.

[110] Hubbs, *Mother Russia*, 44-45.

[111] Propp, *Theory and History of Folklore*, 90.

[112] Naumovska, "The 'Life/Death' Binary Opposition," 545.

[113] Johns, *The Ambiguous Mother*, 163. Referencing Rybakov, Boris A. 1987. *Iazychestvo drevnei Rusi*. Moscow: Nauka, pp. 89-92.

[114] New World Encyclopedia, "Baba Yaga."

[115] Ulasevich, "Баба- Яга: в сказках и в жизни."

[116] Naumovska, "The 'Life/Death' Binary Opposition," 545.

[117] Varga, "Метаморфоза образа Бабы-Яги," 212.

[118] Peskiadmin.ru, "Баба яга."

[119] Varga, "Метаморфоза образа Бабы-Яги," 213.

[120] Ivanova, "The Problem of Mysteriousness of Baba Yaga," 1859.

[121] Varga, "Метаморфоза образа Бабы-Яги," 213.

[122] New World Encyclopedia, "Baba Yaga."

[123] Johns, *The Ambiguous Mother*, 165. Referencing Periañez-Chaverneff, Olga. 1983. "Analyse ethnopsychiatrique de la Baba-Jaga: apport à l'ethnogenàse des slaves." *Reuvuve des Études slaves* 55 (1): 185-195, p.190-192.

[124] New World Encyclopedia, "Baba Yaga."

[125] Ivanova, "The Problem of Mysteriousness of Baba Yaga," 1859.

[126] Ivanova, "The Problem of Mysteriousness of Baba Yaga," 1860.

[127] Johns, *The Ambiguous Mother*, 255. Referencing Ivanitskaia, E.N.1984. " 'Tam stupa s Baboiu-Iagoi…' " *Russkaia rech'* 1984 (2): 112-115.

[128] Nikolskaya, "Baba Yaga the Bony-Legged."

[129] Cooper, "Baba-Yaga, the Bony-Legged," 83.

[130] Adonyeva, "Interpreting the Past, Postulating the Future," 157.

[131] Gradinaru, "Myth and Rationality in Russian Popular Fairy Tales," 7.

[132] Petrova, "Нов прочит на образа на Баба Яга," 440.
[133] Ivanova, "The Problem of Mysteriousness of Baba Yaga," 1858.
[134] Ivanova, "The Problem of Mysteriousness of Baba Yaga," 1863.
[135] Ulasevich, "Баба- Яга: в сказках и в жизни."
[136] Nikolskaya, "Baba Yaga the Bony-Legged."
[137] Ulasevich, "Баба- Яга: в сказках и в жизни."
[138] Bouthillette, "Learning to philosophize with Russian folk tales," 38.
[139] Forrester, *Baba Yaga: The Wild Witch of the East*, 128.
[140] Petrova, "Нов прочит на образа на Баба Яга," 440.
[141] Forrester, *Baba Yaga: The Wild Witch of the East*, 162.
[142]

Forrester, *Baba Yaga: The Wild Witch of the East*, 37-38.
[143] Merisante, "Aloft into the Shining Skies," 5.
[144] Merisante, "Aloft into the Shining Skies," 3.
[145] Merisante, "Aloft into the Shining Skies," 5.
[146] Clarke, *Baba Yaga Slavic Earth Goddess*, 38.
[147] Howard-Hobson, "All Cats are Grey in Russian Folklore."
[148] Dexter, ""Neolithic Female Figures," 86.
[149] Forrester, *Baba Yaga: The Wild Witch of the East*, xliii.
[150] Live Journal, "Фото кота баюна из сказки."
[151] Live Journal, "Фото кота баюна из сказки."
[152] Live Journal, "Фото кота баюна из сказки."
[153] Debicady13, "Cat Bayun."
[154] Live Journal, "Фото кота баюна из сказки."
[155] Damaschin, "Slavic Mythology," 4.
[156] Ivanova, "The Problem of Mysteriousness of Baba Yaga," 1862.
[157] Nikolskaya, "Baba Yaga the Bony-Legged."
[158] Johns, *The Ambiguous Mother*, 262. Quoting Simonsen, Michèle. 1998. "Culture and Symbols. Some Thoughts about Bengt Holbek's Interpretation of Fairy Tales." *Estudos de Literatura Oral* 1998 (4):209-214, p. 213.
[159] From "The Realms of Copper, Silver, and Gold" and other fairy tales.
[160] Scielzo, "Notes on Translating Russian Fairytales,"126.
[161] Johns, *The Ambiguous Mother*, 47.
[162] Bouthillette, "Learning to philosophize with Russian folk tales," 46.
[163] Johns, *The Ambiguous Mother*, 85.
[164] Johns, *The Ambiguous Mother*, 95.
[165] Johns, *The Ambiguous Mother*, 96.
[166] Ulasevich, "Баба- Яга: в сказках и в жизни."
[167] Cooper, "Baba-Yaga, the Bony-Legged," 84.
[168] Dexter, *Whence the Goddesses*, 181.
[169] Polevoï, *Russian Fairy Tales*, 125 (from "The Frog-Tsarevna").
[170] Afanas'ev, *Russian folk-tales*, 338.
[171] Hubbs, *Mother Russia*, 49.
[172] Naumovska, "The 'Life/Death' Binary Opposition," 547.
[173] Engela, "Baba Yaga: A Demon or A Goddess?"
[174] Magic_design, "Баба-Яга."
[175] Engela, "Baba Yaga: A Demon or A Goddess?"
[176] Magic_design, "Баба-Яга."
[177] Magic_design, "Баба-Яга."
[178] Magic_design, "Баба-Яга."

[179] Johns, *The Ambiguous Mother*, 95-96. Quoted from Krivoshapkin, M. F. *Eniseidkii okrug i ego zhizn'*. St. Petersburg: IRGO, 1865 ii 3.

[180] Önal, "The Discursive Suppression of Women," 94.

[181] Ivanova, "The Problem of Mysteriousness of Baba Yaga," 1863.

[182] Matthews, "Baba Yaga Part I."

[183] Matthews, "Baba Yaga Part I."

[184] Ulasevich, "Баба- Яга: в сказках и в жизни."

[185] Staines, "Drawing the Old Woman in the Woods," 339.

[186] Arsenov, "Баба Яга."

[187] Petrova, "Нов прочит на образа на Баба Яга," 440.

[188] Ivanova, "The Problem of Mysteriousness of Baba Yaga," 1859.

[189] Forrester, *Baba Yaga: The Wild Witch of the East*, 178.

[190] Matthews, "Baba Yaga Part I."

[191] Clarke, *Baba Yaga Slavic Earth Goddess*, 13.

[192] Sieff, "Confronting Death Mother," 194.

[193] Nikolskaya, "Baba Yaga the Bony-Legged."

[194] Ivanova, "The Problem of Mysteriousness of Baba Yaga," 1859.

[195] Johns, *The Ambiguous Mother*, 44

[196] Arsenov, "Баба Яга."

[197] Bouthillette, "Learning to philosophize with Russian folk tales," 40.

[198] Propp, *Theory and History of Folklore*, 131.

[199] Dugan, "Baba Yaga and the Mushrooms," 15.

[200] Ivanova, "The Problem of Mysteriousness of Baba Yaga," 1860.

[201] Ivanova, "The Problem of Mysteriousness of Baba Yaga," 1859.

[202] Dugan, "Baba Yaga and the Mushrooms," 11.

[203] Dugan, "Baba Yaga and the Mushrooms," 6.

[204] Ivanova, "The Problem of Mysteriousness of Baba Yaga," 1860.

[205] Andrievskikh, "Food Symbolism," 140.

[206] Ivanova, "The Problem of Mysteriousness of Baba Yaga," 1860.

[207] Arsenov, "Baba Yaga."

[208] Propp, *Theory and History of Folklore*, 128.

[209] Propp, *Theory and History of Folklore*, 129.

[210] Polevoĭ, *Russian Fairy Tales from the Skazki of Polevoi*, 99. (From "The Tsarevna Loveliness-Inexhaustible.")

[211] Polevoĭ, *Russian Fairy Tales*, 45. (From "The Story of the Tsarevich Ivan and of the Harp that Harped without a Harper.")

[212] Forrester, *Baba Yaga: The Wild Witch of the East*, 136-137.

[213] Forrester, *Baba Yaga: The Wild Witch of the East*, 137.

[214] Propp, *Theory and History of Folklore*, 118-119.

[215] Hubbs, *Mother Russia*, 42.

[216] Johns, "Baba Iaga and the Russian Mother," 29.

[217] Rancour-Laferriere, "Slave Soul of Russia," 173.

[218] Stahl, "Releasing the Creative Self," 46.

[219] Johns, "Baba Iaga and the Russian Mother, " 30.

[220] Mendis, "The Role of Women in Russian Fairy Tales," 6.

[221] Rancour-Laferriere, "Slave Soul of Russia," 144.

[222] Johns, "Baba Iaga and the Russian Mother," 30.

[223] Önal, "The Discursive Suppression of Women," 88.

[224] Forrester, *Baba Yaga: The Wild Witch of the East*, 176-177.

[225] Forrester, *Baba Yaga: The Wild Witch of the East*, 177-178.

[226] Johns, *The Ambiguous Mother*, 110.

[227] Johns, *The Ambiguous Mother*, 120.
[228] Johns, *The Ambiguous Mother*, 120.
[229] Ulasevich, "Баба- Яга: в сказках и в жизни."
[230] Ulasevich, "Баба- Яга: в сказках и в жизни."
[231] Ulasevich, "Баба- Яга: в сказках и в жизни."
[232] Forrester, *Baba Yaga: The Wild Witch of the East*, 91-92.
[233] Forrester, *Baba Yaga: The Wild Witch of the East*, xlii.
[234] Hubbs, *Mother Russia*, 49.
[235] Hubbs, *Mother Russia*, 49.
[236] Andrievskikh, "Food Symbolism," 140.
[237] Popławska, "The Female Self," 17. Quoting Estés, C.P. (1995). *Women Who Run With the Wolves: Myths and Stories of the Wild Woman Archetype*. New York: Random House, p. 83.
[238] Stahl, "Releasing the Creative Self," 47.
[239] Popławska, "The Female Self," 18. Referencing Estés, C.P. (1995). *Women Who Run With the Wolves: Myths and Stories of the Wild Woman Archetype*. New York: Random House, p. 111, 118.
[240] Popławska, "The Female Self," 19. Referencing Estés, C.P. (1995). *Women Who Run With the Wolves: Myths and Stories of the Wild Woman Archetype*. New York: Random House.
[241] Cigán, *Priest-King of the Warriors and Witch-Queen of the Others*, 118.
[242] Arsenov, "Баба Яга."
[243] Cigán, *Priest-King of the Warriors and Witch-Queen of the Others*, 121.
[244] Arsenov, "Баба Яга."
[245] Cigán, *Priest-King of the Warriors and Witch-Queen of the Others*, 114.
[246] Cigán, *Priest-King of the Warriors and Witch-Queen of the Others*, 120.
[247] Cigán, *Priest-King of the Warriors and Witch-Queen of the Others*, 119-120.
[248] Cigán, *Priest-King of the Warriors and Witch-Queen of the Others*, 120.
[249] Bouthillette, "Learning to philosophize with Russian folk tales," 39.
[250] Ralston, *Russian Folk-tales*, 144-145.
[251] Ulasevich, "Баба- Яга: в сказках и в жизни."
[252] Mencej, "Connecting Threads," 68.
[253] Mencej, "Connecting Threads," 57. Reference (4) in the quote: This was published in his collection of fairy tales *Severnye skazki* (in translation: Northern tales) from Arkhangelsk and Olonetsk provinces.
[254] Hubbs, *Mother Russia*, 38.
[255] Mencej, "Connecting Threads," 76
[256] Mencej, "Connecting Threads," 68.
[257] Mencej, "Connecting Threads," 70. From Pócs, Éva 2008. Concepts of Time and Space in European Werewolf Mythologies. In: M. Mencej (ed.) *Space and Time in Europe: East and West, Past and Present*. Ljubljana: Oddelek za etnologijo in kulturno antropologijo, pp. 97-98.
[258] "Vasilisa the Fair" in Afanas'ev, *Russian folk-tales*, 111-112.
[259] Nikolskaya, "Baba Yaga the Bony-Legged."
[260] Woodruff, "The Triple God of Old Europe," 9.
[261] Woodruff, "The Triple God of Old Europe," 11.
[262] McNeil, "Who is Baba Yaga?"
[263] Johns, *The Ambiguous Mother*, 164. Referencing Solymossy, Sándor. 1984. "Die Burg auf dem Entenbein." In *Die Welt im Märchen*. Ed. Jürgen Janning and Heino Gehrts. Kassel: Erich Röth Verlag. 123-139.
[264] Forrester, *Baba Yaga: The Wild Witch of the East*, xxvii.
[265] Ganeva, "Bulgarian Folk Costumes," 5.
[266] Clarke, *Baba Yaga Slavic Earth Goddess*, 26-27.
[267] Hubbs, *Mother Russia*, 37.
[268] Rountree, "The Politics of the Goddess," 138.
[269] Dexter, *Whence the Goddesses*, 160.

270 Dexter, *Whence the Goddesses*, 160.
271 Conway, *Maiden, Mother, Crone*, 21.
272 Conway, *Maiden, Mother, Crone*, 22.
273 Conway, *Maiden, Mother, Crone*, 41-42.
274 Dexter, *Whence the Goddesses*, 160, 175.
275 Nikolskaya, "Baba Yaga the Bony-Legged."
276 Conway, *Maiden, Mother, Crone*, 45.
277 Matthews, "Baba Yaga Part I."
278 Conway, *Maiden, Mother, Crone*, 46.
279 Conway, *Maiden, Mother, Crone*, 73-74.
280 Dexter, *Whence the Goddesses*, 160.
281 Gregor, "The Apple and the Talking Snake," 150.
282 Conway, *Maiden, Mother, Crone*, 77.
283 Conway, *Maiden, Mother, Crone*, 79.
284 De Beer, "Honouring the Life Stage of the Crone," 2.
285 Conway, *Maiden, Mother, Crone*, 79-80.
286 Gregor, "The Apple and the Talking Snake," 150.
287 De Beer, "Honouring the Life Stage of the Crone," 2. Referencing Prétat, J.R. 1994.*Coming to Age: The Croning Year and Late-Life Transformation*. Toronto: Inner City Books, p. 44.
288 Interview with shaman Baba Phoenix on September 2, 2022.
289 Clarke, *Baba Yaga Slavic Earth Goddess*, 19.
290 Clarke, *Baba Yaga Slavic Earth Goddess*, 66-67.
291 PianoCzarX, "The Hut on Fowl's Legs."
292 Abramov, "Поседел от встречи с Бабой Ягой."
293 Elderly Attribute, "Реальная встреча с бабой ягой?"
294 Gilbert, "On the Treatment of the Scourge," 236-238.

www.ingramcontent.com/pod-product-compliance
Lightning Source LLC
Chambersburg PA
CBHW061139030426
42335CB00002B/40